outline of international finance:
exchange rates and payments between countries

Reading economics

EDITOR: Geoffrey Denton, Reader in Economics in the University of Reading

outline of international finance: exchange rates and payments between countries

L Sirc

Weidenfeld & Nicolson

London

To the Scottish Universities of Glasgow and Dundee, to my colleagues and students

ISBN 0 297 76720 8. Cased

ISBN 0 297 76721 6. Paperback

Printed in Great Britain by Redwood Burn Limited Trowbridge and Esher.

contents

author's preface

Outline of international finance is the companion volume to the *Outline of International trade,* and the first purpose of this preface is to supply a link between these two partial textbooks on international economics.

The opening chapter of the *Outline of international trade,* in fact its section presenting a simplified illustration of international trade,[1] and again chapter 2, when it discusses the application of price mechanism to the division of production between countries[2], try to explain how exchange rates influence the relationship between domestic prices in international markets. The exchange rates provide the connection between domestic prices in various countries and have to shape their relationship in such a way – either through their own changes or through other 'adjustment mechanisms – that the value of a country's exports becomes equal to the value of its imports or, in a wider framework, that its payments to the world are equal to its international receipts.

Clearly, this need for international equilibrium must have its effects on the functioning of the price mechanism, as is repeatedly stressed in the trade volume. This volume on international finance concentrates on this aspect and follows it through from the description of the ways in which exchange rates can be established, in chapter 1, to a study in chapter 4 of how prices and costs, activity levels and monetary flows, interact and bring about international balance in a highly complex pattern. Chapters 5 to 7 deal with the existing institutions and attempts at reforming them.

International economic relations can be interpreted only in terms of the interplay of prices and costs, expenditure flows and money balances, so that international finance inevitably turns out to be a more complicated branch of economics than many others. In fact, it brings together the findings of most economic disciplines to explain the working of economics in an international context. For this reason it is inevitable that some parts remain fairly complicated despite the efforts to simplify as much as possible.

[1] See L. Sirc *Outline of international trade* London: Weidenfeld and Nicolson 1973, p 6.
[2] See *Outline of international trade,* p 20.

International economics has to investigate the relationship changes in aggregates owing either to employment levels or to growth and changes in costs and prices, because in international operations the economic initiative and responsibility remains in the hands of enterprises, and they receive their clues about what to do mainly from costs and prices. This situation was underlined in the book on trade and is pursued further here. On the other hand, international monetary economics has to interpret in a plausible way the aggregate and microeconomic effects of both expenditure flows; and monetary circumstances, since they often work hand-in-glove, and create problems when they are supposed to work in opposite directions. Furthermore, one can talk in terms of expenditure flows only, while making suitable assumptions regarding money, when dealing with an internal development, but this is hardly possible in view of the prominent role of money in international situations.

In short, international finance is a complex subject which has to be studied in detail to understand even the most basic problems. At present the complexity is worsened by the search for a better institutional framework, which keeps many matters in flux. This fluidity also makes it easier for people to claim that there are perfect or almost perfect answers to international monetary problems, while it would probably be better to admit that there can be hardly any 'final' solution for a most intricate network of international economic relationships. The functioning of such necessarily complex machinery also requires institutional flexibility.

The author will be well satisfied if this book conveys to the reader a feeling of how involved the economic relationships are between countries of the world, and of how inevitable such complexity is if we want to preserve the present high standard of living and improve it at least in the more unlucky areas of the world.

Glasgow, 1973

general reading

M V Clement, R L Pfister and K T Rothwell — *Theoretical issues in international economics* Boston: Houghton Mifflin 1967

A C L Day — *Outline of monetary economics* London: Oxford University Press 1963 (shorter version *The economics of money* 1968)

P T Elsworth — *The international economy* London: Collier-Macmillan 1968

J M Fleming — *Essays in international economics* London: Allen and Unwin 1971

M Friedman — *Dollars and deficits: inflation, monetary policy and the balance of payments* Englewood Cliffs New Jersey: Prentice-Hall 1968

G Haberler — *A survey of international trade theory* Princeton: University Press 1961

G Haberler — *Money in the international economy* London: Institute of Economic Affairs 1965

R F Harrod — *International economics* London: Cambridge University Press 1966

F Hirsch — *Money international* Harmondsworth: Penguin 1969

H G Johnson — *Further essays in monetary economics* London: Allen and Unwin 1973

C P Kindleberger — *International economics* Homewood Illinois: Irwin 1968

A O Krueger — 'Balance of payments theory' *The journal of economic literature* vol VII (1969)

F Machlup — *International monetary economics* London: Allen and Unwin 1966

J E Meade — *The balance of payments, the theory of international economic policy* vol I London: Oxford University Press 1951

R A Mundell	*Theory of international trade* London: Collier-Macmillan 1968
R A Mundell	*Monetary theory: inflation, interest and growth in the world economy* Pacific Palisades: Goodyear 1971
I F Pearce	*International trade* London: Macmillan 1970
P A Samuelson	'An exact Hume – Ricardo – Marshall model of international trade' *Journal of international economics* 1971
W M Scammel	*International trade and payments* Macmillan 1974
T Scitovsky	*Money and the balance of payments* London: Allen and Unwin 1969
B Södersten	*International economics* London: Macmillan 1970
L B Yeager	*International monetary relations* New York: Harper and Row 1966 (shorter version *International monetary mechanism* 1970)

collected readings and papers

American Enterprise Institute	*International payment problems* Washington DC 1966
American Enterprise Institute	*International monetary problems* Washington DC 1972
R E Caves and H G Johnson (eds)	*Readings in international economics* London: Macmillan 1970
M B Connoly and A K Swoboda (eds)	*International trade and money: the Geneva essays* London: Allen and Unwin 1973
R N Cooper (ed)	*International finance* Harmondsworth: Penguin 1969
H S Ellis and L A Metzler (eds)	*Readings in the theory of international trade,* Philadelphia: Blakiston 1949
H G Johnson and A K Swoboda (eds)	*The economics of common currencies* London: Allen and Unwin 1972
R A Mundell and A K Swoboda (eds)	*Monetary problems of the international economy* London: University of Chicago Press 1969
L H Officer and T D Willett (eds)	*The international monetary system: problems and proposals* Englewood Cliffs New Jersey: Prentice-Hall 1969

also the series 'Essays in International Finance', 'Princeton Studies in International Finance' and 'Special Papers in International Economics', all published by the International Finance Section, Department of Economics, Princeton University Press, Princeton, New Jersey.

chapter 1
international payments

1.1 Currencies in international transactions

In modern economic life trade, and for that matter any economic transaction, implies money. Barter between individuals or individual firms is an exception both within countries and internationally.

However, a kind of barter between nations persists in the form of *bilateral trade* entailing clearing payments. Clearing is an arrangement between two countries providing that the proceeds of the sales of goods and services, or any other transaction, from one country to another can be used only for the purchase of goods and services from the same partner. Thus money is used for accountancy purposes, but does not give the seller nation the freedom to look for the best bargains; to buy the goods and services it needs where they can be obtained cheapest and where they are of the best quality. Choice is limited to what the partner country has to offer.

If in addition the partner countries have different political, military and economic weight, the stronger country can pressure its weak partner into accepting unfavourable prices for goods and services and into allowing its currency to be converted into the stronger partner's currency at an unfavourable exchange rate. Clearing can also lead to forced lending if flows of goods and services between the two countries are not matched and the debtor partner refuses to allow the creditor partner to use his surplus on the clearing account to buy goods and services elsewhere.

Before and during the Second World War Nazi Germany used clearing arrangements in this way to the detriment of smaller European countries. Clearing between the Soviet Union and European communist countries has led to similar results.

For this reason full benefit can be derived from international trade only if it is multilateral, that is if the proceeds of sales to one country can be used for purchases from any other country, and if the prices of goods and services are established in the world market. Multilateral trade as sponsored by the GATT, therefore, requires that national currencies be convertible into each other. Full convertibility of the currencies of advanced industrial countries was restored in 1958 within the framework of the International Monetary Fund (IMF), at least for the purpose of paying for current transactions.

International trade and other international transactions do not necessarily involve any kind of international currency. They can be implemented by means of the national currencies of the participants in a transaction, at least so long as the international receipts of residents of a country match their international payments, when the country is said to be in *international equilibrium.* If international receipts and payments of a country are not balanced, the need may arise for so-called *international liquidity* (reserves), as explained in chapter 4 on international adjustment processes.

On the other hand, national currencies used for international transactions have to be converted into each other at some stage, since exporters and other international dealers will have to pay for supplies of goods and services, including factors of production, in their own domestic currency and importers will sell their imports for their domestic currency. Usually the national currencies are changed into each other by the exchange departments of banks. Other possibilities exist: an importer may buy the foreign currency he needs directly from an exporter, or an export-import firm can earn the foreign currency it needs for imports by its own exports.

Internationally as well as nationally, money is not only a means of payment but also a means of preserving value, although this function has been eroded by the now customary inflation. In international transactions it is sometimes necessary to worry about how to preserve value even over short periods because large changes in the value of currencies in terms of each other are possible. Often contracts are concluded well in advance of the actual transactions and it may not always be feasible to convert a currency at the very moment it is received in payment. For this reason international traders often wish their prices and commitments to be stated and the payments to be carried through in a currency they know and trust. If traders lack confidence in and/or knowledge of each other's national currencies they may prefer to conclude the contracts and make their payments in the currency of a third country. A currency used in this way is termed a *commercial* (or sometimes trade or vehicle) *currency* and the obvious candidates for this role are the national currencies of the leading industrial and trading countries, in particular the pound sterling and the dollar. These two currencies are used in many transactions in which residents of their home countries are not involved.

1.2 International contracts or invoices

International traders concluding a contract or issuing an invoice have to be particularly careful about how they state the price and the conditions of payments.

The contract or invoice has to quote the price in either the seller's or the buyer's domestic currency, or in a third currency which is used as an international commercial currency. If the price is quoted in one currency while the actual payment is made in a different currency, the first currency is termed the *quotation currency.* The currency in which the price is paid is the *transaction currency.* The use of a currency for transactions requires that foreign banks or even firms hold working balances of this currency. Historically, the pound sterling was the predominant transaction currency, but it is now estimated that about 33 per cent of international trade is transacted in dollars and 25 per cent in pounds sterling (see p 130).

The businessman whose international business is transacted in his domestic currency does not have to worry unduly about exchange rates since his debts are normally stated in the same currency. This does not mean, of course, that he might not have gained if his claims had been stated in a foreign currency. But the businessman whose business is done in a foreign currency will have to take into consideration exchange rates in addition to the prices of goods and services. This circumstance explains the businessmen's preference for fixed exchange rates as they seem to eliminate this additional business risk. But even if exchange rates are flexible, the risk of their changing can be avoided at least partly, in forward markets (see pp 8–10).

Currencies and exchange rates take on even greater importance if payment is deferred or if the currency received in payment is not immediately passed on (*asset function*).

Since in international trade goods will often be transported over long distance, it is of special importance to state clearly whether and what transport and other costs arising are included in the price quoted. Several expressions and abbreviations have been evolved in international trade usage: *ex* and *franco* (free), *fob* (free on board), *fas* (free alongside the ship), *c & f* (cost (meaning price) and freight) and *cif* (cost, insurance and freight). Some of these formulae have to be further defined. Thus a price quoted 'ex factory' means that any costs incurred outside the factory will be charged to the buyer. 'Franco exporter's border' states that freight as far as the producer's country border is included in the quoted prices. 'Cif importer's port' conveys that insurance, freight and other costs incurred until the landing in the importing country will be at seller's expense.

The statement of the conditions of payment determines who is actually to finance the transactions. The usual formulae are: in advance, cash and carry, upon reception, within one month, within three months. If payment is in advance, the buyer extends credit to the seller and may, at least to some extent, finance the production itself. This arrangement is common in ship-building and aircraft. Under deferred payment the seller gives credit to the buyer and thus finances his stockholding. If payment is 'cash and carry' the goods have to be paid for at the moment when they leave the seller's premises. On the other hand, 'upon reception' means that the buyer has to pay only when the goods reach him, so that the seller finances the goods while in transit.

Short-term credits between buyers and sellers are called *trade credit* and play a considerable role in international competition, since firms that can extend commercial credit to their partners have a competitive edge over their rivals. If a country's currency comes under pressure and there is danger of its devaluation, it is in the interest of the residents to pay their debts denominated in foreign currency as soon as possible, even in advance, and of foreigners owing sums denominated in the currency in danger of devaluation to delay their payments. This situation gives rise to the so called *'leads and lags'* which add to the pressure on the currency (see p 178).

A bank can enter the scene and take over the financing of transactions. In this case it will be in the interest of international buyers and sellers to go for credit to the banks of the country with the lowest interest rates, even if this is a third country. However, British banks are no longer allowed to finance trade between third countries since 1969. In particular when producer goods are involved, the sale may be considerably helped by the extension of long- or medium-term credits. Therefore, many governments have over the last few decades taken a hand in the arrangement of such credits and organized special institutions to support their exporters in this respect, such as the British Export Credit Guarantee Department and the US Import-Export Bank. Of course, this is government intervention in international trade, which is usually listed amongst the 'non-tariff' distortions of international trade flows.[1]

1.3 Methods of payment

The usual methods of payment are: in cash, by bill of exchange or by transfer from one bank account to another. The simplest way of paying is by handing over cash, nowadays banknotes, but previously gold coins. As transport of coins over long distances was cumbersome and sometimes dangerous, Italian bankers began to specialize in payments by *promissory notes,* the original form of a *bill of exchange.* This is a signed statement: 'I promise to pay you so many pounds by a certain date.'

The bill of exchange evolved over time, until it is at present practically identified with a *draft*: an unconditional order in writing signed by the person giving it (the drawer), requiring the person to whom it is addressed (the drawee) to pay on demand (sight) or at a fixed or determinable future time a certain sum to order or to bearer (payee). For instance: 'To Messrs Smith & Co, pay to National Bank or to their order within three months from acceptance £500, value received. Brown.'

The bill of exchange formalizes the relationship between the debtor and the creditor and creates the legal presumption that the debt exists. The document is thus divorced from the transaction that has given rise to it. Therefore, it becomes a negotiable document, a trade bill which can transfer a claim from one person to another.

[1] See *Outline of international trade* p 129.

Often it is required that the bill be submitted to the drawee for *acceptance*, ie for signature, which then binds him in law to honour the bill at the appropriate time. If the debtor himself is not sufficiently well known in business circles he can ask a financial institution to accept the bill in his stead and thus make it a negotiable document. The financial firms specializing in this kind of business are the *accepting houses.* Banks can issue a letter of credit to intimate that they are prepared to extend a credit to some business firm and also accept a bill of exchange on the firm's behalf.

Together with treasury bills, trade bills are part of a bank's liquid assets and good trade bills can be discounted with the central bank at the going bank rate.

Bills of exchange were so important for international transactions that they were the subject of international conferences at the Hague (1910-12) and Geneva (1930-2). The purpose was to work out legal provisions that would be adopted by all participating countries so that the law on bills of exchange would be internationally unified.

The bill of exchange incorporates a credit function: the payee can sell it to somebody else, so as to receive the payment, minus discount (interest), immediately instead of when the bill matures. Usually the bill is passed on together with the *bill of lading,* the shipping document giving access to the merchandise involved. The customary clauses determining when the shipping document has to be handed over to the buyer are: documents against acceptance or documents against payment.

In recent years the bill of exchange has been to some extent replaced by transfers from bank account to bank account for which the order is given in the form of a cheque. A cheque issued by a bank is a banker's cheque. The orders for transfer can be mailed or telegraphed.

Transfer by cheque does not include a credit function. The credits required have to be separately arranged between the seller (exporter) or buyer (importer) and a bank.

1.4 Exchange rates and markets

As pointed out, in international transactions national currencies have to be converted into each other. The exact rate at which this happens is determined in the exchange markets.

Basically, the foreign exchange market is a market like any other. However, what is being bought and sold is a foreign currency instead of a good or a service. Since foreign currencies are ideally homogenous and there is a multitude of buyers and sellers, the foreign exchange market is as close to pure competition as is possible in reality. But although foreign currencies can be bought in order to hold them as an asset for their own sake, the demand for them is usually a derived demand; they are bought in order to buy foreign goods or services or investments.

As a consequence the foreign exchange market is superimposed on markets of foreign goods, services and investments. Any change in the price of foreign currency modifies all foreign prices in that currency when converted into domestic money. In fact, the role of exchange rates is, broadly speaking, to bring average prices in different countries to the same level; to make them comparable, regardless of the relative average efficiencies of these countries.[1]

Physically, the exchange market consists of networks of telephone links between banks acting as foreign exchange dealers. Banks then sell foreign currencies to their customers and buy them from them against the payment of a commission charge.

Under the system of *freely flexible* or *fluctuating* exchange rates, these rates would be determined entirely by the market. If the exchange rates were rigidly fixed by unilateral decree of a government or by international agreement, there would not be any exchange market and the authorities would have to stand prepared to convert any amount of domestic currency and vice versa, or to introduce some kind of rationing. Under the present system of *exchange rates fixed within limits,* the market does function but, if the exchange rate in the market moves to the limits imposed, the responsible authorities (monetary authorities; central bank; Exchange Equalization Account) are obliged to intervene by selling or buying foreign currency so as to prevent the rate from moving beyond the margins.

Under the present IMF system (see p 122),[2] all monetary authorities ought to register the par value or mint parity of their currency, the equivalent of their currency in gold, with the IMF and keep the exchange rate within the margins of 1 per cent (since 1971 2·25 per cent) upwards and downwards of the par value by means of interventionary selling and buying of foreign currencies.

The mint parity of the pound sterling registered with the IMF from the 1967 devaluation till 1970 was 1 ounce of pure gold = £14. As the dollar par value was also registered with the IMF, as 1 ounce of pure gold = $35, in practice the pound exchange rate had to be kept within limits with respect to the dollar. In practice the pound sterling exchange rate was maintained within the limits of $2·38 to $2·42 for £1. In 1971 these figures were changed, but these changes will be discussed later (see p 169).

In the London exchange market the quotations are in units of foreign currency for one unit of domestic currency. In other markets quotations are the other way round – in units of domestic currency for one unit or one hundred units of foreign currency.

The *Financial Times* of 8 October 1970 published the following report (table 1) on foreign exchanges:[3]

[1] See *Outline of international trade* p 53.

[2] Since 1970 the practice of international exchange has been changing fast, so that the bulk of the book refers to the situation in 1970, which is still legally valid, the changes after 1970 are described mainly in the last chapter.

[3] On the day to which the report refers the British bank rate was 7 per cent.

FOREIGN EXCHANGES

Sterling rose $\frac{3}{32}$ cent against the U.S. dollar to \$2.38$\frac{11}{16}$, broadly as a result of the weekly interest rate swing. Conditions were fairly quiet. The 3-month discount on the pound widened $\frac{3}{16}$ cent to $\frac{13}{16}$, the 6-month $\frac{3}{16}$ to 1$\frac{21}{32}$, and the 12-month ¼ to 3$\frac{3}{16}$. Short-term Euro-dollar deposits had an easier tone, though closing above their lowest of the day, and the dollar was softer against some Continental currencies, touching its official floor in Brussels and in Frankfurt.

FOREIGN EXCHANGES

Oct. 7 1970	Bank Rate %	Market Rates Day's Spread	Market Rates Close
New York	8	2.38⅜-⅞	2.38⅝-¾
Montreal.	8½	2.43½-44½	2.43⅝-⅞
Amsr'dam	6	8.58¼-60¼	8.58⅞-59⅜
Brussels...	7½	118.35-55	118.42-52
Copenh'n.	9	17.88-90	17.89-½
Frankfurt	7	8.65¾-67¾	8.68⅛-⅝
Lisbon......	Δ3½	68.00-50	68.25-45
Madrid....	6½††	165.75-166.15	165.95-166.10
Milan.......	5½	1,485½-88½	1,486¾-87¼
Oslo.........	4½	17.04¼-06¼	17.05-½
Paris........	7½	13.16½-18½	13.17-½
Stockh'lm	7	12.36-38	12.36½-37
Tokyo......	6.25	852½-855½	853½-854½
Vienna.....	6	61.55-61.85	61.62-61.67
Zurich.....	5¾	10.32¼-34¼	10.33⅛-⅝

N.B. Bank of England official limits for U.S.\$2.38-42. Δ Bank of Portugal discount rate. †† Basic discount rate under new system.

OTHER MARKET RATES

Australia..	2.1429-1514	Malaysia	7.34-3725
N.Zealand	2.1367-1492	Argentine	♣9.50-9.60
S. Africa..	1.7121-7207		♣¶8½-11
†India.....	5.5280-5.5606	Brazil.....	11.15-11.29
†♠Pakistan	8.737-763		¶12-15
Ceylon.....	1/4[illegible]	France....	¶13.10-30
*H'ngKng	14.530-14.614	W. G'm'y	¶8.63-73
L'xemb'rg	118.42-52	Spain......	¶165-167
Belgium..	¶118½-120	Greece....	71¼-½
Italy.......	♥¶1510-40	Switzerl'd	¶10.25-40

¶ Note rate quoted by specialist dealers. Other rates may be quoted elsewhere. † £'s 100 Rps. ♠ Tourists receive a 45 per cent. bonus on foreign currency surrendered to banks in Pakistan. ♣ Rate for new pesos equal to 100 old. ♥ Rate for denominations under Lr.10,000. Rate for Lr.10,000 denominations and for higher denominations 1,525-50. * Hong Kong dollars to the pound.

U.S., Canada 97.90-95.

FORWARD RATES

—	One month	Three months
New York	$\frac{5}{16}$-$\frac{3}{16}$ c. pm	⅞-¾ c. pm
Montreal.	$\frac{11}{16}$-$\frac{7}{16}$ c. pm	1$\frac{11}{16}$-1$\frac{7}{16}$ c. pm
Amst'dam	1½-1 c. pm	4⅝-4⅛ c. pm
Brussels..	20-05 c. pm	60-35 c. pm
Copenh'n.	Par-5 ore dis	3-7 ore dis
Frankfurt	⅝-⅛ pf pm	2⅝-2⅛ pf pm
Lisbon.....	10 c. pm-35 c. dis	10-60 c. dis
Milan......	4lirepm 6lire dis	3 lire pm-7 liredis
Oslo ...-....	5 ore pm-par	7½-2½ ore pm
Paris.	⅞-⅜ c.pm	2¾-2¼ c. pm
Stockh'lm	2⅞-3⅜ ore dis	5¾-6⅜ ore dis
Vienna. ...	25 gro pm-par	50-10 gro pm
Zurich.	4⅞-4⅜ c. pm	11¼-10¾ c. pm

EURO-CURRENCY

Interest rates

U.S. \$ IN LONDON			£ IN PARIS‡		
Call notice	7-Days notice	3 mths	2 Days notice	Month	3mths
6⅞-7⅛	7-7¾	7⅞-8⅛	8⅛	8⅞	9⅛

The following rates were quoted for dollar certificates of deposit: one month 7$\frac{9}{16}$-7$\frac{7}{16}$ per cent.; three months 8$\frac{3}{16}$-8$\frac{1}{16}$ per cent.; six months 8⅜-8¼ per cent.; one year 8$\frac{7}{16}$-8$\frac{5}{16}$ per cent.

Longer-term dollar certificates were quoted as follows: Bankers Trust 6¾ per cent., February 26, 1971, 8⅜-8¼ per cent.; Credit Lyonnais 6¾ per cent., October 22, 1971, 8$\frac{7}{16}$-7$\frac{15}{16}$ per cent. First National Boston 6.35 per cent., November 8, 1971, 8¼-7⅞ per cent.; Midland and In. 6⅛ per cent., September 25, 1972, 9⅛-3⅛ per cent.; Standard Bank 7¼ per cent., September 18, 1973, 9⅛-8⅞ per cent.

‡ Nominal.

EXCHANGE CROSS-RATES

Oct. 7	Frankfurt	New York	Paris	Brussels	London	Amsterdam	Zurich
Frankfurt	—	3.6393-6403	65.75-80	7.315-320	8.6640-50	100.80-85	83.80-85
N. York...	27.54½-56	—	18.11⅛-⅝	2.0145-52	2.3868-70	27.77-½	23.09½-10
Paris.	152.010-110	5.51975-075	—	11.1225-90	13.1735-1835	153.265-360	127.465-565
Brussels...	13.67-½	49.62½-63	8.98¾-99¼	—	118.45-50	13.78-78½	11.46-½
London....	86⅛-⅝	2.38⅝-¾	13.17-½	118.42-.52	—	8.58⅞-59⅜	10.33⅛-⅝
Am'd'm ...	99.16-21	3.59$\frac{15}{16}$-60$\frac{1}{16}$	65.20½-25½	7.25⅛-⅝	8.59¼-¾	—	83.14-19
Zurich......	119.22-26	4.3292-97	78.42-45	8.72½-73	10.3340-65	120.22-26	—

U.S \$ on Montreal 1.02$\frac{7}{32}$-¼. Canadian \$ on New York 0.9779-9782. Milan on New York 623.00. Milan on London 1487.15.

The two figures under 'Market Rates' indicate dealers' buying and selling rates. They would buy foreign currency at the higher figure (lower price) and sell it at the lower figure (higher price).

The *Neue Zürcher Zeitung* of 7 October 1970 printed the report on foreign exchange rates in the Zürich market on 5 October, reproduced in table 2.

Table 2

Devisen- und Notenkurse in Zürich vom 5. Okt.
Devisen: Dollars 4.32/4.33; 1 Monat Termin 4.30⅝/4.31⅝; 3 Monate Termin 4.29⅜/4.30⅜; £/Fr. 10.30/10.34; 1 Monat Termin 10.25/10.30; 3 Monate Termin 10.20/10.25; £/$ 2.38⅝/2.38⅞; fFr. 78.15/78.50; DM 118.80/119.25; bFr. 8.69½/8.73; Lit. –.6920/–.6955; öS 16.71/16.76; hfl. 119.95/120.30; sKr. 83.15/83.50; dKr. 57.50/57.80; nKr. 60.40/60.65; Pta. 6.18/6.24; Escudos 15.06/15.15; kan. $ 4.22/4.25½; arg. Pesos 106.–/111.–.

Noten: Dollars 4.28/4.34; £ 10.20/10.45; fFr. 77.25/79.25: DM 118.–/120.–; bFr. 8.55/8.75; Lit. –.6700/–.6900; öS 16.60/16.90; hfl. 119.–/121.–; sKr. 81.75/83.75; dKr. 56.50/58.50; nKr. 59.25/61.25; Pta. 6.05/6.35; arg. Pesos 95.–/115.–; Escudos 14.60/15.40: türk. £ –.26/–.31; Cruzeiros –.65/–.95; kan. $ 4.17/4.29; **israel. £ kleine 1.–/1.30; Fmk. 102.–/104.50.**

Here the quotations are direct as opposed to London indirect, so that both London and Zürich will quote £1 = Swiss francs 10·30/10·40. But in Zürich dealers will buy at the lower figure and sell at the higher.

The rates shown in table 1 under the heading 'Foreign Exchanges' are *spot rates,* ie the rates paid at present for immediate delivery of foreign exchange. If the spot rate is different from par value, as the spot rate of the pound sterling was on 7 October 1970, when £1 = $2·38 ⅝ – ¾, than it is said that the currency that fetches less than par value is *at a discount,* and the other currency *at a premium.* On 7 October the pound sterling was at a discount of 1¼ cents versus the dollar.[1]

In addition to spot rates, there are *long rates* and *forward rates.* Long rate is the rate paid at present for foreign currency delivered at some future date. Long rates are always at a discount with respect to spot rates, because the dealer who delivers currency later can earn interest on the amount in the meantime.

Forward rate is the rate fixed in a contract on future delivery of both currencies. Usually, the delivery is within one month or three months. If forward rates are

[1] Terms used to indicate a divergence of the spot rate from the par value are *agio* for premium and *disagio* for discount.

different from spot rates the terms used are *forward premium* (deport) and *forward discount* (report).

The *Financial Times* report on the London exchange market quotes forward premia and discounts for one or three months under the heading 'Forward Rates'. The quotation for New York three months was $^7/_8$ – $^3/_4$ cents premium. The higher premium is far selling, the lower premium for buying, and in a market with indirect quotation of spot rates the premium has to be deducted from the appropriate spot rate. As the selling spot rate is \$2·38 $^5/_8$, this rate minus the dollar premium gives the selling forward rate of 2·37 ¾. If a currency's forward rates are at a discount, like the forward rate of the Portuguese escudo on 7 October 1970, the discount has to be added to the spot rate, the lower discount figure to the selling rate, and the higher discount figure to the buying rate.

If forward rates could be isolated they would be determined by the present demand for and supply of foreign currency at some future date (present contracts on future exchange transactions). It is one of the banks' functions to bring demand for and supply of foreign currencies in the future together.

But forward rates are linked to spot rates. If interest rates were equal in all countries and there were the same confidence in all currencies, forward rates would be equal to spot rates. If they were not, it would pay to buy spot the currency to which the forward rate is favourable and sell it forward at a premium, keeping it deposited in the meantime at the going interest rate. This operation is called *time arbitrage.*

If interest rates are different, the difference will be reflected in forward rates. Assuming that the forward rate is equal to the spot rate, it will pay to buy spot the currency of the country with higher interest rates, sell it forward and earn higher interest rates in the meantime (*interest arbitrage*). The currency with higher interest rates will thus be at a forward discount equal to the difference in interest for the period.

A third kind of arbitrage is *space arbitrage,* which is not connected with forward markets but which keeps spot rates in different financial centres in line. It can be two-point arbitrage, if it profits from difference in spot rates in two financial centres, and three-point or triangular if it profits from difference in cross-rates in three financial centres.

Whatever the forward rate, the existence of forward markets makes it possible for foreign traders to eliminate risks because of changing exchange rates in the sense that there is no uncertainty for them about the rates at which they will buy or sell foreign currency in the future. This precludes not only losses but also gains as a consequence of movements of exchange rates over time. Since fluctuations of exchange rates can be wider and more uncertain under a system of freely flexible exchange rates, forward markets play a particularly important role under this adjustment system.

The elimination or reduction of risk by means of forward markets is called *covering* and *hedging.* Covering eliminates risk altogether. An operator is in a *covered position* if his foreign assets are equal to his foreign liabilities. If he want to *speculate,* an operator can take a *long position* when his foreign assets are larger than his foreign liabilities, or a *short position* when his foreign assets are smaller than his foreign liabilities. Covering is possible only if the asset or liability involved refers to a definite amount maturing at a definite date. If that is not so only hedging is possible, that is, taking a speculative risk in order to offset another speculative risk (difficult to assess) in ths opposite direction.[1]

Arbitrageurs do not run any risks – they only have to be well informed and exploit any space or time differences in exchange rates or interest rates.

On the other hand, speculators by definition run risks by relying on their informed guesses about what the future development is going to be. A forward market speculator sells foreign currency he does not possess forward, expecting that at the time of delivery he will be able to buy it cheaper spot, or buys foreign currency he does not need forward, expecting that he will be able to sell it at a higher spot rate on delivery. If their guesses are correct speculators also help to keep spot and forward rates in line and iron out fluctuations. If they are wrong, speculators accentuate fluctuations, but then they also lose money.

Official intervention in forward markets can help to smooth fluctuations, but it can also be used to conceal the weakness of a currency, thus reducing the present loss of reserves by postponing them. [2]

Hot money movements are international short-term capital movements in search of arbitrage or speculative gain.

Multiple exchange rates exist when different rates have to be paid for foreign currency according to the purpose for which it is bought. Clearly this requires official intervention in exchange markets. Britain has multiple exchange rates in so far as there is a separate market for the so-called *investment dollar,* and for foreign exchange stemming from sales of foreign investment or intended for the purchase of foreign investment. The quotation is for a *dollar premium,* a percentage that has to be paid on top of the going exchange rate if foreign currency is being bought for investment purposes, or which is paid in addition to the exchange rate for foreign currency proceeds of the disposal of investment abroad.

[1] Paul Einzig 'The relations between practice and theory of forward exchange' *Banca Nazionale del Lavoro Review* vol 15 1962 p 231.

[2] See E B Chalmers (ed) *Forward exchange intervention* London: Hutchinson 1971.

further reading

R Z Aliber (ed)	*The international market for foreign exchange* New York: Praeger 1969
E B Chalmers (ed)	*Forward exchange intervention* London: Hutchinson 1971
B J Cohen	*Balance-of-payments policy* Harmondsworth: Penguin 1969
B J Cohen	'Sterling and the City' *The Banker* (1970)
P Einzig	*A textbook on foreign exchange* London: Macmillan 1966
P Einzig	'The declining use of sterling as a trading currency' *Westminster Bank review* (1968)
H E Evitt	*A manual of foreign exchange* London: Pitman 1966
F Machlup	'The theory of foreign exchanges' in *International Monetary Economics* London: Collier-Macmillan 1966
R V Roosa and F. Hirsch	*Reserves, reserve currencies, and vehicle currencies: an argument* Princeton: University Press 1966
E Sohmen	*The theory of forward exchange* Princeton: University Press 1966
R Weisweiller	*Foreign exchange* London: Allen and Unwin 1972
D P Whiting	*Finance of foreign trade* London: Macdonald and Evans 1964

chapter 2
accounts of foreign transactions and capital

2.1 Balance of payments

When the determinants of trade flows were discussed[1] it was said that, in order to link the general equilibrium systems of two countries, it has to be postulated that the value of exports of each country has to be equal to the value of its imports. This is true as long as it is assumed that goods only, or goods and services only, are being exchanged between countries (meaning 'between the residents of the countries, including firms and the government'). If the assumption that goods and services only are exchanged between countries is dropped and all possible sorts of international transactions are included, the items to be added are purchases and sales of capital and unilateral transfers. This addition does not however alter the fact that exchanges between countries can continue only if both sides of the balance have the same value. The difference is that, with all transactions included, some operations can be on credit, and the giving of credit may be considered short-term investment.

It was mentioned that the part of international economics called 'international finance' deals with the question of how to match the value of exports with the value of imports, or better the value of transactions in one direction with the value of transactions in the opposite direction, and that the exchange rate has the task of making this equality possible. If it is decided that the whole burden of adjustment should fall on the exchange rate, or more precisely on the alterations of the exchange rate, any disturbance of the balance between the value of transactions in both directions will be reflected in the exchange rate. This will change all prices of goods, services and investment in one country in terms of the currency of the other country, and will thus also alter their demand and supply, and this change will subsequently show in the demand for and supply of the currencies themselves.

If it is decided however that the exchange rate should be fixed within narrow limits, then it is possible that at a given exchange rate, other things being equal (meaning that other adjustment mechanisms do not work), the supply and demand of foreign currency in the exchange market are not equal and that monetary authorities have to

[1] See *Outline of international trade* p 21.

intervene by selling or buying foreign currency, as the case may be. What is called the 'market balance of payments',[1] then, means that at a given exchange rate the value of transactions in and out of the country is equal and that the supply of foreign currency is equal to the demand for it. If it is not, there is an exchange market deficit or surplus. Such a deficit or surplus is the first symptom that something is amiss and that further measures may have to be taken.

Transactions in and out of a country can also be recorded by what accountants call double-entry book keeping. If those accountancy entries referring to payments to abroad and from abroad are then assembled in a separate account or balance, what is usually known as the balance of payments, or to be more precise the 'accountancy balance of payments', is obtained. Since it is a flow account it has to refer to a period of time, normally a year. Thus the accountancy balance of payments is a record of all international payments to and by a country within a year. To illustrate, the UK balance of payments in 1969[2] is reproduced in table 3.

It has to be kept in mind that the balance of payments is exactly what it says: a record of payments. Therefore it contains only that part of transactions and accountancy entries that represents payments. The other side of these transactions and entries, the fact that a country has received goods or services or even land or entire factories or shares or bonds, is recorded elsewhere, as will be shown below. For this reason the signs given to entries may seem peculiar. Imports are given a – sign although the UK has received goods. Even more peculiarly, British private investment abroad has a – sign, although it increases British assets abroad, and a government loan from the US Export-Import Bank a + sign, although it raises indebtedness abroad. But when looking at a balance of payments we wish to know exclusively how purchasing power (or cash or liquidity) has flowed in and out, regardless of what the other effects of these flows were.

Year after year there are millions of transactions between countries and, accordingly, millions of payments. If the authorities and other users of statistics wish to gain an overall view of what foreign transactions have taken place, individual entries have to be added together in some way at some level of generality. The way in which this is done depends on the purpose of a particular presentation. We may want to know what the balance of payments is with another particular country or with respect to a special kind of operation. We may wish to know how exports and imports of particular kinds of goods, for instance food or machinery, have fared.

At the summary level, exports of all goods and imports of all goods, exports of all

[1] See Fritz Machlup 'Three concepts of the balance of payments and the so-called dollar shortage' in *International monetary economics* London: Collier-Macmillan 1966.

[2] For further UK balance-of-payments statistics see table 6, p 23, and table 12, p 46.

Table 3
Summary UK balance of payments 1969 (millions of pounds)

	+ inflows, receipts, credits	– outflows, payments, debits
imports (fob)		–7,153
exports and re-exports (fob)	+7,013	
visible trade balance		–140
net adjustment for recording of exports	+43	
payments for US military aircraft		–61
visible balance		–158
government services and transfers (net)		–457
private services and transfers (net)	+509	
interest, profits and dividends (net)		
private sector	+801	
public sector		–329
invisible balance	+524	
current balance	+366	
official long-term capital (net)		
loans from Export-Import bank (net)	+11	
other (net)		–106
private investment (net)		
outward (private investment abroad)		–593
inward (private investment in UK)	+709	
balance of long-term capital	+21	
balance of current and long-term capital transactions	+387	
balancing item	+182	
balance of monetary movements		–569

Source *Economic Trends* (March 1970)

services and imports of all services, sales of securities to foreigners and purchasers of securities by residents and so on will usually be added together and compared with each other. Sometimes inflows and outflows of payments belonging to the same category will not only be compared but will be netted out: inflows and outflows belonging to the same category will be added, taking account of their accountancy signs, and the result given the accountancy sign of the larger items. Taking the very top three entries of the UK balance of payments in 1969, we can abbreviate by putting imports (fob) and exports with re-exports (fob) as '(net) −140 million', which implies the calculation:

$$+ 7{,}013 \quad - 7{,}153 \text{ million} \quad = \quad - 140 \text{ million.}$$

But to make a balance of payments manageable, it is not sufficient to add entries of the same category at some level of generality; they have to be grouped so as to help users to understand them. The division between consumption and capital accumulation is common in economics, and it is also the usual first way of grouping entries in the payment accounts of various countries. Consequently, the balance of payments consists of a current account and capital accounts. Payments for producer goods bought abroad for instalment at home are also included in the current account. From an international payments point of view they are 'consumed' because they move into the domestic sphere and do not produce additional foreign currency income, although they may give rise to returns in domestic currency. The purchase of foreign securities or bonds, on the other hand, will be entered in the capital account of the balance of payments because these foreign assets produce returns in foreign currency which are then entered as dividends or interest, ie current income from abroad, in the current account.

In the UK balance of payments the current account contains a 'visible balance' (imports and exports of goods) and an 'invisible balance'. 'Invisible' include sales to foreigners and purchases from foreigners of services: tourism, transport, bank commissions, insurance premiums, dividends, interest, profits and unilateral transfers. Dividends, interest and profits can be considered payments for the services of investment and management abroad.

International unilateral transfers are similar to transfer payments in national income statistics. The latter are payments by citizens or the government of a country to other citizens of the same country without a *quid pro quo.* The former are payments by residents or by the government of a country to residents or governments of other countries also without a *quid pro quo,* in other words gifts across borders, including international government aid in the narrow sense of the term.

If receipts (received payments, credits or inflows) on current account are smaller than payments (payments out of a country, debits or outflows), there is a deficit on current account. But excess payments must come from somewhere and they can come only from the capital account in the form of a reduction of previously accumulated investments (assets) by residents and the government of the country, or of a rise in the investment owned by foreigners in the country, which means a rise in the country's liabilities. If on the other hand receipts of a country surpass payments out of it, both on current account, there is a surplus on this account, which necessarily means that its foreign assets have risen or its foreign liabilities diminished.

Not all accumulated assets are equally easy to use for payments; some assets are easy to liquidate and are, therefore, described as *liquid.* Bank balances (deposits) can be used for payments immediately (at sight) or, at the utmost, within a short time; treasury bills and trade bills can be turned into cash within a short time or immediately against a discount; trade credits are not extended for more than a few months. On the contrary, if a person wishes to liquidate a bond of some duration, so as to obtain cash, he may have to sell it at a loss, ie for less than the fixed amount stated on the bond. If the market rate of interest is higher than the rate to which the bond entitles, the current price of the bond will be less than its nominal value, and to sell the bond at the time cash is required may incur losses. This danger of loss is even more true in the case of equity capital (risk capital). The stock market price of shares depends not only on a comparison between dividends paid out and market interest rates, but on many other circumstances, so that the danger of loss is very great if they have to be liquidated at short notice to produce foreign cash. The additional danger is that an attempt to sell a large amount of shares at one time will in itself depress their price.

It is therefore customary to distinguish between liquid and non-liquid assets in international accounts just as in domestic banks or other companies' balance sheets. The distinction has to be drawn along an arbitrary line; fixed nominal amount claims with a maturity under a year are liquid; fixed nominal amount claims with more than a year maturity, and risk capital, are non-liquid. Parallel to liquid and non-liquid, the terms *short-term* and *long-term* are frequently used.[1] Accordingly, in the UK balance of payments, the capital account used to be divided, up to 1969, into the long-term capital account and the short-term capital account (the latter also called the account of monetary movements, since liquid assets are, in part, money and near money).

The UK balance of payments then consisted of

current account
long-term capital account
short-term capital account.

[1] But it should be noted that the US balance of payments as presented in table 5 includes 'non-liquid short-term private capital flows'. The explanation is that 'short-term' refers mainly to short maturity, while 'liquid' refers to marketability, so that there can be short-term claims that are not readily marketable, hence non-liquid. A different concept of liquidity was used in the US balance of payments and US international investment position until the change in presentation in 1971 (see p 30).

This division had nothing to do with the distinction between autonomous or spontaneous transactions, on the one hand, and accommodating, compensatory or induced transactions, on the other. *Autonomous* or *spontaneous transactions* are those undertaken for their own sake, not in order to keep the balance of payments in equilibrium or the market exchange rate within the prescribed margin from the parity. If autonomous transactions do not balance at the fixed exchange rate, the rate would have to change were the authorities not to intervene by using their own reserves for this purpose or obtaining means for intervention by borrowing from other central banks or the IMF. The related changes in monetary authorities' assets and liabilities indicate *compensatory transactions,* ie transactions undertaken to support the fixed exchange rates.

Transactions are undertaken for their own sake with the aim of profit, of keeping foreign working balances, of maintaining dependants (unilateral private transfers), giving aid for moral or political reasons, etc. Such transactions can be implemented by private persons or institutions or by governments who can obviously act for other purposes than keeping the exchange rate within official limits.

On the other hand, can private persons or institutions act in compensatory way? On the whole they cannot. Even if they believe that the fixed exchange rate is going to be maintained, and they therefore buy the currency the rate of which falls below its parity, they do not do it for reasons of accommodation but out of the speculative motive, hoping that they will gain when the market exchange rate moves back to parity. However, foreign monetary authorities can keep their reserves in the form of balances with private banks primarily in the UK and US. In that case compensatory transactions of foreign monetary authorities will be reflected in the changes of private foreign liabilities in the UK and US.

This possibility induced the IMF originally, in its presentation of the balance of payments of member countries to divide the capital account (movements of capital and gold) into two parts, one dealing with non-monetary sectors (private – excluding banking institutions), the other with monetary sectors (official and banking institutions). The second part thus comprised changes in short-term assets and liabilities of the central bank and commercial banks, the first part all the rest.[1] The IMF presentation has changed since: in the standard presentation the capital account is now divided into capital flows and official reserves and reserve items; the former is then subdivided into non-monetary and monetary, the latter with a section for private institutions and another for official institutions. The IMF analytic presentation contains five headings in addition to totals: goods, services and unrequited transfers; capital movements;

[1] See IMF *Balance of payments yearbook,* particularly 'General principles' in the issue for 1938^{n} 46/7.

commercial bank capital; allocation of SDRs (special drawing rights); and official monetary movements.

It is obvious that there is considerable scope for variation in the layout of the balance of payments, and as a consequence in the definition of surplus or deficit; and presentations vary from country to country, as IMF publications themselves stress. It is also possible to interpret accommodating or compensatory movements in a different way. It can be said that accommodating movements are not only those movements of short-term funds that are expressly intended to keep the fluctuation of market exchange rates within limits, but also those that come about in response to credit conditions which changed as a result of the working of adjustment mechanisms or balance-of-payments policy. In such cases private funds do move in pursuit of gain, but this gain is offered to them to entice them to move in a compensatory way.

The pre-1971 and present presentations of the US balance of payments are shown in tables 4 and 5. In the old presentation the most important difference between the British and American layouts was that changes in US private short-term assets abroad were taken out of what corresponded to the UK account of monetary movements and added to the US private capital flows (short-term and long-term) under (3). As will be shown in section 2.2, this had implications for the definition of the balance-of-payments deficit. Since 1971, however, US private short-term flows have been treated as part of monetary movements, but by that time the British presentation had changed (see p 22).

2.2 Definition of the balance-of-payments deficit/surplus

When looking for a definition of the balance-of-payments deficit or surplus we are searching for a figure that would give an indication of how the payments have gone in the period under consideration. But since in double entry bookkeeping entries on both sides must balance, to find such a figure the balance of payments must be divided into two parts according to some principle so that the resulting imbalance in the two parts indicates what we wish to know. The position of the dividing line[1] will then depend on what figure is believed to give the best idea of the *liquidity* or cash *position* of a country. This position is of interest because it tells us what the prospects are for a country to remain financially solvent, ie able to meet its short-term liabilities resulting either from purchases of goods, services and capital abroad in excess of analogous foreign purchases in the country or from the liquidation of foreign short-term assets in the country. Since short-term obligations can be met, at a moment's notice, only from short-term assets, the figure we are looking for is supposed to indicate losses or gains over a year in precisely these assets, possibly in combination with increases or

[1] This dividing line is the origin of the expressions 'above the line' and 'below the line'.

Table 4
US balance of payments: presentation till 1971 (millions of dollars)

	1960	1963	1964	1965	1966	1967	1968	1969	1970
export of goods and services	26,974	32,339	37,009	39,147	43,039	45,756	50,662	55,514	62,962
import of goods and services	–23,205	–26,442	–28,637	–32,203	–37,937	–40,989	–48,129	–53,564	–59,291
balance on goods and services	3,769	5,897	8,462	6,944	5,102	4,768	2,493	1,949	3,672
remittances and pensions	–672	–867	–896	–1,024	–1,010	–1,276	–1,121	–1,190	–1,389
1 balance of above	3,097	5,030	7,566	5,120	4,092	3,492	1,372	759	2,285
2 government fund and capital flow, net	–2,775	–3,381	–3,560	–3,375	–3,446	–4,210	–3,975	–3,828	–3,235
3 US private capital flow, net		–4,456	–6,542	–3,743	–4,132	–5,504	–5,412	–5,233	–6,351
4 foreign capital flow, net, excluding change in liquid assets in US	–3,552	689	685	275	2,512	3,185	8,701	4,131	3,861
5 errors and unrecorded transactions	–683	–352	–949	–415	–383	–532	–514	–2,841	–1,274
SDRs (seignorage)									867
A balance on liquidity basis	–3,913	–2,670	–2,800	–1,335	–1,357	–3,571	171	–7,012	–4,715**
change in liquid assets in US*								9,217	–6,511
B balance on basis of official reserve transactions		–2,044	–1,549	–1,304	225	–3,405	1,641	2,700	–10,686**

* not the *exact* difference between A and B
** excluding SDRs (see p 158).

Source: *Federal Reserve bulletin*

Table 5
US balance of payments: presentation since 1971 (millions of dollars)

	1968	1971	1972
merchandise trade balance	624	–2,689	–6,816
military transactions, net	–3,140	–2,894	–3,541
travel and transportation, net	–1,558	–2,432	–2,583
investment income, net	6,220	7,995	7,901
other services, net	344	748	819
balance on goods and services	2,489	727	–4,219
remittances, pensions and other transfer	–1,168	–1,529	–1,557
balance on current account	1,321	–2,847	–7,983
US government capital flows, net	–2,262	–2,378	–1,367
long-term private capital flows, net	–1,198	–4,079	107
balance on current account and long-term capital	–1,349	–9,304	–9,243
non-liquid short-term private capital flows, net	–231	–2,386	–1,634
allocation of SDRs	–	717	710
errors and omissions	–493	–11,031	–3,806
net liquidity balance	–1,610	–22,002	–13,974
liquid private capital flows, net	3,251	–7,763	3,677
official reserve transaction balance	1,641	–29,765	–10,297
excluding SDRs			
net liquidity balance		–22,719	–14,684
official reserve transaction balance		–30,482	–11,007

Source: Federal reserve bulletin

reduction in foreign short-term liabilities.

The very presentation of the UK balance of payments up to 1969 led to the dividing line being drawn so that current account and long-term capital account were above the line, and account on monetary movements below the line. The balance of current and long-term capital transactions was also called the *basic balance* and should in principle have been exactly matched by a balance of monetary movements with opposite sign. Both should have indicated the balance-of-payments deficit (basic balance –sign, balance of monetary movements + sign) or surplus (signs the other way round).

But normally the two balances did not match for the simple reason that data were collected from different sources (eg for exports and imports from customs statistics, for monetary movements largely from banks). To make them equal, a *balancing item* was inserted representing errors and omissions. In US terminology the figure inserted is, indeed, called *errors and unrecorded transactions.* It is impossible to know exactly what this item stands for, since *known* errors and omissions could be corrected.

However, random errors and omissions should cancel out over the years, so that, when this proved not to be the case in Britain, research was instituted on why errors and omissions were leaning to the + side. It was found that exports tended to remain under-recorded, and the balance of payments for 1969 therefore contained a 'net adjustment for recording of exports'.

Basic balance and balance of monetary movements, then, showed differences, but since the reports by banks may be assumed to be more precise than other statistics, as the banks must keep precise accounts for their own sake, it is normally assumed that the balance on monetary movements represents the balance-of-payments deficit. It must be pointed out, however, that monetary movements also contain, under 'miscellaneous capital', changes in holdings of trade credit, trade bills and local government short-term borrowing.

The balance of monetary movements, which until 1969 was identical with the usual definition of the balance-of-payments deficit, described more precisely as *on the basis of net liquidity position,* or even on the basis of the *change* in the net liquidity position, hence comprised the following:

rise (–) or reduction (+) in gold reserves

rise (–) or reduction (+) in { official / private } foreign short-term assets

reduction (–) or rise (+) in { official / private } foreign short-term liabilities

The sum of all these changes indicates a surplus, if – prevails, or a deficit, if + prevails.

The signs have been explained earlier, but most UK balance-of-payments statistics (see eg p 47) have a footnote stating: 'Assets: increase –/decrease +. Liabilities: increase +/decrease –.'

The US definition of the balance-of-payments deficit *on liquidity basis* had not been entirely identical with the UK definition bearing a similar name. The difference was that in the US, as the description of the entry under (3) in contrast with that under (4) in the US balance of payments makes clear, the deficit did not include changes in private short-term assets owned by US citizens and firms abroad. The change in them was included 'above the line'. The reason for this arrangement was that US short-term assets abroad are, on the whole, working balances needed for the operations of American businesses outside the US, so that they will not be repatriated and can be considered long-term investment, although they have the form of short-term capital. But as pointed out on p 18, in 1971 US-owned short-term capital assets abroad were moved to 'liquid private capital flows'. Comparing the old and the new presentations (tables 4 and 5), one sees that the new layout turned the 1969 surplus on liquidity basis of \$171 million into a deficit of \$1,610 million. This is, of course, a consequence of the alteration in the treatment of changes in the US-owned liquid assets and indicates that in 1968 US liquid assets abroad were used to finance US purchases of goods, services and capital abroad to the tune of \$1,610 million + \$171 millions = \$1,727 million.

The second US definition, *on basis of official short-term transactions,* transfers above the line all short-term private liabilities. The rationale seems to be that the movement of short-term funds into the US is also a rather stable transaction, so that a sudden outflow is not to be expected. But figures seem to belie this assumption. In 1966 a liquidity deficit of \$1,357 million becomes a surplus of \$225 million on official transactions basis; in 1969 even a liquidity deficit of \$7,012 million is turned into an official transaction surplus of \$2,700 million. Obviously, funds had been flowing into the US in a big way, to a large extent possibly because of the flourishing Euro-Dollar market (see p 136). But in 1970 a liquidity deficit of \$3,852 million became an official transaction deficit of \$9,821 million. The flow of funds had been reversed, perhaps in anticipation of the 1971 crisis (see p 168).

In 1970 the UK changed to a presentation of balance of payments which shows only a deficit or surplus, defined similarly as the US deficit/surplus on basis of official short-term transactions, although the term is not used. The official *United Kingdom balance of payments* now publishes a summary[1] as shown in table 6.

The entry under 'investment and other capital flows' now contains the previous long-term capital account and all private short-term capital movements. *Total currency flow* is the previous basic balance plus balancing item plus private short-term capital flows, the balance of which has to be *officially financed* by borrowing or using reserves.

It should be understood that there is no 'best' or 'correct' definition of the balance-of-payments deficit or surplus. Any definition has its advantages and disadvantages for the simple reason that it is impossible to express all the complexities of the balance-of-payments situation in one single figure. The balance-of-payments deficit on a net liquidity position basis, for instance, hides the possible adverse influence that private short-term capital movements have on the official reserve, and the deficit calculated on the basis of official financing conceals the help that official reserves can be

[1] For further UK balance-of-payments statistics see table 12, p 46.

Table 6
Summary UK balance of payments (millions of pounds)

	1961	1962	1963	1964	1965	1966	1967	1968	1969	1970	1971
current account											
visible trade	–152	–102	– 80	–519	–237	– 73	–557	– 648	–143	+ 12	+ 299
invisibles	+158	+224	+204	+137	+188	+157	+242	+ 377	+587	+ 669	+ 741
current balance	+ 6	+122	+124	–382	– 49	+ 84	–315	– 271	+444	+ 681	+1,040
currency flow and official financing											
current balance	+ 6	+122	+124	–382	– 49	+ 84	–315	– 271	+444	+ 681	+1,040
investment and other capital flows	–316	– 3	– 99	–305	–332	–574	–600*	–1,007*	–106	+ 547	+1,839
balancing item	– 29	+ 73	– 83	– 8	+ 28	– 57	+244	– 132	+405	+ 59	+ 349
total currency flow	–339	+192	– 58	–695	–353	–547	+671	–1,410	+743	+1,287	+3,228
allocation of SDRs (+)	–	–	–	–	–	–	–	–	–	+ 171	+ 125
Gold subscription to IMF (–)	–	–	–	–	–	– 44	–	–	–	– 38	–
Total	–339	+192	– 58	–695	–353	–591	–671	–1,410	+743	+1,420	+3,353
Financed as follows											
net transactions with overseas monetary authorities	+370	–375	+ 5	+573	+599	+625**	+556**	+1,296	–699	–1,295	–1,817
official reserves (drawing on +/ additions to –)	– 31	+183	+ 53	+122	–246	– 34	+115	+ 114	– 44	– 125	–1,536

* Including EEA loss on forward commitments.
** Including transfer from dollar portfolio to reserves.

given by an inflow of private funds. Obviously, any analysis of the balance-of-payments situation of a country must go beyond the single figure for the deficit and look at more detailed data.

In Britain trade figures are published monthly in the official *Trade and industry journal,*[1] and so are figures on official reserves in *Financial statistics.* But these monthly data have to be handled with care, because they do not give the whole picture. In particular, figures for the movements of reserves can hide heavy borrowing from various sources. Full quarterly balance-of-payments figures are published at the end of the following quarter in *Economic trends.* In any case, flow figures should not be entirely isolated from stock figures. The figure for reserves is of course a stock figure and the change in it from month to month a flow.

2.3 Balance of foreign assets and liabilities

A systematic account of foreign stock figures, assets and liabilities at a point in time, is given in the balance of foreign assets and liabilities (see tables 7, 8 and 9). This balance sheet has to be read in conjunction with the balance of payments. It was mentioned (p 13) that only the payment part of any transaction is recorded in the balance of payments, while it does not and cannot show what happened to the goods or capital purchased with that payment. If the payment was used to buy shares or bonds (portfolio investment) or entire plants (direct investment), the increase in assets thus achieved is shown in the figures under long-term assets. The same happens if the government extends a loan to a foreign government, which is identical with the purchase of bonds although it may not take that form. If foreign residents buy shares or bonds, etc., in Britain this appears as an increase in British liabilities; if shares or bonds are sold instead of bought the opposite happens.

If on the other hand purchasing power is used only to deposit the proceeds in foreign banks, or to buy short-term credit instruments (treasury bills, trade bills, local government bills), short-term assets increase. Short-term liabilities increase if foreigners deposit money in domestic banks or buy domestic credit instruments.

If purchasing power is used for buying goods or services or implementing unilateral transfers, then these items are 'consumed', at least from an international point of view (see p 15), which means that they do not appear in any account of foreign assets and yield no new income from abroad. However, in some cases imported goods can still have a bearing on the development of the balance of payments. If goods are not physically consumed but are stocked, imports may slow down later because inventories are being used up. In 1964 the British balance-of-payments deficit was exceptionally large because firms were buying goods for inventories, particularly in view

[1] See sources of data at the end of this chapter.

Table 7
UK external assets and liabilities: presentation until 1970 (millions of pounds)

external assets — end:	1962	1966	1968
monetary (short-term)			
official			
reserves	1,002	1,107	1,009
dollar portfolio	(360)	(180)	–
UK subscription IMF	696	871	1,017
	(2,060)	(2,160)	2,025
private			
in sterling and sterling area currencies	672	981	1,322
in foreign currencies	1,221	3,208	7,326
suppliers' credit on exports	474	712	(852)
	(2,375)	(4,900)	(9,500)
long-term			
official	(710)	(985)	(1,115)
private investment abroad			
portfolio	(3,000)	(3,450)	(5,800)
direct (except oil, insurance and banking)	(3,410)	(4,500)	(5,630)
oil companies	(1,100)	(1,475)	(1,650)
insurance companies (US only)	(375)	(425)	(475)
	(7,885)	(9,850)	(13,555)
total	(13,030)	(17,895)	(26,195)

external liabilities — end:	1962	1966	1968
monetary (short-term)			
official	3,045	4,485	6,125
private	2,765	5,005	(9,015)
long-term			
official	(2,670)	(2,580)	(2,995)
private investment in UK			
portfolio	(1,050)	(1,100)	(2,200)
direct (except oil, banks, insurance)	(1,430)	(2,170)	(2,570)
oil companies	(700)	(850)	(1,150)
borrowing by UK concerns	(5)	(90)	(165)
	(3,185)	(4,210)	(6,085)
total	(11,665)	(16,280)	(24,220)

Figures in brackets are precarious estimates and/or known to be incomplete.

Source: *Bank of England quarterly bulletin* (1969)

Table 8
UK external assets and liabilities (millions of pounds)

	external assets					
end:	1962	1968	1969	1970	1971	1972
private sector						
private UK investment abroad:						
direct investment (excluding oil, insurance and banking)*	3,405	5,585	6,100	6,415	6,875	8,070
oil companies' net assets abroad*	1,100	1,650	1,800	1,950	2,050	2,150
banks' and insurance companies' direct investment in the US**	365	515	475	475	475	500
portfolio investment†	3,200	6,150	5,650	5,550	5,500	7,800
total private investment abroad	8,070	13,900	14,025	14,390	14,900	18,520
UK banks' assets:						
advances and overdrafts in						
sterling	318	370	414	423	415	609
overseas currencies	1,031	6,894	11,601	14,281	16,332	23,606
commercial bills discounted and acceptances	329	1,086	1,491	1,833	2,109	2,566
suppliers' trade credit on exports	487	968	1,070	1,089	1,080	1,063
other known assets held abroad by UK companies	55	105	145	140	95	125
total banking and commercial claims	2,220	9,425	14,720	17,765	20,030	27,970
total external assets of the private sector	**10,290**	**23,325**	**28,745**	**32,155**	**34,930**	**46,490**
public sector						
intergovernment loans by the UK	398	739	791	875	963	1,017
subscriptions to international financial organisations (excluding the IMF)	141	199	244	269	312	358
government holdings of Suez Finance Company shares†	27	25	25	20	20	25
other official assets	145	166	170	172	191	204
total public sector lending etc	710	1,130	1,230	1,335	1,485	1,605

	external liabilities					
end:	1962	1968	1969	1970	1971	1972
private sector						
overseas investment in the UK private sector						
direct investment (excluding oil, insurance and banking)*	1,430	2,720	3,000	3,330	3,715	3,980
overseas oil companies' net assets in the UK*	700	1,150	1,250	1,350	1,600	1,700
portfolio investment in UK companies' sterling securities†	1,000	2,350	2,200	1,900	2,550	2,700
portfolio investment in foreign currency securities issued by UK companies†	30	105	110	200	290	435
direct borrowing abroad by UK companies	5	180	275	425	565	690
total overseas investment in the private sector	3,165	6,505	6,835	7,205	8,720	9,505
UK banks' liabilities in						
sterling	1,532	1,745	1,839	2,207	3,130	3,047
overseas currencies	1,148	7,194	12,025	15,215	17,605	25,460
overseas sterling deposits with finance houses	98	51	57	119	136	22
suppliers' trade credit on imports	100	285	382	445	549	724
total banking and commercial liabilities	2,880	9,275	14,305	17,985	21,420	29,255
total external liabilities of the private sector	**6,045**	**15,780**	**21,140**	**25,190**	**30,140**	**38,760**
public sector						
intergovernment loans to the UK	1,930	2,226	2,232	2,137	1,906	1,802
loan from Deutsche Bundesbank	–	21	23	23	–	–
overseas investment in the UK public sector						
British government stocks†						
by overseas monetary authorities	985	880	1,105	1,180	1,355	1,320
by others	780	870	730	705	950	980
local authorities' securities and mortgages	110	50	50	55	75	75
foreign currency securities issued by public corporations and local authorities†	–	–	60	60	71	71
other foreign currency borrowing by public corporations and local authorities	–	–	22	20	82	82
other public sector capital						
overseas holdings of Treasury bills and notes§	1,096	615	533	541	904	1,001
import deposits received from overseas	–	1	60	28	–	–
IMF gold deposits	–	17	17	13	11	–
overseas deposits with local authorities	93	71	97	56	118	262
total public sector borrowing (other than official financing)	4,995	4,750	4,930	4,820	5,470	5,595

/continued

Table 8 *(continued)*

			external assets			
end:	1962	1968	1969	1970	1971	1972
reserve assets						
official reserves	1,002	1,009	1,053	1,178	2,526	} 2,167(*d*)
reserve position in the IMF	179	–	–	–	–	
official swaps with overseas monetary	–	–	–	–	864	–
government portfolio of dollar securities†	360	–	–	–	–	–
total reserve assets	1,540	1,010	1,055	1,180	3,390	2,165
total external assets of the public sector	**2,250**	**2,140**	**2,285**	**2,515**	**4,875**	**3,770**
total of identified external assets	**12,540**	**25,465**	**31,030**	**34,670**	**39,805**	**50,260**

– nil or less than £½ million
* estimated book value of net assets
** derived from US Department of Commerce estimates; these include market valuation of securities held by insurance companies
† at estimated market value
‡ offical reserves were redefined in July 1972 to include the reserve position in the IMF

of the expected devaluation. In 1965 and 1966 imports were more limited and the deficit reduced *inter alia,* because inventories were being reduced. This is of course a normal business cycle occurrence, which influences the balance of payments. Similarly, imported new plant, which at one stage burdens the balance of payments, may later help, if it produces for export expansion or import substitution.

Inventories and imported plant can thus still remain relevant for the balance of payments, but they are an exception. The great bulk of imports will be consumed. This leads to an important difference between a balance-of-payments deficit caused by a deficit on current account and one caused by a deficit on capital account. The former in fact reduces net assets abroad; the latter simply means a reshuffling within the assets themselves, leading to a 'change in portfolio', as it is called. Long-term assets replace short-term assets, or private assets replace government assets. And any kind of asset is still there to be used in some way, even if it does not yield income from abroad. Of course, net assets can be increased only if a country has a surplus on

	external liabilities					
end:	1962	1968	1969	1970	1971	1972
official financing liabilities						
net drawings on the IMF excluding gold tranche §§	–	880	850	678	123	–
liabilities to other monetary authorities in						
sterling	–	2,018	1,410	399	–	–
foreign currencies	–	211	150	–	–	–
total official financing liabilities	–	3,110	2,410	1,075	125	–
total external liabilities of the public sector	**4,995**	**7,860**	**7,340**	**5,895**	**5,595**	**5,595**
total of identified external liabilities	**11,040**	**23,640**	**28,480**	**31,085**	**35,735**	**44,355**

§ excludes official financing liabilities; includes liabilities to the IMF arising from accumulated charges in sterling

	1962	1967	1969	1970	1971	1972
§§ net drawings on the IMF of which	–	1,134	1,104	970	415	–
gold tranche	–	254	254	292	292	–
	–	880	850	678	123	–

Source: Bank of England quarterly bulletin (June 1973)

current account (roughly speaking if it exports more than it imports), which also requires additional domestic savings.

The difference between short-term and long-term assets was explained earlier (see p 16).

When discussing the cash or liquidity position, ie the financial solvency of a country, the analyst is naturally primarily interested in short-term assets and liabilities. Furthermore, since private short-term funds may not be used for compensatory transactions if they are not profitable, the authorities can take only funds which they own (reserves), or which they can borrow, as the first line of defence should there be a balance-of-payments deficit or should foreigners begin repatriating their short-term investment. That is why one normally compares total short-term liabilities with short-term assets officially owned. The statistics on the US international investment position (see p 30) used to be arranged in a way that took account of this approach. The table was not divided into short-term and long-term assets and liabilities as was the British balance

Table 9
US international investment position, 1960, 1969, 1971 (billions of dollars)

	assets			liabilities		
	1960	1969	1971	1960	1969	1971
non-liquid						
private						
long-term	44·4	96·0	115·5	18·4	41·0	49·6
short-term	5·0	14·1	14·7 (+4·0)*	1·0	2·9	3·8
	49·4	110·2	130·2	19·4	43·9	53·4
government	17·0	30·7	34·2	0·3	4·9	1·5
	66·4	140·8	164·4 (168·4)*	19·6	48·9	54·9
liquid						
reserves	19·4	17·0	12·2			
private assets			4·0*			
to official				12·4	13·0	57·2
to private				9·1	28·9	10·5
total	85·8	157·8	180·6	41·2	90·7	122·8
net position	44·6	67·0	57·8			

* As mentioned on pp 18 and 22, the treatment of US-owned liquid private assets in the balance of payments was changed in 1971: as a consequence it was also changed in the investment position tables. According to the old presentation, the figure would have been included where it is in brackets.

Source: October issues of *Survey of current business* published by US Department of Commerce

of foreign assets and liabilities, but into liquid and non-liquid assets and liabilities, and liquidity was looked at from the government's point of view. Liquid liabilities are those liabilities to foreigners that can be presented for payment, and therefore internationally for conversion at sight, while liquid foreign assets are only those the government itself can use at a moment's notice. (But see p 16, footnote).

Privately owned short-term funds were counted together with long-term investment as 'non-liquid' from the government's point of view. This was entirely in line with the US definition of balance-of-payments deficit or liquidity basis where US-owned short-term assets abroad were also included as part of total 'US private capital'. In this way in 1969 liquid assets thus defined were given as $17·0 billion as compared with $41·9 billion of liabilities, a ratio of 1:2·5, a marked deterioration in comparison with 1960, when it was almost 1:1. The deterioration continued until 1971. In that year $67·7 billion worth of liquid liabilities were facing $12 billion liquid assets, a ratio of about

1:5. At that time, in line with the change in the balance-of-payments presentation (see p 18), some short-term private assets were moved from the non-liquid to the liquid part of the inventory. However, even with this addition, the ratio between liquid assets to liquid liabilities remained 1:4.

The corresponding British figures, ie official short-term assets as compared with short-term liabilities to official and private holders, but excluding British potential borrowings from IMF, in 1968 amounted to £1,009 million versus £15,140 million, that is 1:15, while the ratio in 1962 had been 1:4·3. However, the composition of liabilities changed considerably since 1962. £1,028 million worth of short-term liabilities (about 17 per cent) were denominated in foreign currencies, while by 1968 this kind of liabilities rose to £7,110 million (about 47 per cent). The presentation for the year 1969 changed as shown in table 8, again in line with the change in the balance of payments. The distinction between short-term and long-term was abolished, so that the main division is now between private sector and public sector. For this reason the state of external financial solvency is not immediately visible. A note in the *Bank of England quarterly bulletin* of December 1970, under the title 'A revised presentation of external liabilities and claims in sterling', explained the revision. The nature of the items included since the 1930s in the statistical series of external liabilities and claims in sterling ('sterling balances' for short) had changed so that they no longer provided the intended measure of 'short-term' or 'liquid' liabilities. This was due to the development of new types of liabilities and assets denominated in sterling, some of which had arisen out of international financial arrangement, particularly the Basle Facility (see p 131). On the other hand, movements of funds across internal company accounts[1] defeat the short-term/long-term and autonomous/compensatory categorizations, hence the change in the presentation of both the balance of payments and balance of external assets and liabilities.

It has to be emphasized again that the ratios noted above were concerned with the international cash position and international financial solvency and not with the comparison of total foreign assets versus total foreign liabilities, which can be termed international real solvency. Although financial insolvency is an awkward corner, the awkwardness is much reduced if there are at least long-term assets to fall back upon in difficult times. That is precisely what the British government did during the Second World War when they requisitioned British private portfolio assets in the US to finance current war expenditure. Some of the requisitioned securities remained in British government hands till the 1960s when they were gradually sold off to finance the balance-of-payments deficit, as the British balance on foreign assets clearly shows. As pointed out, massive selling of shares and bonds could have depressed the stock exchange

[1] See the section on multinational companies in *Outline of international trade* p 143.

Table 10
Summary input-output transactions matrix, 1963 (millions of pounds)

purchases by / sales by		agri-culture, fores-try and fishing	coal min-ing	other min-ing and quarry-ing	food, drink and tob-acco	min-eral oil refin-ing	other chemi-cals and allied indus-tries	metal manu-fac-ture	engin-eering and allied indus-tries
		1	*2*	*3*	*4*	*5*	*6*	*7*	*8*
agriculture, forestry and fishing	*1*	–	5	–	571	–	–	–	–
coal mining	*2*	1	–	1	14	–	156	12	14
other mining and quarrying	*3*	–	–	–	3	2	9	14	15
food, drink and tobacco	*4*	*315*	–	–	–	–	35	–	–
mineral oil refining	*5*	20	1	1	10	–	80	21	21
other chemicals and allied industries	*6*	91	9	7	125	48	–	85	238
metal manufacture	*7*	–	48	–	5	–	26	–	1,143
engineering and allied industries	*8*	36	37	7	67	2	83	76	–
textiles, leather and clothing	*9*	4	8	–	13	–	14	2	86
other manufacturing	*10*	61	45	4	91	12	80	15	438
construction	*11*	30	18	–	13	–	11	8	33
gas, electricity and water	*12*	16	25	3	42	5	60	60	133
services	*13*	250	47	49	440	67	331	255	816
public administration, etc*	*14*	–	–	–	–	–	–	–	–
imports of goods and services	*15*	157	5	1	605	284	213	308	213
sales by final buyers to one another	*16*	–	–	–	3	–	2	62	24
goods and services *((1)* to *(16))*	*17*	981	248	73	2,002	420	1,100	918	3,174
taxes on expenditure *less* subsidies	*18*	–270	12	7	1,353	15	31	36	98
income from employment	*19*	353	535	47	*545*	25	387	501	2,759
gross profits and other trading income**	*20*	605	117	34	464	38	284	268	953
total input *((17)* to *(20))*	*21*	1,669	912	161	4,364	498	1,802	1,723	6,984

* Public administration and defence, public health and educational services, ownership of dwellings, domestic services to households and services to private non-profit-making bodies serving persons.

** Before providing for depreciation but after providing for stock appreciation.

Source: National income and expenditure London: HMSO 1966

tex-tiles, leather and cloth-ing	other manu-facturing	con-struction	gas, elec-tricity and water	ser-vices	public admin-istra-tion, etc*	total inter-mediate out-put ((1) to (14))	final buyers					total final out-put ((16) to (20))	total out-put ((15) plus (21))	
							current expenditure		gross domestic capital formation		ex-ports			
							per-sonal sector	public auth-orities	fixed	stocks				
9	*10*	*11*	*12*	*13*	*14*	*15*	*16*	*17*	*18*	*19*	*20*	*21*	*22*	
28	9	–	–	–	–	613	965	16	9	24	42	1,056	1,669	*1*
16	51	–	345	37	–	647	209	26	21	–23	32	265	912	*2*
–	44	47	–	7	–	141	–	–	–	–	20	20	161	*3*
2	3	–	–	101	–	456	3,584	43	–	55	226	3,908	4,364	*4*
7	19	21	32	52	–	285	67	27	8	2	109	213	498	*5*
26	145	111	22	161	–	1,068	262	109	–	–19	382	734	1,802	*6*
2	15	124	29	28	–	1,420	–	1	40	–27	289	303	1,723	*7*
25	100	182	70	683	–	1,368	867	817	1,753	137	2,042	5,616	6,984	*8*
–	104	8	–	87	–	326	1,076	25	–	13	438	1,552	1,878	*9*
16	–	417	25	832	–	2,036	692	75	42	11	308	1,128	3,164	*10*
7	14	–	8	117	–	259	400	303	2,141	32	15	2,891	3,150	*11*
35	83	9	–	236	–	707	680	81	131	–	4	896	1,603	*12*
159	492	247	161	–	–	3,314	6,726	748	450	1	1,667	9,592	12,906	*13*
–	–	–	–	–	–	–	1,430	2,741	–	–	–	4,171	4,171	*14*
463	441	150	18	781	–	3,639	1,689	163	276	17	176	2,321	5,960	*15*
3	3	2	–	35	–	134	31	–145	–87	–	67	–134	–	*16*
789	1,523	1,318	710	3,157	–	16,413	18,678	5,030	4,874	223	5,817	34,532	50,945	*17*
28	69	53	68	435	–	1,935	1,371	52	114	–	–	1,537	3,472	*18*
769	1,165	1,364	371	6,234	3,065	18,120	–	–	–	–	–	–	18,120	*19*
292	407	415	454	3,080†	1,106	8,517	–	–	–	–	–	–	8,517	*20*
1,878	3,164	3,150	1,603	12,906	4,171	44,985	20,049	5,082	4,898	223	5,817	36,069	81,054	*21*

Note: during the printing of this book, the statistical office has published input-output tables for the United Kingdom, 1968, *Studies in Official Statistics No. 22.* The new tables are 90 by 90 prices, so the handling of the situation required some delicacy.

With respect to total solvency, the United Kingdom and especially United States are in a very good position. In spite of the selling of enormous foreign investment by Britain to finance both world wars, the UK continues to hold about £2 billion worth foreign assets more than liabilities. The US net position kept rising until the crisis year of 1971, which will be discussed in chapter 7.

2.4 Foreign transactions in input-output tables[1]

Input-output tables were devised by Leontieff to give a picture of flows of goods and services between various industries (*inter-industry flows*) and other sectors of the economy. Reprinted in this section are two tables from the UK *National income and expenditure.* They refer to 1963; tables for a later year have not yet been calculated.

Columns 1-14 of table 10 indicate how much in value terms individual industries *buy from* other industries (rows 1 – 16) and how much they pay to the owners of labour (row 19) and of capital (row 20) and also in indirect taxes to the government (row 18). Rows 1 – 16 tell us how much various industries *sell to* other industries (columns 1 – 14) and how much of their product is used for personal consumption (column 16), collective consumption (column 17), gross domestic fixed capital (column 18), stock formation (column 19) and exports (column 20).

Imports of goods and services are entered in row 15, so the figures in this row tell us the import content of the production value of individual industries. For instance, the total production of the food, drink and tobacco industry is worth £4,364 million, which includes imports worth £605 million. This import content (see p 35) of the product of the food, drink and tobacco industry can be expressed also as a percentage as in table 11. There we find that imports participate with 18 per cent in the total output of this industry.

From columns 15 and 21 of table 10 we find that in 1963 a total of imports worth £3,639 million was used in production and £2,321 million as final output. But final output has to be split into consumption (£1,689 million personal and £163 million public), gross domestic capital formation, of which £276 million was fixed investment and £17 million in stocks, and £176 million worth of re-exports. These figures are important to the question of whether government controls can reduce imports more efficiently than general fiscal and monetary policy can. This question is dealt with on p 69, but it can be said immediately that, in so far as some inputs have to be imported, the curtailment of their import may prevent production altogether.

Of course, there is no simple answer to the question of what *must* be imported.

[1] See J N Robinson *Planning and forecasting techniques* (London: Weidenfeld and Nicolson 1972) for a basic treatment of the subjects referred to in this section.

Those goods and services that cannot be produced at home at all obviously have to be imported; on the other hand, if some goods and services cost more to produce at home than abroad, then home production of them will reduce the gain from trade. These aspects are treated in the companion volume.[1]

Unfortunately, table 10 does not give us any information about what happens if prices or exchange rates are altered. It is based on the assumption of constant domestic and world prices and existing exchange rates. Under this assumption, it tells us that at a total final output at factor prices of £34,532 million, the British economy will import goods and services worth £5,960 million, so that its average propensity to import (see p 60) is 17·4 per cent.

This does not even tell us what the *marginal* propensity to import would be. Nevertheless, input-output tables are often used to calculate, for instance, by how much imports would have to be raised if total final output rose by a certain percentage, or if the output of any industry rose by a given percentage. Of course, input-output tables make it possible to calculate not only the rise in direct requirements of imports by an industry that increases final production, but also the indirect requirements, that is requirements in imports of other industries that would have to increase their production in order to supply inputs required by the first industry. But these calculations are still based on the assumption that input relationships or *technical coefficients* do not change, which requires not only that prices do not change, but also that technology does not change either.

Column 20 in table 10 lists the value of exports contributed by individual industries under the existing conditions. However, we do not learn anything about what determines these figures, that is, primarily, the world demand at given prices and exchange rates, and the domestic supply elasticities. But the total figures for imports of goods and services, £5,960 million, and for exports of goods and services, £5,817 million, do give us the data from which to calculate the deficit on current account which should be matched by the corresponding figure in the balance of payments. There are no figures, however, on either long-term or short-term capital flows which could, *inter alia,* substantially influence exports and imports.

The table itself enables us to calculate changes in requirements if total output or parts of it change, provided everything else changes proportionately. However, if we wish to take account changes in prices, exchange rates and capital flows, these have to be assessed independently. This, of course, considerably limits the usefulness of calculations on the basis of input-output.

Another shortcoming is the need for aggregation. No input-output table can take account of the properties of all the millions of goods and services produced. Many

[1] *Outline of international trade p* 79.

Table 11
Total requirements per £100 of final industrial output in terms of net output, 1963* (pounds)

		agriculture, forestry and fishing	coal mining	other mining and quarrying
		1	*2*	*3*
agriculture, forestry and fishing	*1*	60	–	–
coal mining	*2*	1	73	1
other mining and quarrying	*3*	–	–	50
food, drink and tobacco	*4*	6	–	–
mineral oil refining	*5*	–	–	–
other chemicals and allied industries	*6*	3	1	2
metal manufacture	*7*	1	3	1
engineering and allied industries	*8*	3	3	4
textiles, leather and clothing	*9*	–	1	–
other manufacturing	*10*	4	3	3
construction	*11*	1	1	–
gas, electricity and water	*12*	1	2	2
services	*13*	16	7	25
imports of goods and services	*14*	19	4	6
taxes on expenditure *less* subsidies	*15*	–15	2	6
total	*16*	100	100	100

Source: National income and expenditure London: HMSO 1966

* Each entry represents the value of the net output (including depreciation) of the 'row' industry required to produce £100 of final output by the 'column' industry. The input-output coefficients have been derived from table 10.

food, drink and tobacco	mineral oil refining	other chemicals and allied industries	metal manufacture	engineering and allied industries	textiles, leather and clothing	other manufacturing	construction	gas, electricity and water	services
4	*5*	*6*	*7*	*8*	*9*	*10*	*11*	*12*	*13*
8	–	–	–	–	1	–	–	–	–
1	1	7	2	1	1	2	1	16	1
–	–	–	1	–	–	1	1	–	–
24	–	–	–	–	–	–	–	–	–
–	13	1	–	–	–	–	–	–	–
2	4	38	2	2	1	2	2	1	1
–	–	2	47	8	–	1	2	2	1
2	1	4	3	55	1	3	4	4	3
–	–	1		1	57	2	1	–	–
2	2	4	2	4	1	51	7	2	4
–	–	1	–	1	–	–	57	1	1
1	1	2	2	2	1	2	1	52	1
11	13	17	14	13	8	14	10	10	75
18	61	19	23	10	27	18	11	6	9
31	4	4	4	3	2	4	3	6	4
100	100	100	100	100	100	100	100	100	100

production lines have to be aggregated in one industry. There are rules about how to aggregate, but they are so stringent that they cannot possibly be taken into account when we construct tables of 22 columns by 21 rows or even 800 by 800, the largest table feasible so far. Because of aggregation, technical coefficients are averaged not only with respect to the size of output, but also over the production of many goods.

Input-output tables are the simplest version of linear programming.[1] A more complex version could take into account choice in consumption and choice of techniques and express them in terms of changing prices. But most deficiencies, particularly the need for aggregation, would still remain. Non-linear programming could overcome some of these deficiencies, but would make matters so complex that it would hardly be of any practical value.

In spite of all these qualifications, quantitative methods are used in international economics, although on a rather rough and ready basis, to estimate import and export demand relationships, to measure elasticity of substitution in international trade, to estimate international capital movements, to measure trade dependence and interdependence, to analyse export growth on the basis of constant market-shares and to estimate the welfare effects of trade liberalization.[2] There are also more ambitious econometric models and the IMF has even constructed a model for the calculation of equilibrium exchange rates (see p 112).

[1] See *Outline of international trade,* p 38.

[2] Cf E E Leamer and R M Stern *Quantitative international economics* Boston: Allyn and Bacon 1970.

further reading

'The balance of payments: methods of presentation' *Bank of England quarterly bulletin* (1964)

B J Cohen — *Balance-of-payments policy* Harmondsworth: Penguin 1969

IMF — *Balance of payments concepts and definitions* Washington DC: IMF Pamphlet Series No 10, second edition 1969

W Lederer — *The balance of foreign transactions: problems of definition and measurement* Princeton: International Finance Section 1963

'Which balance of payments' *Westminster Bank review* (1965)

Some sources of data on foreign transactions and investment

United Kingdom

Trade and industry published by Department of Trade and Industry HMSO, weekly. Contains *inter alia* overseas trade value (monthly), unit value and volume indices (monthly), balance of payments (quarterly)

Financial statistics published by Central Statistical Office HMSO, monthly. Contains balance of payments, UK account with IMF, exchange rates, etc

Overseas trade statistics in UK published by Department of Trade and Industry/HMSO, quarterly. Contains detailed trade statistics

Economic trends published by the Central Statistical Office/HMSO, monthly. Contains *inter alia* an analysis of the quarterly balance of payments at the end of the following quarter in March, June, September and December

UK balance of payments published by Central Statistical Office/HMSO, yearly in October. Contains detailed balance-of-payments statistics

Bank of England quarterly bulletin publishes yearly, in June or September, the UK external assets and liabilities

United States

Federal reserve bulletin published by the Board of Governors of the Federal Reserve System, monthly. Contains *inter alia* balance of payments, exchange rates, gold reserves, gold production in the world

Survey of current business published by the US Department of Commerce, monthly. The October issue contains the US international investment position

International

Yearbook of international trade statistics Statistical Office of the United Nations

International financial statistics International Monetary Fund, monthly.

Balance of payments yearbook International Monetary Fund, supplied monthly in loose leaves.

chapter 3
international economic equilibrium

3.1 Elements in international equilibrium

After the survey of various definitions of a balance-of-payments deficit (or surplus) in a country's external accounts, the question arises: what changes in the economies participating in international economic activities lead to such imbalances? It must be pointed out again that the imbalances take the form of deficits or surpluses only when exchange rates are fixed, as they usually[1] are under the present international monetary system, while with completely flexible exchange rates any changes in the balances will be reflected in alterations of these exchange rates themselves. Deficits and surpluses are the obverse sides of the same situation since one country's deficit must be another country's surplus, so that the answers to the two sides of the question are connected and run in opposite direction.

The international economy consists of national economies linked through exchange rates which used to be fixed. Therefore, any change in any of the circumstances determining supply and demand curves can disturb the international equilibrium to some extent as it does the internal equilibrium (see p 45). But as detailed changes tend to offset each other, the magnitudes that in most instances have to be aligned in order for the international system to be in equilibrium are of an aggregate nature. The average price/cost and activity levels of a country appear to be linked to the world price/cost and activity levels (as a synthesis of average price/cost and activity levels of all other countries) through the exchange rate:

domestic price/cost level
(domestic productivity)
domestic activity level
↕
exchange rate
↕
world price/cost level
(world productivity)
world activity level

[1] See chapter 7 for a description of the complexity of the present situation caused by *ad hoc* changes in the system.

In a way, this simple model of international equilibrium deals only with surface symptoms. It is possible to go deeper and indicate on what price/cost levels depend. Thus Joan Robinson says:

> In any given situation, there is an equilibrium [exchange] rate corresponding to each rate of interest and level of effective demand, and any rate of exchange, within very wide limits, can be turned into the equilibrium rate by altering the rate of interest appropriately. Moreover, any rate of exchange can be made compatible with any rate of interest provided the money wages can be sufficiently altered.[1]

Mrs Robinson links the exchange rate, interest rate, level of effective demand and money wages. Two of these magnitudes are the same as in the simple model. Money wages are the most important part of costs and, related to product units, also embrace productivity. The interest rate however can be looked at from three aspects: as a part of costs, as determining the domestic money supply and demand, and as determining international capital movements. International capital movements have been assumed away in our simple equilibrium model. They will be brought back into the picture later (see pp 48 and 87). In so far as the interest rate is a part of costs it will co-determine their level, while as the determinant of money supply and demand it will co-determine prices and wages. In this way, we return to the simple model after taking notice of some deeper influences on the aggregates included in it.

Returning to the model which simply features the price-cost relationship as a single element, one has to remind oneself that one of the effects of international trade is the equalization (or at least a tendency to equalization) of commodity prices.[2] For this reason it would seem impossible for the internal prices of goods and services that enter international exchanges substantially to differ from the world price level, if transport costs and trade barriers are disregarded. Prices of international goods[3] remain closely aligned with world prices; the alignment of prices of quasi-international goods will be less close, but their variation is limited. Domestic goods and services are not exposed to international competition, so their prices can move freely. These domestic prices, therefore, reflect the disequilibrium, but as particular prices of domestic services vary from country to country anyway (see p 109) it is impossible to disentangle to what extent their level is a consequence of disequilibrium and to what extent it is the result of other causes.

Thus the price level of domestic goods and services is a bad indication of what the external equilibrium situation is, but the average price level of both domestic and

[1] J Robinson 'The foreign exchanges' in Ellis and Metzler (eds) *Readings in the theory of international trade* p 00.

[2] See *Outline of international trade* p 79.

[3] See *Outline of international trade* p 16.

traded goods serves this purpose even less well. Nevertheless, price levels are often referred to when equilibrium is discussed. As an abbreviation so to speak, it is said that an increase in the average price level of a country leads to international imbalance if world prices remain the same.

What happens in reality is more complex. If domestic prices begin to rise because of excessive demand, the prices of traded goods will soon come under pressure because of foreign competition and will not be able to rise further. The prices of non-traded goods will however increase without hindrance from abroad and even rise further because of the lagging behind of prices of traded goods. The rising prices will give firms producing non-traded goods higher profits, so they will expand and also raise their wages. In all probability their wage increases will spread, on the basis of wage parity, to the trade sector, where the prices cannot rise. Therefore the marginal firms may run into difficulties and close down, dismissing workers. Some of these workers may find employment in the booming non-traded goods sector but others may not. This is of course not Keynesian unemployment, but structural unemployment. One could almost call it quasi-structural unemployment, as it is the result not of genuine structural changes, but of the fact that, given the exchange rate, domestic and world prices are out of gear.

The unfortunate consequences of a tendency of domestic prices to rise, in particular quasi-structural unemployment, appear even faster if the reason for price increases are rising costs, especially wages. Changes in price-cost relationships are especially relevant in this context.

When costs rise for exogenous reasons, they reduce even sooner the profit margins on international and quasi-international goods that are exposed to international competition, so that eventually their output has to contract. Their exports diminish or competing imports increase, depending on the initial situation. As pointed out, prices of domestic goods rise without hindrance from foreign competition. In this way, they influence the cost of living and may contribute to further demands for higher wages, that is to a further increase in costs (see further, p 71).

Of course, costs have to be considered with respect to units of production. Factor rewards can increase if productivity is simultaneously increasing. It has to be kept in mind however that wage and salary rises in manufacturing, where according to the experience of the recent years productivity increases are concentrated, spread to other sectors under the influence of comparability: the tendency that jobs requiring similar qualifications command comparable pay. Therefore, increases in wages in step with productivity changes in individual enterprises may still lead to a rise in the average cost level.

3.2 Transitional and fundamental disequilibria

If as a result of a disequilibrium a deficit develops in a country's external accounts, it has to be financed. The source of financing is the gold and currency reserves of the country plus the foreign currency holdings of its private firms and residents and the willingness of foreigners to extend credits to them.

These sources of financing are not unlimited and it is therefore important to distinguish between *transitional* disequilibria, which are merely temporary and may even reverse themselves, and *fundamental* disequilibria, which are continuous and may be progressively deteriorating.

Transitional deficits have causes that do not last, for example bad harvests or strikes. They are only a limited drain on the source of financing and it can be hoped that some change working in the opposite direction will again replenish the reduced reserves and holdings.

If the cause is reversible, as are all causes connected with internal cyclical movements of the economy, then the balance of payments will pass from a deficit to a surplus and back to a deficit and a new surplus, so that a drain on the financing resources will alternate with their replenishment. Increases in stocks or inventories, for instance, lead to the stepping-up of imports but later make it possible for imports to be reduced when firms decide to use material from the stocks and reduce them to their normal volume.

It is difficult to determine whether a deficit is transitional or fundamental, in the terminology of the IMF, without looking at a series of figures. If the position has been deteriorating over some years, the conclusion must be that the balance-of-payments deficit is fundamental. But it must be stressed that a fundamental disequilibrium can come about only if adjustment mechanisms are not allowed to work. What this means will be explained in detail at the end of this and in later chapters, but it has to be said here that there is at least a tendency for any deficit to trigger off one or more adjustment mechanisms. Governments however, can, prevent these mechanisms from working.

The UK balance of payments in the 1950s and 1960s is a case in point. Looking at the summary of this balance for 1952–67, we find that the peaks of surpluses were £95, £215 and £89 million; the peaks of deficits £156, £158 and £728 million. Also, while in earlier years surpluses of two or three years' duration alternated with deficits of the same duration, the deficit that had set in in 1963 did not reverse itself into a surplus but only into a lower deficit and then began deteriorating again. This was an indication that the British deficit was fundamental and that in 1967 corrective action had to be taken to bring about adjustment (see figure 1 and table 12).

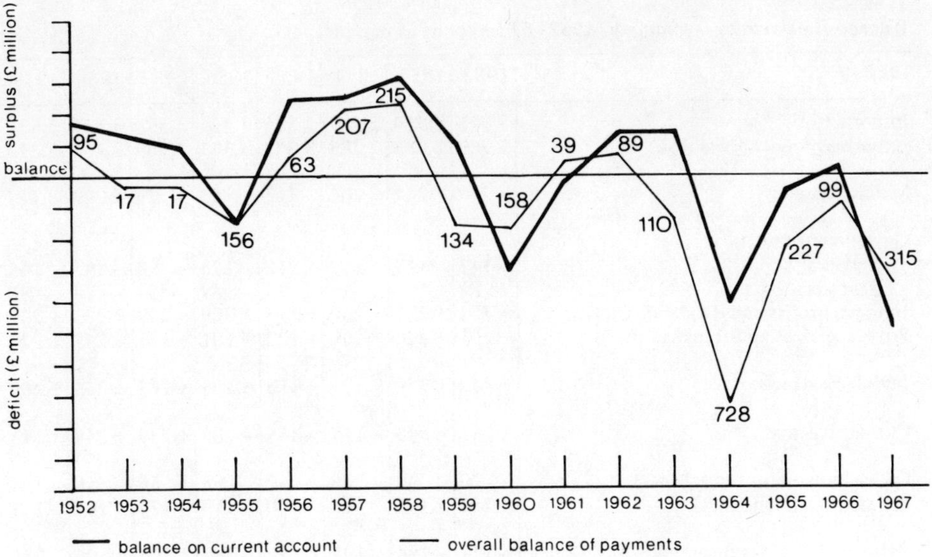

figure 1. UK balance-of-payments deficits and surpluses, 1952-67

3.3 Causes of fundamental disequilibria

It was mentioned at the beginning of this chapter that when the system is initially in equilibrium any change in the circumstances that determine supply and demand can disturb the balance, but that such changes normally tend to offset each other. However, if this offsetting does not occur a serious foreign trade disturbance may develop. This is particularly true if a country's foreign trade is largely dependent on one commodity or on a limited number of commodities. In such a case a shift in the international demand for that commodity, or the appearance of a new competitive supplier, can plunge the country in a fundamental disequilibrium. Changes in the circumstances determining demand and supply are called structural changes.

In the modern world the economies are never at rest; underlying circumstances such as tastes, factor quantities, and technology, and with them costs and prices, continue to change, so that every economy must be very flexible. It must be ready to abandon some lines of production and switch to others or to alter techniques. If it does not, it is overtaken by events: it becomes saddled with declining industries and finds it more and more difficult to pay for imports. *Structural deficiencies* can thus become a cause of continuous and even progressive external imbalance.

Changes in economic aggregates are more obvious causes of fundamental disequilibria.

Table 12
Balance-of-payments – summary, 1952–67 (millions of pounds)

1952–9	1952	1953	1954	1955	1956	1957	1958	1959
Imports (fob)	3,048	2,927	2,989	3,386	3,324	3,538	3,377	3,639
Exports and re-exports (fob)	2,769	2,683	2,785	3,073	3,377	3,509	3,406	3,522
Visible balance	−279	−244	−204	−313	+ 53	− 29	+ 29	−117
Government (net):								
Services	−147	−119	−112	−115	−128	− 90	−145	−145
Transfers	+ 86	+ 53	− 19	− 23	− 47	− 54	− 74	− 82
Interest, profits and dividends (net)	+ 252	+ 229	+ 250	+ 174	+ 229	+ 249	+ 293	+ 260
Private services and transfers (net)	+ 251	+ 226	+ 202	+ 122	+ 101	+ 157	+ 241	+ 227
Invisible balance	+ 442	+ 389	+ 321	+ 158	+ 155	+ 262	+ 315	+ 260
Current balance	+ 163	+ 145	+ 117	−155	+ 208	+ 233	+ 344	+ 143
Official long-term capital (net)	− 20	− 49	− 28	− 62	− 68	+ 66	− 50	−124
Private investment (net)	−114	−145	−163	− 60	−119	−172	−146	−131
Balance of long-term capital	−134	−194	−191	−122	−187	−106	−196	−255
Balance of current and long-term capital transactions	+ 29	− 49	− 74	−277	+ 21	+ 127	+ 148	−112
Balancing item	+ 66	+ 32	+ 57	+ 121	+ 42	+ 80	+ 67	− 22
Balance of monetary movements[1]	− 95	+ 17	+ 17	+ 156	− 63	−207	−215	+ 134

1960–7	1960	1961	1962	1963	1964	1965	1966	1967
Imports (fob)[2]	4,138	4,043	4,095	4,362	5,001	5,037	5,203	5,562
Exports and re-exports (fob)	3,732	3,891	3,993	4,282	4,466	4,777	5,108	5,023
Visible trade balance[2]	−406	−152	−102	− 80	−535	−260	− 95	−539
Payments for US military aircraft	–	–	–	–	− 2	− 12	− 41	− 98
Visible balance[3]	−406	−152	−102	− 80	−537	−272	−136	−637
Government (net):								
Services	−188	−214	−239	−250	−269	−270	−282	−269
Transfers	− 94	−118	−121	−132	−163	−177	−179	−184
Interest, profits and dividends (net)	+ 231	+ 252	+ 333	+ 394	+ 413	+ 470	+ 422	+ 410
Private services and transfers (net)	+ 192	+ 228	+ 241	+ 179	+ 157	+ 158	+ 190	+ 276
Invisible balance	+ 141	+ 148	+ 214	+ 191	+ 138	+ 181	+ 151	+ 233
Current balance	−265	− 4	+ 112	+ 111	−399	− 91	+ 15	−404

Table 12 *(continued)*

1960-7	1960	1961	1962	1963	1964	1965	1966	1967
Official long-term capital								
Loans from Export-Import Bank (net)	–	–	–	–	–	–	+ 51	+ 76
Other (net)	–103	– 45	–104	–105	–116	– 86	–132	–133
Private investment (net)	– 89	+ 113	+ 6	– 43	–254	–117	– 23	– 29
Balance of long-term capital[1]	–192	+ 68	– 98	–148	–370	–203	–104	– 86
Balance of current and long-term capital transactions	–457	+ 64	+ 14	– 37	–769	– 294	– 89	–490
Balancing item	+ 299	– 25	+ 75	– 73	+ 41	+ 67	– 10	+ 175
Balance of monetary movements[1]	+ 158	– 39	– 89	+ 110	+ 728	+ 227	+ 99	+ 315

[1] Assets: increase –/decrease +. Liabilities: increase +/decrease –.
[2] Excluding US military aircraft and missiles.
[3] Including payments for US military aircraft and missiles.

Source: UK balance of payments HMSO 1968

Inflation, both of demand-pull and cost-push variety, produces a tendency towards external imbalance. But any rate of inflation has this effect only if there is no inflation elsewhere. If on the other hand inflationary tendencies prevail everywhere, those countries with higher *differential rates of inflation* than the rest are apt to develop a balance-of-payments deficit of a permanent nature.

The usual explanation is that their price level is rising faster than in other countries and that this makes them less competitive. But as pointed out previously, the possibilities for a rise in the prices of traded goods are narrowly circumscribed, so that higher rates of inflation will show mainly in the prices of non-traded goods and in the cost level. The rising cost level makes unprofitable the production of marginal output in export- and import-competing industries or, in the best case, prevents the further expansion of these production lines. Investment and managerial talent are shifted towards the more profitable output of non-traded goods and services. Again the result is a fundamental disequilibrium.

However, even in the absence of inflation, *different rates of real growth* in different countries can lead to external disequilibrium, provided growth is expressed in rising incomes and constant prices, as opposed to constant incomes and falling prices.

The simplest case is a situation in which one country grows and the rest of the world stagnates. Out of the growing incomes, a part (depending on the propensity to import – see p 60) is spent on additional imports. These imports should be paid for by exports, but the other countries have not grown, their incomes have not increased and therefore their demand for imports has not risen, so that the growing country will not be able to sell its exports. The result will be a balance-of-payments deficit. Strictly speaking, the growing country will be hard put to obtain its imports since the other countries have not been growing and thus cannot increase their exports at constant prices. They will have to be enticed to do so by the offer of higher prices for their exports. But more exports at higher prices will increase their demand for imports from the growing country. Thus a disequilibrium will only develop if, at constant prices, the additional exports of the growing country are not sufficiently attractive. The disequilibrium will be fundamental if prices in the growing country are inflexible downward, as is often the case at present. Prices can be reduced if incomes increase more slowly than productivity; or if the increases in productivity are particularly large in the export sector, while incomes in this sector rise only in proportion with the average rise in productivity of the country.

The situation becomes more complicated if it is assumed that all countries grow, but some faster than others. In such a case it is not the growth rate itself that is decisive but the *growth rate of demand for imports,* which is determined by the growth rate multiplied by the propensity to import. The country with the highest increase in the demand for imports may find itself in external difficulties even if its rate of GNP growth is not the highest.

A special case of 'real growth' occurs if a country's economy moves from a lower to a higher level of employment. This rise also steps up the demand for imports, but the chances are that other countries have some degree of unemployment too; that is, some of their capacities are idle. Therefore increased demand for their exports will move them towards a higher employment level so that their demand for imports will augment in turn and the external disequilibrium will not ensue, even without price changes. Changes in employment tend in any case to be cyclical and will thus not lead to fundamental disequilibria.

The discussion of the next possible cause of fundamental disequilibrium has to be conducted in terms of the link between the balance of payments and the balance of external assets and liabilities. If for any reason the authorities or resident firms and individuals of a country decide to invest abroad, domestic purchasing power will pass into foreign hands. As a consequence either foreigners will hold more domestic currency or some foreign currency held by residents will be returned to foreigners. The net balance of foreign assets and liabilities will not be altered, but the composition of the country's foreign assets and liabilities will change. A parallel development occurs if foreigners withdraw their investment from the country.

If new investment abroad is short-term, made to profit from higher foreign short-term interest rates or from the possibility of an increase in the price of foreign currency (changes in the exchange rate), this movement does not show as a change in the net liquidity position or, in fact, as a balance-of-payments deficit. But private short-term investment abroad will draw down official short-term foreign assets and thus affect the balance of payments defined on the basis of official reserve transactions. If short-term funds are flowing abroad in response to normal changes in short-term interest rates, the movement is cyclical and should not create fundamental balance-of-payments difficulties. If it is a consequence of speculation regarding a change of the exchange rate, it can and does become a fundamental problem, or rather it intensifies a fundamental problem resulting from some other part of the balance-of-payments.

Long-term capital investment flows to the countries with a high marginal efficiency of capital, or moves to escape unsettled political conditions in the home country. The conditions that have to be fulfilled in order to prevent a fundamental disequilibrium as a consequence of such an outflow are treated under the heading of the *transfer problem* (see p 87). But under present economic circumstances these conditions often do not obtain, so that a fundamental disequilibrium will ensue if the capital outflow continues over a few years, which can happen if a part of savings is invested abroad year after year. On the other hand, if the foreign investment decision is a once-for-all stock decision, that is a decision to substitute foreign long-term assets for domestic short-term assets, the resulting deficit is inherently temporary. At any rate, a balance-of-payments deficit caused by investment abroad is of a different kind from a deficit caused by excessive current consumption in so far as, in the first case, foreign assets of the country increase and will even provide new earnings from abroad given time, while in the second case, short-term assets are used to pay for current consumption; that is, dissaving is involved. However, in spite of its long-term benefits, investment abroad can create balance-of-payments difficulties.

Government and private transfers abroad, handing over purchasing power to foreign residents or governments without repayment or current earnings, create similar problems to investment abroad but without its advantages.

Finally, external disequilibrium can develop because a government changes the legal framework of foreign transactions, either unilaterally or in agreement with other governments. For instance an agreed reduction of tariffs, such as in the Kennedy Round, will tend to increase the demand for imports in the previously higher-tariff countries, *ceteris paribus,* by more than in the originally lower-tariff countries. Any relaxation of government foreign trade rules may work in this way.

In summary, fundamental disequilibria can be caused by structural deficiencies, differential rates of inflation, differential growth rates, long-term investment and other capital transfers abroad, and by changes in government rules affecting foreign transactions. These reasons can work in different directions and partly cancel each other out. As pointed out, any of these occurrences will trigger off an adjustment mechanism.

but these mechanisms may not be allowed to work under the present conditions of inflexibility of commodity and factor prices downwards or even rising factor prices regardless of economic circumstances.

3.4 Fundamental disequilibria and internal money supply

Whatever the original cause of a balance-of-payments deficit, it will be connected with an outflow of purchasing power because purchases of goods or investment abroad have to be paid for; if they are supplied on credit this credit will finally have to be repaid. Johnson[1] expresses this necessity as an excess of foreign payments over foreign receipts:

$$B = R_f - P_f$$

where B is the balance of payments, R_f foreign receipts and P_f foreign payments. If foreign payments exceed foreign receipts the balance will be negative, meaning that there will be a balance-of-payments deficit. But since domestic receipts are by definition equal to domestic payments, the balance of payments is also equal to the difference between total receipts and total payments of a country:

$$B = R - P$$

provided receipts and payments of the monetary authority in exchange for gold and currency reserves are not considered as domestic receipts or payments but as cancelling and creating domestic money.

Thus a deficit means that some domestic money is used for purchases abroad. If foreigners are prepared to accept domestic money in payment of their claims, some domestic money will pass into foreign hands and will in this way be taken out of domestic circulation. If the foreigners are not prepared to accept domestic money, it will have to be converted into foreign currency, which means that either private holdings of foreign currency will be drawn down or that the monetary authorities will have to intervene in the exchange market, and that their gold and monetary reserves will be reduced while they acquire domestic currency. This last event takes money out of circulation provided the monetary authorities do not automatically put it back into the hands of the public. Thus the British monetary authority automatically relend any domestic money acquired in exchange for gold and monetary reserves. If this is the arrangement (cf. p 91), the domestic economy is insulated and the adjustment mechanism does not work. If, instead of official reserves, private holdings of foreign currency are drawn down, the liquidity of the domestic economic system is

[1] H G Johnson 'Towards a general theory of the balance of payments' in *International trade and economic growth* London: Allen and Unwin 1965, reprinted in R N Cooper (ed), *International finance*

also reduced, in particular since foreign currency holdings are mostly in the hands of banks, and monetary authorities always stand ready to convert foreign currency into domestic money, so that foreign currency holdings supplement domestic cash.

The consequence is that cash balances in the hands of residents are reduced and a moment comes when the remaining cash balances will only just satisfy their liquidity preference, so that they are no longer prepared to part with more cash to pay for foreign purchases. Thus, while in the first instance a balance-of-payments deficit can be fed by dishoarding, the willingness to dishoard eventually comes to an end and therefore the balance-of-payments deficit also has to stop.

The only possibility for the balance-of-payments deficit, whatever its origin, to continue indefinitely is the policy of monetary authorities' allowing domestic credit expansion. For this reason Johnson claims that a balance-of-payments deficit is *essentially a monetary phenomenon.* It can come about only if the velocity of circulation increases (dishoarding) or if the supply of money is maintained regardless of its outflow (credit creation). Since there are limits to the speeding up of velocity, a fundamental disequilibrium can be only a consequence of credit expansion, that is, the maintenance or even increase in the supply of money by the monetary authorities.

Looking back at section 3.3, we find that these 'real causes' could not produce a continuous disequilibrium without the connivance of the authorities. In the case of inflation, this seems self-evident. With real growth, the outflow of purchasing power would lead to a situation where growth would be expressed partly in rising incomes and partly in falling prices, which would be enough to make additional exports flow abroad. The prices of export goods would have to fall sufficiently to match the value of increased exports at lower prices with the value of increased imports at higher prices. Without an increase in the supply of money, the conditions for making goods follow the export of capital would be satisfied, so that a balance-of-payments problem would not arise (cf. p 107).

If the deficit is caused by structural changes, the authorities' refusal to replace the outflow of money by an expansion of credit is also bound to restore external equilibrium at some level. The revival of foreign transactions will depend on the adjustment of production to the changed demand or to the more efficient production methods of competitors. A similar development wipes out the balance-of-payments deficit following an alteration of the government legal framework, for example a reduction of tariffs, provided the authorities do not maintain the money supply.

Johnson concludes that the problem of external disequilibrium 'is associated fundamentally with the power of national banking systems to create money which has no internationally acceptable backing'. If this is true, why do countries not keep in external balance by appropriate monetary policies?

3.5 Multiple economic goals

The reason is that balance-of-payments equilibrium is only one of the goals of governments. An OECD (Organization for Economic Co-operation and Development) Report[1] states:

> Each country seeks to achieve a number of economic and social objectives, including full employment and a satisfactory rate of growth, reasonable price stability and an equitable distribution of income, and balanced regional and sectoral development.

Some or even all of these goals can be in contradiction with the aim of external equilibrium.

In particular, full employment, or as the OECD Convention formulates it 'the highest sustainable employment', as the predominant aim may work directly against the balance in foreign operations. This has not always been the case. Before the First World War, the main economic concern of governments was the stability of their currencies in terms of other currencies. The internal money supply had to serve this purpose, so that deflation followed inflation and vice versa, all in order to maintain the external equilibrium. Commodity and factor prices fluctuated in accordance with the needs of external balance. Their movements did cause unemployment every now and then, but this was thought to be a necessary concomitant of adjustment and to be only temporary, since changes in commodity and factor prices were bound to re-establish the internal full-employment balance at some level.

Between the two wars however, conditions changed. The number of independent entrepreneurs, particularly farmers and artisans, diminished and the number of employees increased. While independent owners had to accept a decrease in their money incomes if prices fell, since there was nothing to cushion them from the market, employees, especially after they had organized themselves in trade unions, could refuse to allow their pay to be lowered when there was pressure on prices in the market[2]. As a consequence the brunt of the situation had to be born, in the first instance, by ever larger enterprises, which cannot reduce their prices because they cannot reduce their costs. This rigidity may have been strengthened further by full-cost pricing, the habit of larger firms to calculate their prices simply by adding a customary profit margin to the total costs, instead of adjusting prices in response to the market pressures.

[1] OECD *The balance-of-payments adjustment process* no 3 Paris 1966 p 9.

[2] This passage should not be interpreted as claiming that reducing wages is sufficient to bring the economy back to full employment. Axel Leijonhufvud, for instance, describes in his *Keynes and the Classics* (London 1971 p 35) how a breakdown of communications may keep the system in an unemployment state although the money wage is 'right' from the standpoint of overall equilibrium.

Thus a shrinking money supply no longer brings about a fall in commodity and factor prices to a new external equilibrium level, but rather a deficiency in effective demand at constant prices. The consequence of such a deficiency is a fall in employment. Through industrialization and concentration almost everybody has become an employee and the proportion of people endangered by unemployment is very high. Therefore, it has become an accepted rule, especially since Keynes explained the nature of the connection between full employment and effective demand, that the government will rekindle effective demand as soon as the employment rate exceeds a given low percentage of the labour force. Rekindling of effective demand requires financing which means monetary expansion.[1]

Therefore, the outflow of money caused by a balance-of-payments deficit no longer serves to reduce the domestic money supply, and consequently cash balances, to a level at which residents are not prepared to part with more of their liquidity. Since reduction in wages is resisted, for the authorities to allow a reduction in money supply would be equivalent to allowing unemployment. The effect of the outflow of purchasing power is therefore usually countered by new injections of money, so that the deficit can continue.

Moreover, since the Second World War another aim prominent in the minds of both government and governed has been 'the highest sustainable growth'. Some economists and policy-makers believe that growth can be fostered by a degree of inflation, and one result of so much stress on growth has been that the population expects, as of right, the yearly distribution of the fruit of increased productivity in the form of higher incomes, regardless of whether growth in output per head has actually been achieved or not. In addition, the pressure for higher money wages (real wages depend on the actual increase in productivity) is stronger the lower the level of unemployment: a relationship expressed in the so-called Phillips curve.[2] Thus the more successful the authorities are in running the economy at full speed, the greater will be the pressure for rises in wages. Of late, the situation has become so entangled that even in periods of falling output and increasing unemployment the inflationary pressure on wages remains.

Although the behavioural patterns described are widespread, there remain differences in their intensity. The demand for periodical increases in wages is stronger in some countries than in others where either the connection between wages and productivity

[1] See D Croome and J N Robinson *Understanding the economy: an introduction to macro-economic theory* Weidenfeld and Nicolson 1972.

[2] See ibid chapter 8 and A W Phillips 'The relation between unemployment and the rate of change of money wage rates in the United Kingdom (1861–1957) *Economica* vol 25 1958. reprinted in R J Ball and P Doyle *Inflation* Harmondsworth: Penguin 1969.

is better understood or wage demands are better restrained by some kind of incomes policy. The acceptable rates of inflation also vary from country to country: the rate of inflation needed for the normal functioning of one economy may be considered disruptive in another. Thus there are differential rates of inflation with consequential balance-of-payments difficulties.

The multitude of government aims and the conflict between them has led to a situation in which monetary policy is subordinated to the internal goals of full employment and growth. In many respects the internal economic situation has been cut off from external economic developments. But real divorce between them is not feasible under a system of fixed exchange rates. Sooner or later, the external imbalance catches up with the economic authorities of the country and confronts them with the need to find a solution. That is what has been happening over the last few years and has precipitated one 'crisis' after another, as will be described in chapters 6 and 7.

further reading

H G Johnson	'Towards a general theory of the balance of payments' *International trade and economic growth* London: Allen and Unwin 1965, also in Cooper *International finance* p 50
F Lutz	*The problem of international economic equilibrium* Amsterdam: North Holland 1962
OECD	*The balance of payments adjustment process* Paris: OECD 1966
J Robinson	'The foreign exchanges' Ellis and Metzler *Readings in the theory of international trade*
T Scitovsky	*Money and the balance of payments* London: Allen and Unwin 1969.

chapter 4

international adjustment processes

4.1 Financing

Strictly speaking, financing a balance-of-payments deficit is not an adjustment process, but a holding operation which makes it possible for the actual adjustment to be postponed. In a wider sense, financing can be described as any movement of short-term funds qualifying as accommodating (see p 17); in a narrow sense, as the use of gold and foreign exchange reserves that the government of a country in balance-of-payments deficit either owns or borrows from the International Monetary Fund or the appropriate authorities of another country. Under the system of fixed exchange rates, this financing takes the form of the government selling or buying foreign currency, *intervention currency,* in order to maintain the exchange rate within the prescribed limits. Possibly, one could also term 'financing' the intervention of the government in foreign exchange markets under freely fluctuating exchange rates when the government is trying to iron out short-term fluctuations of the rate.

If the balance-of-payments deficit is cyclical or temporary (see p 44) financing may be all that is required. But if it is fundamental, then financing is only a temporary expedient and something more is required to put things right again. Financing cannot continue indefinitely, as the deficit country is bound to run out of owned reserves and to exhaust the borrowed reserves to which it is entitled from the International Monetary Fund or which other countries are prepared to put at its disposal.

Financing cannot continue indefinitely from the viewpoint of surplus countries, either, although their situation of course is much easier. A surplus country accumulates short-term claims against a deficit country. The deficit country pays its debts in dollars, or pounds, or SDRs and then the whole question of international liquidity and of confidence in such liquidity appears (see p 142). If the deficit country is a *key currency country* (see p 128), Britain or the United States, the short-term claims have the form of sterling or dollar balances from the beginning, and when the imbalance continues over years, as it did in the 1960s, the claims become of an ever worse quality. The claims are bad because as they increase it becomes less and less probable that the deficit country will be able to honour its debts without changing its exchange rate, which would mean reducing their value in terms of other currencies when the debts are denominated in the deficit country's currency. Accumulation of claims also means that the surplus country is using its savings to lend to another country instead of perhaps investing them itself more profitably.[1]

As long as interest is paid on short-term debts, there is some kind of compensation for this loss of a country's own investment. Hence, the alternative of an excessive accumulation of gold in a surplus country is not a rational policy. Gold does not bring in any returns unless its price is raised, as it is commodity money and not an interest-yielding asset. Therefore the amount of gold, or for that matter any other kind of reserve a country holds, should be the minimum required for financial solvency.

If, as in many cases, more is required for a solution then merely financing, why do governments persist in applying this temporary remedy? Because they are usually pursuing other economic goals (see p 52) and the automatic working or deliberate use of adjustment mechanisms could interfere with this pursuit. Governments even attempt to give themselves more latitude in this respect by schemes to increase international liquidity (see p 139). But adjustment is finally required if there is a persistent deficit or surplus.

4.2 Adjustment mechanisms

If international imbalance means that domestic price/cost level and income/activity level are out of line with the world price/cost and activity levels as connected to them through the exchange rate (see p 41), it follows that balance can be re-established by bringing precisely these levels back into line, by changing them, or by changing the exchange rate. If the government is deliberately working the mechanisms, it can on the whole influence only the domestic values, while the spontaneous functioning of adjustment mechanisms has effects on both domestic levels and on levels in all other countries.

The main adjustment mechanisms are then: the price–specie flow mechanism, the income change mechanism and the exchange rate change mechanism. The last mechanism works automatically if foreign currency is freely sold and bought in the exchange market and it is worked deliberately, as a policy measure, if the government fixes a new parity. The other two mechanisms both work automatically under the influence of inflows and outflows of purchasing power if the government takes a passive role, and are operated by fiscal and monetary policies if the government deliberately uses them as its policy. Which of the two mechanisms or what mixture of the

[1] Johnson calls reserves 'low-yield or negative-yield loans to foreigners' and adds that inflation is an implied 'tax on reserve-holding'. H G Johnson *'Inflation and the monetarist controversy'* Amsterdam: North Holland 1972 pp 25-6 and 87.

two mechanisms works depends on the degree of flexibility of commodity and factor prices.

The three mechanisms mentioned above all function by changing the signals the economy provides for the decisions of individual firms. The government can overrule such signals by directly telling the firms what to do or by altering the signals. In this way government orders or controls can also act as an adjustment mechanism of sorts, but they act either by transferring at least a part of economic decisions from the firms to the government (for example, by ordering a limitation of imports regardless of profitability) or by making imports more expensive by imposing taxes and exports cheaper by paying subsidies.

Since prices are per unit of commodity and costs per unit of factor, the relationship between prices and costs per unit of commodity depends also on factor productivity. Thus if international imbalance occurs because domestic costs are rising, while prices cannot rise because of international competition (see p 42), adjustment could be also brought about by improved productivity. However, productivity changes are not considered an adjustment mechanism because productivity cannot be changed at will and in a short time. It has to be assumed that productivity is whatever it is because people do their best under the impact of competition and their wish to have maximum incomes. Of course there is always some scope for improving productivity with greater effort, but this limited possibility can hardly be considered a normal way of adjustment although it can help the normal adjustment processes if it comes about.

a *price–specie flow mechanism*

This mechanism is usually associated with the gold standard, but it works with any kind of transmittable purchasing power provided prices are flexible. It was described as early as 1752 by David Hume in the essay entitled 'Of the balance of payments'.[1] Assume that there are two countries with no mobility of labour and other factors of production between them and that they both use the same gold coins as means of payment, a situation which actually existed in the past. If the prices are such that one country will buy more from the other than vice versa, a flow of gold coins will follow and the country with an export surplus will increase its money supply. The result will be a rise in its prices, while the prices in the country losing gold will fall. Of course, this smacks of the quantity theory of money, but it can hardly be doubted that an increasing supply of money finally leads to a rise in prices, albeit maybe not a proportionate one, and that a decreasing supply of money, in the end, brings down either prices or employment if prices of commodities and factors are inflexible downwards.

[1] Reprinted in R N Cooper (ed) *International finance* Harmondsworth: Penguin 1965.

This is the simplest kind of price–specie flow mechanism (specie meaning precious metal). A more complicated form will be described when the historical institution of the gold standard is discussed (see p 119). In equilibrium there will be no excess inflow or outflow of purchasing power from country to country although there will be flows in both directions. The quantities of money in both countries in a balanced position then determine equilibrium prices and through them equilibrium wages. Wages determined in this way also measure relative efficiencies, since these depend not only on physical productivities but also on the demand patterns and co-operating factors.

b *income–change mechanism*

If prices are inflexible downwards, exactly the same basic mechanism, excess inflow or outflow of purchasing power, triggers off income changes. One could speak of an income–specie flow mechanism if there were a historical justification for such a term as there is in the case of price changes. As it is, the term would probably be misleading because the original Keynesian multiplier works without money–specie, or rather assumes that money will be forthcoming if there is an expansion of income, whereas here the income change process is described under the original macroeconomic assumptions. It has to be kept in mind, however, that in reality the process is more complicated, and the relation between income and money has to be taken into account.

The main macroeconomic assumption[1] is that commodity and factor prices are not flexible downwards the opposite is true of assumptions of price theory in microeconomics), so that all adjustments have to occur through changes in production, the level of activity. Some further assumptions follow from the assumption of constant prices and wages. Prices and wages can remain constant only if there is less-than-full employment, at least in a static system. Only if there is less-than-full employment do changes in money incomes correspond to real changes and the system not run into inflation. Constant prices also imply constant consumption and saving propensities and, in the international context, constant import propensity. The assumption of less-than-full employment further makes it possible to assume that the composition of any increase in demand will be matched by the structure of unemployed capacities, so that there will be no structural problems. As mentioned, financing is assumed not to be a limiting factor on the changes of income, the interest rate is kept constant by assuming adjustable supply of money, and investment and government expenditure are autonomous, that is are not determined by savings that are dependent on the level of income. It is assumed that changes happen instantly or that there is enough time for them to work themselves out.

[1] About macroeconomics in general see D Croome and J N Robinson *Understanding the economy* London: Weidenfeld and Nicolson 1973.

There can be hardly any doubt that these assumptions have to be relaxed if it is desired to bring the model nearer to reality, but in spite of this reservation the model is a useful first approximation to the working of an economy when prices and wages become less flexible or inflexible because of the behaviour of organized labour and corporations with high fixed costs and full-cost pricing.

The foreign trade multiplier is parallel to the domestic investment or government expenditure multipliers. In fact, these latter two will have foreign trade effects if they work in an open economy.

To show in a simple way how the foreign trade multiplier works, it can be assumed, to start with, that there is an autonomous increase in exports, E, which increases the income of the country by the same amount in the first round. If government is ignored for the moment, those people to whom such income accrues partly save it and partly spend it on domestic goods, of which, since the economy is open, some are imports. The results of this distribution of additional income are summarized in the propensity to save, s, the propensity to consume, c, and the propensity to import, m. However, imports from abroad are not the only difference between an open and a closed economy. When an open economy is discussed, it has to be taken into account that an increase in the country's exports implies an increase in the imports of its partner countries in the rest of the world. In the same way, since an increase in exports creates additional demand, and hence additional income, an increase in imports means a reduction in demand (incomes pass to the partner countries) and therefore a reduction in income.

Thus, the multiplier is no longer dependent only on the propensity to consume and the propensity to save. Besides saving, there are also leakages through increased domestic imports and reduced world imports from the country. The multiplier[1] is no longer $k = \frac{1}{s}$, because $1 - c = s$ no longer holds. The domestic propensity to import, m_d, and world propensity to import from the country, m_w, must be included. However, while m_d is the propensity to import out of the domestic increase in income dY, m_w is the propensity to import out of the world increase or decrease in income dY_w. But the foreign trade multiplier relates E to dY and, if m_w is to be included, it has to be corrected for the difference between dY and dY_w. Both the increase in dY and the reduction $-dY_w$ start from E, meaning in the first case an autonomous increase in exports and in the second an autonomous increase in imports. Therefore, neglecting further influences,

$$dY = E\frac{1}{s_d} \quad \text{and} \quad dY_w = E\frac{1}{s_w}$$

[1] See Croome and Robinson *Understanding the economy,* pp 60–4

As a consequence,

$$dY_w = \frac{s_d}{s_w}\,dY \quad \text{and} \quad m_w dY_w = m_w \frac{s_d}{s_w}\,dY$$

To relate it to dY instead of to dY_w, m_w has to be multiplied by s_d/s_w; then $1 - c = s_d + m_d + m_w\,(s_d/s_w)$. The foreign trade multiplier thus becomes:

$$k = \frac{1}{1-c} = \frac{1}{s_d + m_d + m_w\,(s_d/s_w)}$$

The original autonomous increase in exports is used up, when the multiplier works itself out, by the increase in savings, $s_d\,dY$, increase in domestic imports, $m_d\,dY$, and fall in the world imports from the country, $m_w(s_d/s_w)\,dY$. Expressed as an equation:

$$dY\,[s_d + m_d + m_w\,(s_d/s_w)] = E$$

Under our assumptions, an autonomous increase in exports does not bring about an improvement in the balance of payments, dB, by an amount equal to the autonomous increase in exports, as it triggers off changes in imports and exports through domestic and world propensities to import.

$$dB = E - [m_d + m_w\,(s_d/s_w)]\,dY$$

which means that the income-change mechanism automatically cancels a part of the balance-of-payments gain through increased exports, or for that matter, of the balance-of-payments loss through increased imports, since it can work in reverse and in such a case reduces domestic imports and raises world imports from the country. If there were no domestic propensity to save, the income-change mechanism would cancel the whole balance-of-payments improvement because of larger exports, through increased income and, hence, increased imports.

It also follows that $dB = s_d dY$, meaning that, starting from a balance of payments in equilibrium, an autonomous increase in exports generates just enough savings to finance the country's final excess of exports over imports following an autonomous increase in exports. In other words, the additional savings will be sufficient to finance loans, presumably short-term loans, to the world which make it possible for the world to buy the excess of such exports on credit. On the other hand additional savings may be hoarded, which requires that the new excess of exports over imports be financed from some other source, for instance from the previously acquired reserves of the rest of the world.

Instead of relating a marginal improvement in the balance of payments to marginal savings and investment, one can generalize by considering the total income flow and relating total savings and investment to an external imbalance. For an equilibrium income flow it is still required that savings, S, be equal to investment, I, but investment can be divided into investment at home, I_d, and investment abroad, I_f, so that $S = I = I_d + I_f$. Investment abroad is equal to the difference between exports and imports, $I_f = X - M$. This makes $S = I_d + X - M$ and $S + M = I_d + X$. In other words; leakages through savings and imports must be equal to injections through investment at home and exports. From this it follows that $X - M + S - I_d = I_f$. As long as there are no long-term capital transfers, $X - M$ is also equal to the balance-of-payments surplus on liquidity basis, $+B$ (see p 21). With a balance-of-payments deficit, $-B$, foreign investment in our country has to be equal to the excess of imports over exports. This borrowing is not necessarily used for increased investment at home, however, but may be used for increased consumption (see p 49). When long-term capital transfers are included, or if external imbalance is defined on an official transactions basis, the approach remains the same in principle but becomes more complex.

If we wish to bring in the monetary side, we have to relate $B = X - M$ to Johnsons's formula $B = R - P$ (see p 50).

In the first instance, income changes were followed through beginning from an autonomous increase in exports. Now it is necessary to show what happens to the foreign trade multiplier if the starting point is an autonomous increase in domestic investment, dI, as this occurrence also has external repercussions in an open economy. The difference is that there is not going to be any leakage because of the initial reduction of the world income dY_{wi}, which would be equal to this reduction $(E/{}^{s}w)$ multiplied by the world propensity to import from our country. Since this leakage does not take place, the final increase dY, if we begin with an autonomous increment in domestic investment, will be that much larger. But to correct the multiplier formula for this magnitude, it has to be expressed in terms of the domestic initial increase in income, dY_i, which is taken to be equal to I_d/s_d. Thus we obtain:

$$m_w \; dY_{wi} = m_w \frac{s_d}{s_w} \; dY_i = \frac{m_w}{s_w} Id$$

and further

$$dY = I_d \left[\frac{1}{s_d + m_d + m_w \dfrac{s_d}{s_w}} + \frac{\dfrac{m_w}{s_w}}{s_d + m_d + m_w \dfrac{s_d}{s_w}} \right]$$

$$dY = I_d \frac{1 + \frac{m_w}{s_w}}{s_d + m_d + m_w \frac{s_d}{s_w}}$$

It was stressed at the beginning of this section that the multiplier is construed under certain assumptions and that, even disregarding these assumptions, it is a simplified representation of reality. So far government activity has been left out, but in fact government taxation is a leakage just like saving or imports, and government spending is an injection like investment or exports. However, taxation and budget spending are to a large extent subject to deliberate decisions, so that the government can use them to strengthen or counteract other leakages or injections that are far more difficult to alter since they depend on great numbers of microeconomic decisions. Thus the government can try to influence income flows by fiscal and monetary policies. This device also gives the government the possibility of influencing the working of the income-change mechanism and, indeed, of other adjustment mechanisms, as will be discussed in chapter 5.

On the other hand, it has to be kept in mind that macro-magnitudes based on microeconomic decisions are in no way preordained but can change, as decisions by economic units change, as a result of variations in 'tastes', 'preferences' or 'behaviour'. Even government activities themselves can alter non-government 'propensities'. Thus taxation can change the propensity to save, or the substitution of government spending for private expenditure can change the propensity to import, as the government is much less inclined to buy goods from abroad.[1]

The multipliers shown above are both 'simultaneous' multipliers, which assume either that everything happens instantly or that there is enough time for them to work themselves out. Time can be brought back into the picture by tracing how expenditure flows change from stage to stage as with the 'period' multiplier, or by showing how expenditure flows are influenced by injections repeated at regular intervals.

The Keynesian multiplier considers such a short time period that investment only starts expenditure flows without yielding any output. If the period in the model is made long enough for the investment gestation to be completed, the problem is no longer only to push activity up to full-employment level, but in addition to increase demand sufficiently to take the new production off the market. This is a dynamic situation with which demand-oriented growth models are trying to cope. The 'problem' of additional output does not arise in the case of government spending since

[1] Cf *Outline of international trade* p 129

it provides public goods that do not come within the purview of aggregate demand. At the first glance the same seems to be true of exports, but only if the exporting country is prepared to make a gift of them to the other country. If it is not, it will be obliged at some time to repatriate this investment abroad and/or the returns on it (see p 56). Thus it will eventually find it necessary to reverse the trade flows.

At this stage, it must be mentioned that there is no clear-cut line between unemployment and full employment. If the structure of potential output were exactly geared to the structure of potential demand, if industrial branches were perfectly harmonized or if factors or production were instantly mobile, such a border line could exist. But bottlenecks appear because some branches reach their full capacity output (though even this cannot be uniquely defined) before others, so that in some sectors inflation sets in before others come anywhere near full employment. Simultaneously, the pressure on costs begins to build up before full employment is reached, so that instead of having a line dividing under-employment from inflation or growth, there is a transitional zone.

c *exchange rate alteration mechanism*

Depending on whether the system of fixed-but-adjustable or flexible exchange rates (see p 115) is in operation, the alteration is brought about by a decision of monetary authorities or by market forces. In both cases the price of domestic currency in terms of foreign currency is either reduced (depreciation, devaluation) or increased (appreciation, revaluation upward) and vice versa for the price of foreign currency in terms of domestic currency.

As a consequence, in the case of devaluation domestic prices, when converted into foreign currency, have to be multiplied by a smaller figure, which means that domestic goods become cheaper for foreigners; and foreign prices, when converted into domestic currency, also have to be divided in a smaller figure, which, on the contrary, means that foreign goods are made more expensive for domestic buyers. The presumption is that foreigners will buy more of the cheaper domestic goods and domestic buyers less of the more expensive foreign goods (and vice versa with revaluation upward).

When expressing depreciation or appreciation as percentages, it has to be remembered that the same absolute figures do not represent the same percentages when added to or subtracted from the same base figures. When the pound was devalued from £1 = \$2·80 to £1 = \$2·40, ie by \$0·40, this was a devaluation by (0·40/0·028) = 14·3 per cent. If, on the other hand, the pound were revalued from £1 = \$2·40 to £1 = \$2·80, ie also by \$0·40, this would be a revaluation by (0·40/0·024) = 16·6 per cent. A similar difference in percentages arises if devaluation or revaluation upward is calculated on the bases of indirect and direct exchange rate quotations (see p 8) If the pound sterling indirectly quoted is devalued from £1 = \$2·80 to £1 = \$2·40, ie by 14·3 per cent, the equivalent alteration in terms of direct quotation is from \$1 = £0·357 to \$1 = £0·417, which means by (0·06/0·036) = 16·6 per cent.

d *government controls*

As described in the introduction to this section, government controls or orders can be employed as an adjustment mechanism either by using them to change the price signals on which individual enterprises base their foreign trade decisions (qualitative controls) or by substituting, at least partly, government decisions for enterprises' decisions on quantities imported or exported (quantitative controls). The methods used to achieve these results are the same as the methods for government intervention in general which is understandable since all these methods also have a balance of payments effect.

The government can operate either on the commodity side of foreign trade by tariffs and subsidies (qualitative controls) or by quotas (quantitative control), or on the monetary side by a rise or reduction in the average multiple exchange rates (qualitative) or allocation of currency for various purposes (quantitative). A uniform rise in multiple exchange rates has, of course, the same effects as devaluation, and a uniform reduction the same effects as a revaluation upward. Generally, changes in commodity prices or quotas or changes in multiple exchange rates and allocation of foreign currency can achieve the same balance-of-payments effects.

Instead of using controls affecting prices or quantities of imports or exports for adjustment, the government may try to obviate the need for adjustment by applying controls such as price control and incomes policy on domestic developments that create external imbalance (see p 41). This may be necessary if incomes and prices are set without regard for actual economic conditions and restrictive fiscal and monetary policy leads only to unemployment.

4.3 Effects and interactions

a *effects of imbalance*

So far we have been dealing with effects of the opening of international trade and of the imposition of protective measures. The opening of trade moves the country towards a foreign trade optimum, the value of exchanges that maximizes the gain from trade, while the imposition of protective measures moves it in general away from this optimum.[1] If a tariff is imposed on imports (or exports) the value of foreign trade shrinks below the optimum level and the gain from trade does not achieve its full potential; if subsidies are granted on exports (or imports) the value of trade expands beyond the optimum point so that some foreign trade operations cause a welfare

[1] See *Outline of international trade* pp 79 and 119.

loss and the gain from trade is again not maximized.

All this occurs, provided a balance in foreign trade is somehow maintained. The trade can be balanced at the optimum level, but also at a less than optimum level. When there is an imbalance the two sides of foreign trade, imports and exports, move away from the optimum or sub-optimum points in opposite directions. With a balance-of-trade deficit imports are excessive and exports insufficient; and it is the other way round for a balance-of-payments surplus. What is required to correct imports and expand exports (or stabilize imports and expand exports, or reduce imports and stabilize exports) in the case of deficit, and vice versa in the case of surplus? In the following, deficits will be mainly discussed, keeping in mind that what applies to them also applies, *mutatis mutandis,* to surpluses. As pointed out on p 57, a deficit can persist only if there is a constant outflow of purchasing power and, as a consequence, if monetary authorities allow continuous credit expansion. This monetary policy also has to be reversed if the deficit is to be corrected. The obverse is true in the case of a surplus.

The immediate reason for the disharmony between the value of imports and the value of exports is that price signals are wrong and firms therefore take the wrong decisions from a national point of view. The deeper reasons for fundamental imbalance have been discussed in chapter 3. Except when the reasons for a deficit are structural changes and possibly changes in government policy, it is not relative prices that are wrong but the absolute level of domestic prices as compared with world prices. However, as the price level of domestically produced traded goods (exportables and importables) is linked to the world price level (see p 42), it is, in fact, the level of traded good prices that has to be compared with the level of non-traded good prices.

If the imbalance because of a higher differential rate of inflation (see p 47) is taken as an example, prices of non-traded goods rise, the more so as prices of traded goods cannot rise since there is competition from abroad. The rise is a consequence of the increased nominal expenditure which on one hand raises the prices of non-traded goods and on the other spills over into demand for additional imports, especially if the country is too small for its increased demand to cause a rise in prices also in the world markets. But since output at certain prices is in the end always equal to income out of the production at those prices, there can be excessive demand for imports only if there is expenditure in excess of incomes, which can happen only with constant credit expansion. The higher prices of non-traded goods also pull up the rewards to factors engaged in their production if the inflationary impulse does not come from them anyway. The higher factor rewards spread to the traded goods sector and make its marginal production units unviable. Its factors of production move into the production of non-traded goods or, if they are immobile, become unemployed. This of course is structural unemployment, rather than unemployment for lack of demand (see p 43).

The description here only indicates the direction in which things will move and does not pretend to be complete. The movement will continue until inflation stops (see p 71) and adjustment comes about. It does indicate, nevertheless why the profitability of production of exportables and importables is reduced or turned into losses and why the production of non-traded goods becomes more profitable. The situation is worsened if the communication between domestic and foreign markets is imperfect and domestic prices of traded goods rise to some extent over world prices. Then enterprises will find it more profitable to sell exportables at home instead of exporting them. This is true of quasi-international goods (see p 42).

The opposite will happen if the country has a lower rate of inflation than the rest of the world. Then the production of traded goods is more profitable than the production of non-traded goods.

In both cases, the lower or higher relative profitability of traded goods is artificial as it is due to the wrong price signals. Since the external imbalance cannot continue for a long time (see p 56), this kind of profitability or unprofitability of enterprises should not be taken as a real symptom of their viability or non-viability.

To summarize the effects of a foreign deficit: production shifts from traded to non-traded goods; consumption from non-traded to traded goods, meaning to imports. There is a redistribution of income from traded goods producers, some of whom may become unemployed, to non-traded goods producers and even from foreign consumers to domestic consumers. Since this last shift requires foreign short-term loans which will have to be repaid, it is not really a redistribution between foreigners and residents but between the present and the future, when loans will have to be paid back by restricting domestic consumption. Since only the relative prices of traded and non-traded goods change, this does not necessarily affect unit terms of trade which compares the prices of exportables and importables. There may be structural unemployment, but there is no reason for unemployment because of insufficient demand. Any attempt to correct the imbalance requires the reversal of all these effects.

So far, only the effects of a foreign imbalance on the domestic economy have been described, while similar although obverse effects will necessarily take place abroad, in the world economy. Unless it is assumed that there is such a difference in size between the domestic economy and the world economy that the effects abroad can be neglected, the discussion has to be conducted in terms of a world general equilibrium system, including the monetary side of it.

According to the way in which international adjustment mechanisms correct a foreign imbalance, they can be divided into three groups: a mechanisms altering the relationship between the prices of traded and non-traded goods, b those working through the domestic level of activity and c mechanisms relying on quantitative orders by the government.

Group a includes the price-change mechanism, which works through the changes in domestic prices, the exchange-rate-alteration mechanism, which functions through the change in the price of foreign currency in terms of domestic currency, and qualitative government controls, interposing government between buyers and sellers. These three mechanisms have in principle the same effects with the possible exception of qualitative controls. Bringing domestic prices down by, say, 10 per cent has the same effect as raising foreign prices for domestic buyers and sellers by devaluing by the same percentage. This is also true of the combination of a 10-per-cent tariff on imports and a 10-per-cent subsidy on exports.

The difference regarding government controls is that they can be used in a different way. The foreign balance can also be brought into equilibrium, other things being equal, by imposing a tariff of 20 per cent instead of a tariff of 10 per cent and a subsidy of 10 per cent, but this procedure will have different effects. It will correct the balance by restricting imports without encouraging exports and thus take the country away from foreign trade optimum. By altering the relationship between prices of exportables and importables, it improves the terms of trade at the danger of retaliation. Distribution of income in the country will be changed away from producers of exportables and non-traded goods and from consumers of importables. A one-sided tariff has the fiscal effect of providing government with revenue. In short, it has all the effect of a protective measure although it also achieves the balance-of-payments effect required. Government controls also may be not uniform but discriminating among goods and countries.

On the other hand, a uniform tariff-cum-subsidy does not even have a fiscal effect, since the revenue collected from tariffs has to be spent on subsidies. In fact, some such system is used, or was used, in East European countries which, apparently for prestige reasons, stick to exchange rates that grossly overvalue their currencies. The very large profits on imports are used to subsidize exports, while the relative levies and subsidies are expressed in terms of 'multiplicators' or 'import and export factors'.

Since the three adjustment mechanisms relying on the alteration of the relationship between price levels of traded and non-traded goods work in an almost identical way, the discussion of how they influence the balance of payments is to be conducted using one of them, alteration of the exchange rate, as an example. But in view of the fact that a surplus is the obverse of a deficit and their effects are a mirror image of each other, the investigation here will also be limited to finding out how a balance-of-payments deficit can be corrected.

b *effects of income-change mechanisms and government controls*

If the exchange rate is fixed, if domestic factor and commodity prices are inflexible downwards, and if the government does not wish to use direct controls, the only way of bringing the balance of payments into equilibrium, starting from a deficit, is to reduce income, ie the level of activity. This result can be achieved either by allowing the foreign-trade multiplier to work in reverse or by deflationary government policy. The preceding sentence again underlines the link between a deficit, income flows and monetary flows. For the income-change mechanism to work, either the deficit must be allowed to reduce money supply through outflow or the government must deliberately use deflationary policies.

As domestic income is reduced, imports are reduced by an amount equal to the reduction of income multiplied by the fractional propensity to import out of this income. At the same time, exports may not be reduced as they do not depend on domestic demand but on foreign demand, which is assumed constant. Thus the deficit is eliminated and external equilibrium re-established when the reduction in imports becomes equal to the deficit, but this happens at the expense of creating domestic unemployment.

Prices of neither traded nor non-traded goods change; both production and consumption are curtailed, but consumption more than production so as to eliminate the overhang of demand for foreign goods. There is no redistribution between those who remain employed, but the unemployed of course lose their income from employment. Possible structural unemployment (see p 43) in traded goods industries is also transformed into unemployment for lack of demand. Structural unemployment is a consequence of the low mobility of factors between traded and non-traded goods sectors, but the reduction in domestic income also reduces the output of non-traded goods so that the factors would no longer find employment there even if they were mobile.

The effects of this method for curing a foreign deficit are far from welcome, so that it is often said, even by economists, who on the whole are not in favour of direct government intervention, that it is better for the government to use direct controls than to bring about foreign balance by creating unemployment. What is suggested is that the government should change the propensity to import rather than reduce the level of activity in order to reduce imports. If the government achieves this result by qualitative controls, tariffs and subsidies, then the result is the same as in the case of devaluation, and all one can say is that devaluation would be much simpler. If quantitative controls are employed, some difficulties may arise. The government cannot know the elasticities of demand for imported goods and will therefore order the reduction of imports in an arbitrary way. With imported consumer goods such arbitrary reductions lead to welfare losses and changes in their relative prices. With imported intermediate and capital goods, the reduction of their availability may easily affect production and thus lead also to a reduction in the level of activity. But it was mentioned above that a balance-of-payments deficit resulting from the wrong relationship between the prices of traded and non-traded goods has as a consequence structural unemployment in traded goods branches. Quantitative limitations on imports as a means of correcting a balance-of-payments deficit could therefore bring these unemployed resources back into use so that they could replace the prohibited imports, though at a higher price.

There is however no need for workers and entrepreneurs to accept unemployment passively. In particular, marginal firms that are being pushed out of business may try to become more efficient either in their production or in their sales techniques, meaning that they reduce their unit prices without reducing factor awards. This can keep them in business and obviate unemployment. If efficiency cannot be increased, firms can also stay in employment if the factors are prepared to accept lower payments. In this case, however, the income-change mechanism changes into a domestic price-change mechanism and no longer works in the same way.

c *effects of devaluation*

Devaluation, either automatic or by government order, does change the relationship between the prices of traded and non-traded goods in spite of the possible inflexibility of domestic factor and commodity prices downwards. If these prices are flexible, however, the same result can be achieved by lowering the prices of non-traded goods and factors instead of pushing up the prices of traded goods expressed in the national currency, which is what devaluation does.

If the devaluing country is small and does not abnormally concentrate on the export or import of certain goods, it will hardly influence the world prices and its domestic prices of traded goods rise by the approximate percentage of devaluation. A large country may possibly bring down the world prices of its exports by putting additional exportables in noticeable amounts on to the world market and the world prices of its importables by reducing its demand for them. Nevertheless, its relative domestic prices of traded goods do increase, even if not by the full percentage of devaluation.

This change in relative domestic prices will shift production towards traded goods and consumption away from them. These effects should be sufficient to eliminate any overhang of demand for imports and thus remove the balance-of-payments deficit. It is sometimes said that devaluation has a protective effect because it makes it possible for the production of importables to expand. But this is necessary so as to equilibrate imports and exports at the optimum international trade point. Thus the newly produced importables are in fact cheaper than imports competing with them.

Devaluation also has a redistribution effect away from factors engaged mainly in the production of non-traded goods towards factors engaged mainly in the production of traded goods. This may at least partly take the form of reabsorbing in the traded goods sector resources that are structurally unemployed because of the deficit.

In principle, there is no need for the unit price terms of trade to change in order to make devaluation effective, as the crucial point is to change the relationship between the prices of traded and non-traded goods. The prices of importables and exportables expressed in domestic currency can rise in step by the same percentage and their prices expressed in foreign currency can even remain the same as before devaluation (but see p 86).

Devaluation is bound to generate inflationary pressures. The very fact that it eliminates, or at least reduces, a balance-of-payments deficit stops or reduces the flow of money and expenditure abroad. If it turns a deficit into a surplus it even induces the flow of money and expenditure into the country. At any rate, this change increases the level of activity and pushes the price level up when full employment of capacities is reached. In fact, this effect is due to an *interaction* of the two adjustment mechanisms: the alteration of the exchange rate and the income-change mechanism.

On the other hand, even disregarding this interaction, devaluation pushes up the relative prices of importables and exportables while the prices of non-traded goods at best remain the same, which means that the average price level of the devaluing country by necessity rises.

This second inflationary effect of devaluation is unavoidable because prices of traded goods must be realigned with prices of non-traded goods and factors in this way, if prices are not flexible downwards. For this reason it may be better not to use the term 'inflationary' in this context at all because a correction of relative prices is involved and must not lead to upward changes in the prices of non-traded goods, and especially prices of factors wages, if devaluation is to succeed at all.

It has been described (see p 42) how domestically generated inflation raises the prices of non-traded goods and factors, while it cannot raise the prices of traded goods because of foreign competition. If domestic inflation stopped the excess demand would be reduced through money and expenditure flows abroad, and prices and factors would have to fall to a level in line with the prices of traded goods, upon which the deficit would be cured. But if we assume prices to be inflexible downwards, the only thing that can be done is to bring prices of traded goods up to the level of the prices of non-traded goods and factors through an alteration in the exchange rate, and of course to stop further domestic inflation. The operation presupposes the use-of-money illusion – the relative prices are in the end the same without, however, any change in money wages. If there is insistence on unaltered real wages as opposed to money wages, and if rising prices of traded goods are countered by higher wage claims, devaluation cannot work under any circumstances. In other words, the elimination of a deficit does not require a change in the unit price terms of trade (see above) but it does require a change in the factoral terms of trade; that is, the quantity of traded goods a wage can buy has to be reduced.[1]

In so far as this is not obvious from the need for the realignment of prices, it must be obvious from the need to bring in line domestic output and consumption in the widest sense of the word, including investment and government consumption. Later in this chapter this wider consumption is called absorption and also simply expenditure (see p 83). As long as there is a foreign deficit, national expenditure is larger than national output so that a part of the goods and services used is brought in from other countries without equivalent exports.

The link between such excessive imports and wages is easy to see if inflation is 'cost-push', that is originates from excessive wage claims. Of course, real incomes cannot in principle be larger than real output since incomes are paid out of the proceeds of output. However, firms can, at least temporarily, pay out incomes larger than their revenue by either drawing on their reserves, dishoarding or taking on credit, in the hope that prices will follow incomes. Usually, this happens because a refusal by monetary authorities to top up the money supply would cause unemployment and failures. When prices are lagging behind wages, the temporary gains from inflation are going largely straight to wage-earners so that they consume more than they produce. Therefore real wages have to be brought into line, in other words reduced, when the necessary measures are taken.

Inflation may not stem from incomes larger than output but from expenditure larger than incomes normally equal to output. That can be the result if there is dishoarding, but since the scope of dishoarding is limited, it is normally a consequence of the behaviour of monetary authorities allowing more credit expansion (see p 51) than is required for maintaining prices constant in a growing economy. In this case the government uses inflation as a particular kind of taxation on money-holders and gains in the first place. If wages are lagging behind prices, profits increase too. Nevertheless, the inflationary process bestows some benefits from the excessive imports on wages. They are pulled up with the prices of non-traded goods in contrast with the prices of traded goods which are pinned down by foreign competition. Thus some reduction of real wages is required although relatively less, in comparison with government spending and profits, than in the case of cost-push inflation.

The need for reducing real incomes can be obviated only if we change from a static to a dynamic framework, and allow for the possibility that rising prices at full employment are taken as a sign that demand is increasing and that an expansion of production through investment in new capacities is called for. But under no circumstances can real incomes rise in step with increasing production, since a part of output must be switched to foreigners in order to close the gap between the value of imports and

[1] See *Outline of international trade* p 94.

exports.

If incomes are temporarily larger than output, or expenditure larger than incomes and output, an overspill of excessive demand abroad, hence a deficit, is inevitable. This deficit is necessarily reflected in prices, since prices do reflect quantities – prices of non-traded goods and factors rise in relation to prices of traded goods. Devaluation itself brings prices of traded goods into line with prices of non-traded goods and with prices of factors, particularly wages, this last relationship depending on their value productivities; but it is the authorities and their monetary and fiscal policies that have to bring output, incomes and expenditure into harmony. On the other hand, price relations have to change in order to give individual firms guidance about what to do.

Elasticities condition. In the 1930s, when scepticism regarding the working of the price system in general was rife, strong doubts prevailed about whether the response to the changes in export and import prices through devaluation was sufficient to correct an external imbalance. Abba Lerner therefore elaborated on a formula previously enunciated by Albert Marshall and known as the elasticities condition for the working of devaluation, and now also as the *Marshall–Lerner condition.* The formula states that devaluation at least reduces a balance-of-payments deficit if the sum of the elasticity of demand for exports and elasticity of demand for imports is larger than one.

The starting point for the derivation of the elasticities condition is

$$B = V_x - V_m$$

where B = balance-of-payments deficit or surplus according to the sign, V = value, subscript x refers to exports and subscript m refers to imports.

$$dB = dV_x - dV_m$$

$$V_x^* = V_x + dV_x$$

$$V_m^* = V_m + dV_x$$

where d = change in and * indicates magnitudes after devaluation.

$$V_x^* = Q_x^* P_x^* = (Q_x + dQ_x)(P_x - dP_x) = P_x Q_x + P_x\,dQ_x - Q_x\,dP_x - dQ_x\,dP_x$$

$$dV_x = P_x\,dQ_x - Q_x dP_x$$

where Q = quantity, P = price.

($dQ_x dP_x$ is neglected because it is insignificant if changes are small.)

$$dV_x = P_x Q_x \left[\frac{dQ_x}{Q_x} - \frac{dP_x}{P_x}\right]$$

similarly

$$dV_m = P_m Q_m \left[-\frac{dQ_m}{Q_m} + \frac{dP_m}{P_m}\right]$$

and hence

$$dB = V_x \left[\frac{dQ_x}{Q_x} - \frac{dP_x}{P_x}\right] - V_m \left[-\frac{dQ_m}{Q_m} + \frac{dP_m}{P_m}\right]$$

At this stage, it has to be decided whether the calculation is to be in domestic currency of the devaluing country or in that of another country. Some assumption also has to be made regarding elasticities of supply: if it is assumed that the elasticities of supply are infinite (costs of production constant or supply curves horizontal) then the domestic price of exportables remains the same and so does the world price of importables.

With calculation in domestic currency, the domestic price of exportables does not change because of the assumed perfect elasticity of supply, but the price in foreign currencies does because domestic prices are converted into foreign prices at a different exchange rate. And the export quantity demanded is in response to the foreign price, so that the value of exports in domestic currency changes because of changed quantity, but not because of changed price. With imports, both the quantity and the price in domestic currency change. Thus we obtain:

$$dB = V_x \frac{dQ_x}{Q_x} - V_m \left[-\frac{dQ_m}{Q_m} + \frac{dP_m}{P_m}\right]$$

Beginning from a balance-of-payments deficit, the balance of payments will improve (the deficit will be reduced, eliminated or turned into a surplus) if V_x* increases and V_m* decreases, or if V_x* increases by more than V_m*. (The opposite argument would be true if we started from a surplus which has to be 'improved' by a revaluation upward.) Now

$$|\epsilon_c| = \left|\frac{\frac{dQ}{Q}}{\frac{dP}{P}}\right|$$

where ϵ = elasticity and c refers to demand.

If

$$|\epsilon_{cm}| > |1|$$

the proportional reduction in the quantity of imports demanded is greater than the proportional increase in their price because of devaluation, so that the reduction in $V_m{}^*$ only strengthens the rise in $V_x{}^*$. Should, however,

$$|\epsilon_{cm}| < |1|$$

$V_m{}^*$ increases. In that case, the balance of payments improves solely if

$$V_x \frac{dQ_x}{Q_x} > V_m \left[- \frac{dQ_m}{Q_m} + \frac{dP_m}{P_m}\right]$$

$$V_x \frac{dQ_x}{Q_x} + V_m \frac{dQ_m}{Q_m} > V_m \frac{dP_m}{P_m}$$

Assuming that $V_x = V_m$, which means that $B = 0$ or at least that the deficit is very small and, hence, the difference also, it turns out that for a devaluation to work

$$\frac{dQ_x}{Q_x} + \frac{dQ_m}{Q_m} > \frac{dP_m}{P_m}$$

That is, calculating in domestic currency, the proportional increase in the quantity of exports and the proportionate reduction in the quantity of imports together must be larger than the proportional rise in the price of imports, which under simplifying assumptions is equal to the percentage of devaluation.

If the inequality is divided by the proportional change in price, we obtain

$$\frac{\frac{dQ_x}{Q_x}}{\frac{dP_m}{P_m}} + \frac{\frac{dQ_m}{Q_m}}{\frac{dP_m}{P_m}} > \frac{\frac{dP_m}{P_m}}{\frac{dP_m}{P_m}}$$

and

$$| \epsilon_{cx} | + | \epsilon_{cm} | > 1$$

This is the elasticities condition.

But it has to be pointed out that

$$\frac{\frac{dQ_x}{Q_x}}{\frac{dP_m}{P_m}} = \epsilon_{cm}$$

only if

$$\frac{dP_m}{P_m} = \frac{dP_x}{P_x}$$

which is approximately true so long as the percentage of devaluation is small, so that there is not much difference between whether direct or indirect quotation of exchange rates is used (see p 64). That is another reason (the first is the omission of dQdP in the derivation) for saying that the elasticities condition holds for *small* changes in the exchange rate.

Elasticity pessimism. The mood prevailing in the second quarter of this century may be termed 'elasticity pessimism'; a contention that devaluation would not work because elasticities were insufficient and, presumably, that the only solution, unless unemployment was accepted, was direct quantitative government controls or, perversely, that an upward revaluation should be used instead of a devaluation.

Defenders of the price system combated this defeatist view by trying to show both that the elasticities condition is excessive and that the attempts at actual measurements of elasticities were faulty.[1]

[1] See in particular Fritz Machlup 'Elasticity pessimism in international trade' in his *International*

One line of argument, that the elasticities condition overstates its case, is based on the possibility, indeed probability, that V_m is not equal to V_x when devaluation is applied. Then

$$V_x \frac{dQ_x}{Q_x} + V_m \frac{dQ_m}{Q_m} > V_m \frac{dP_m}{P_m}$$

becomes

$$\frac{V_x}{V_m} \frac{dQ_x}{Q_x} + \frac{dQ_m}{Q_m} > \frac{dP_m}{P_m}$$

and

$$\frac{V_x}{V_m} \epsilon_{cx} + \epsilon_{cm} > 1$$

Thus the conclusion imposes itself that $\epsilon_{cx} + \epsilon_{cm}$ may be smaller than 1 to the extent that $V_x > V_m$, and vice versa.

But calculating in foreign currency and assuming perfect elasticity of supply, the result is exactly opposite; then the price of imports does not change and we obtain

$$dB = V_x \left[\frac{dQ_x}{Q_x} - \frac{dP_x}{P_x}\right] - \left[V_m \quad -\frac{d\,Q_m}{Q_m}\right]$$

For an improvement of the balance-of-payments the following is then needed:

$$V_x \frac{dQ_x}{Q_x} - V_x \frac{dP_x}{P_x} + V_m \frac{dQ_m}{Q_m} > 0$$

$$\frac{V_m}{V_x} \frac{dQ_m}{Q_m} + \frac{dQ_x}{Q_x} > \frac{dP_x}{P_x}$$

$$\frac{V_m}{V_x} \epsilon_{cm} + \epsilon_{cx} > 1$$

monetary economics London: Allen and Unwin 1966 and Guy H Orcutt 'Measurement of price elasticities in international trade' in Caves and Johnson (eds) *Readings in international economics* London: Macmillan 1968.

With the calculation in foreign currency, the sum of elasticities may be smaller than 1 and devaluation still work if $V_m > V_x$.

The results of calculations in domestic and foreign currency are different, as devaluation, of course, changes the rate at which the deficit or surplus in domestic currency is converted into the deficit or surplus in foreign currency; in fact it reduces this rate (exchange rate indirectly quoted), so that the domestic currency figure has to be reduced by proportionately less than the foreign figure. The foreign currency figure will be reduced even if the domestic figure increases, provided it increases by less than the percentage of devaluation.

There is no final answer to the question of which imbalance figures, in domestic or in foreign currency, are preferable. Since most countries have to cover any deficit from their reserves of gold and foreign currency, the figures in foreign currency seem to be more relevant. On the other hand, for many countries, in particular Britain and the United States, deficits mean to a considerable extent an increase in the foreign holdings of their domestic currency (see p 128), so that figures in domestic currency are as relevant and are in fact usually published.

If the assumption of infinite supply elasticities is abandoned, the elasticities condition becomes less stringent. Both import and export prices now vary, so that no change in price can be eliminated. Hence, devaluation works when

$$V_x \left[\frac{dQ_x}{Q_x} - \frac{dP_x}{P_x} \right] > V_m \left[-\frac{dQ_m}{Q_m} + \frac{dP_m}{P_m} \right]$$

Now, if calculating in domestic currency, one has to bear in mind that the change in the price of exports in domestic currency is not the change in price to which demand for exports reacts, since foreign buyers are interested in the price in their own currency. If less than perfectly elastic supply forces the domestic price of exports up, the price in foreign currency continues to be lower than before devaluation so long as the domestic price does not go up by more than the percentage of devaluation.

Thus we obtain

$$V_{xd} \left[\frac{dQ_x}{Q_x} + \frac{dP_{xd}}{P_{xd}} \right] > V_{md} \left[-\frac{dQ_m}{Q_m} + \frac{dP_{md}}{P_{md}} \right]$$

where subscript d indicates values in domestic currency and

$$V_{xd} \frac{dQ_x}{Q_x} + V_{xd} \frac{dP_{xd}}{P_{xd}} + V_{md} \frac{dQ_m}{Q_m} > V_{md} \frac{dP_{md}}{P_{md}}$$

Under the assumption that $V_{xd} = V_{md}$, this inequality means that the devaluation will succeed if the proportional changes in the quantity of exports plus in the quantity of imports plus in the domestic price of exports, added together, are larger than the proportional change in the domestic price of imports. And the domestic price of imports will presumably not rise by the whole percentage of devaluation, since the elasticity of their supply may be less than infinite so that the foreign price of imports will fall if the demand for them in the country is reduced.

Calculating in foreign currency and assuming again $V_{xf} = V_{mf}$, we obtain

$$\frac{dQ_x}{Q_x} + \frac{dQ_m}{Q_m} + \frac{dP_{mf}}{P_{mf}} > \frac{dP_{xf}}{P_{xf}}$$

where subscript f indicates values in foreign currency.

These inequalities can also be expressed in terms of elasticities of supply of and demand for imports and exports if we substitute, for example, in the above inequality using foreign currency:

$$|\epsilon_{cx}| = \frac{\frac{dQ_x}{Q_x}}{\frac{dP_{xf}}{P_{xf}}} \qquad |\epsilon_{cm}| = \frac{\frac{dQ_m}{Q_m}}{\frac{dP_{md}}{P_{md}}}$$

$$\epsilon_{sx} = \frac{\frac{dQ_x}{Q_x}}{\frac{dP_{xd}}{P_{xd}}} \qquad \epsilon_{sm} = \frac{\frac{dQ_m}{Q_m}}{\frac{dP_{mf}}{P_{mf}}}$$

$$\frac{dP_{xd}}{P_{xd}} = -\frac{dP_{xf}}{P_{xf}} + \frac{dr}{r} \qquad \frac{dP_{md}}{P_{md}} = -\frac{dP_{mf}}{P_{mf}} + \frac{dr}{r}$$

where r = exchange rate (direct quotation).

The result of these substitutions reads:

$$\frac{|\epsilon_{cm}|(\epsilon_{sm}+1)}{|\epsilon_{cm}| + \epsilon_{sm}} + \frac{\epsilon_{sx}(|\epsilon_{cx}| - 1)}{|\epsilon_{cx}| + \epsilon_{sx}} > 0$$

This means that the Marshall–Lerner condition in its simple form, leaving out elasticities of supply, overstates the requirements for a successful devaluation. It has nevertheless to be kept in mind that less-than-perfect supply elasticities help devaluation to work only so long as the demand elasticities are each less than one. If they are each larger than one, the devaluation yields the better results the more perfect are the elasticities of supply. The reason is that less-than-perfect supply elasticities influence supply prices while perfect elasticities allow them to remain constant. If then, calculating in domestic currency, the domestic price of imports goes up because of devaluation and reduces the quantity demanded, it helps if the reduction in quantity demanded leads to a reduction of foreign supply price because this fall in price will further reduce the value of imports, as the percentage reduction in the supply price will be larger than the subsequent percentage correction of quantity since $\frac{dQ_m}{Q_m} < \frac{dP_m}{P_m}$. And in the same way, a rise in the domestic supply price of exports will increase the value of exports in domestic currency by more than it will be reduced because of the subsequent change in quantity.

If, on the contrary, the price elasticities of demand are greater than one, the change in quantity prevails over the change in quantity. Thus a reduction in the foreign price of imports after devaluation leads to a larger percentage increase in quantity, so that the value of imports is reduced by less than without such a reduction. And a rise in the domestic supply price of exports, and hence also in the foreign price of exports after devaluation, will entail a larger percentage reduction in quantity so that the value of exports will fall.

This finding about the importance of supply elasticities poses the question of what supply elasticities are in reality. It is highly improbable that the devaluing country can substantially change the world prices unless it is a giant or concentrates on the production and export of a particular good. This means that the elasticity of the world's supply of imports to one country may be regarded as infinite and the domestic supply of exports to the world as relatively very small in spite of the possible structural unemployment in traded goods industries because of imbalance (see p 43). The prices in foreign currency thus tend to remain the same, while the prices in domestic currency tend to go up by the full percentage of devaluation. In consequence, the quantity exported will at worst stay the same, and the quantity imported will be at least somewhat reduced because of the higher domestic price of imports.

As a result, in foreign currency the value of exports will stay the same and the value of imports will fall; in domestic currency the value of exports increases by the full percentage of devaluation and of imports by less than this percentage. The assumption of unchanged world prices appears to bring us nearer to what happens in reality than the assumption of perfect elasticities of supply.

Under dynamic conditions, when all countries are growing, the value of exports will be increasing even if the price in foreign currency remains the same. That will happen because of the propensity to import out of increased income, reflecting income elasticity of demand for imported goods. On the other hand, even if the devaluing economy is growing at an equal rate, the rise in its value of imports will be slowed down: the propensity to import is based on constant prices, but the domestic prices of imports in the devaluing country will rise as a consequence of devaluation, which necessarily alters not only the country's marginal but also its average propensity to import.

Something on these lines seems to have happened in the case of the British devaluation of 1967 when the visible deficit for the year was £566 million. In domestic currency the value of both exports and imports shot up in 1968, but after 1969 the rise in the value of imports slowed down, so that the values were almost equal in 1970 and the value of exports was larger by about £300 million in 1971. In dollars, the value of exports even fell in 1968, but then speeded up so as to catch up with and surpass the value of imports. It has to be taken into account in the British case that a large proportion of foreign trade contracts are denominated in pounds sterling, so that changed import and export prices prevail with a delay.

It is important to realize that devaluation may take time to produce effects not simply because of the extant contracts (in particular those expressed in domestic currency), but also because of the possible need for restructuring and new investment to take advantage of new possibilities. It also has to be remembered that a devaluation does not influence only visible trade, but also invisible trade and capital movements.

It was mentioned on p 76 that past attempts at actual measurement of elasticities were criticized – especially by Orcutt and Machlup – apparently rightly so.

One line of criticism applies to the measurement of elasticities in general. There is no way of finding out what the demand curve is at any given moment. All that can be done is to establish the relationship between quantity demanded and price at two different points in time and assume that they lie on the same curve. But it could well be that they are not on the same curve at all, because the curve shifted between one measurement and the other. Thus the conclusion may be that the elasticity of demand is low, where in fact the elasticity of the actual demand curves is high. Points on two different demand curves have been erroneously placed on a spurious demand curve as illustrated in figure 2.

Solid lines represent actual elastic demand curves; the discontinuous line (linking two points measured at different times) represents the assumed less elastic demand curve.

Elasticities of demand for exports or imports are of course the averages of a host of elasticities of demand for different goods exported and imported. Such 'aggregative' elasticities can therefore be very misleading, as Machlup shows using a very simple example. Suppose there are only two goods imported into a country in equal quantities Of these two goods the demand for A is relatively elastic, its elasticity being –2·0, the

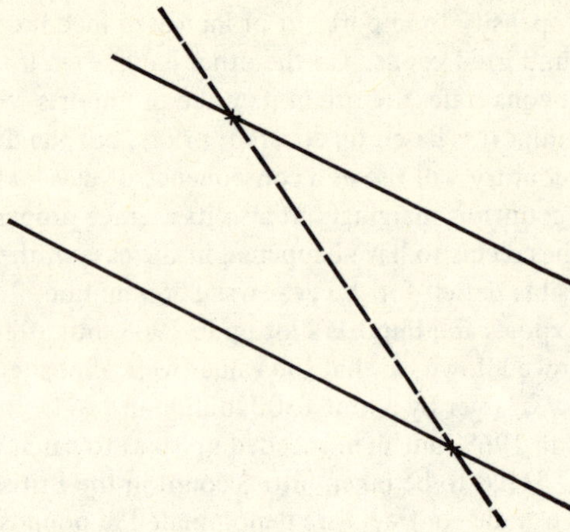

figure 2

demand for B relatively inelastic, its elasticity being –0·5. The researcher observes the response to price changes over a certain period. It so happens that over that period only the price of B falls, by 10 per cent, while the price of A does not. As a result he calculates that the average price has been reduced by 5 per cent and the average quantity demanded by 2·5 per cent, as the increase in the quantity demanded of B has increased by 5 per cent, and this percentage must be halved to obtain the average change in the quantity demanded. Thus the 'aggregative elasticity of demand for imports' of the country turns out to be –0·5 per cent, which is equal to the elasticity of demand for B.

In the calculation of aggregative elasticities, the component elasticities are weighted not only for their value in the aggregate of imports (or exports) but also for the chance price changes during the period of observation. And it has to be expected that prices of the goods for which demand is less elastic will change more than of those for which it is more so. The calculated aggregative elasticity is even more seriously wrong if, during the period of observation, some prices move down but others up.

In addition, a change in the exchange rate may lead to the import or export of additional goods, or to the cessation of previous imports or exports, both of which are not taken into account at all in the calculation of 'aggregative elasticities'.

But even if it were possible to calculate correct 'aggregative elasticities', there is no reason to assume that the elasticity figures obtained in one period could be applied to predict the working of devaluation in another period under entirely different conditions of income levels, their distribution, range of price changes, etc.

Absorption approach. After the Second World War there was so much dissatisfaction with the elasticities approach that Alexander tried to replace it with what he called the income-absorption approach.[1] The salient feature of Alexander's analysis is his stress on the need for the domestic real absorption (equal to what is usually called real expenditure) to be reduced, with respect to the domestic real output, for a balance-of-payments deficit to be reduced; in fact, the two magnitudes have to be brought in line if the balance-of-payments deficit is to be eliminated. The relationship between output, incomes and expenditure has already been mentioned on p 70.

Alexander's starting point is the identity of the foreign balance B with the difference between the total production of goods and services Y and the total absorption of goods and services A.

$$B = Y - A$$

He denotes *changes* in these quantities by the corresponding small letters, so that

$$b = y - a$$

This formula he calls his 'fundamental identity'. The first question that arises is how the devaluation affects the two terms y and a. Alexander claims that the relationship holds in both real and money terms, but proceeds to discuss the changes in real terms.

In his view, the absorption of goods and services depends on real income, which is equal to the output of goods and services, and may also depend on the price level and other factors related to the devaluation, so that:

$$a = cy - d$$

where c = the propensity to absorb, equal to the propensity to consume plus an analogous effect of income on investment, which may be called the propensity to invest; and d = the direct effect of devaluation on absorption, expressing whatever tendency there may be for the devaluation to induce a change in the amount of real absorption at any given level of real income.

Thus, in the above equation cy is the change in real consumption plus real investment that is induced by the change in real income resulting from the devaluation, and d is the change in absorption that results other than through the income effect.

[1] Sidney Alexander 'Effects of a devaluation on a trade balance' *IMF staff papers* vol II (April 1952) pp 263–78

Substituting $cy - d$ for a in the 'fundamental identity', we obtain

$$b = (1-c)\ y + d$$

Alexander then investigates the changes in y, c and d, stressing however that a summary of the main ideas, rather than a precise formulation of the relationships, is in question.

He comes to the tentative conclusion that there are two 'effects of devaluation on income' which he calls the 'idle-resources effect' and 'terms-of-trade effect', and several 'direct effects on absorption' which he enumerates as the 'cash-balance effect', the 'redistribution-of-income effect', 'money illusion' and three more 'miscellaneous direct-absorption effects'.

Machlup[1] criticized Alexander's 'income-absorption approach' for failing to consider substitution effects in addition to income effects, or, put in a different way, to add the 'resource-reallocation effect' of devaluation to the 'idle-resources effect' and the 'terms-of-trade effect'. Johnson[2] believes that Machlup's criticisms of Alexander's argument were valid in detail, but that he did not sufficiently appreciate the main point of Alexander's contribution, namely to view the balance of payments as a relation between the aggregate receipts and expenditure of the economy rather than as a relation between the country's credits and debits on international account. Johnson underlines that, since 1945, a new (though still Keynesian) approach to balance-of-payments theory has been emerging, an approach that is better adapted to post-war conditions than the 'foreign-trade-multiplier theory' and 'elasticity analysis' in two major respects; first, it poses the problems of balance-of-payments adjustment in a way which highlights their policy implications; and secondly, it allows for conditions of full employment and inflation.

In fairness to Machlup, it has to be said that he pleads for the roles of both aggregate spending and relative prices to be given scope and repeatedly underlines the importance of monetary policy. Johnson, in fact, in his own words, attempts a reconciliation of the two approaches in a broader framework of analysis by replacing Alexander's fundamental identity of $B = Y - A$ with his own

$$B = Y - E$$

derived from his $B = R - P$ (see p 50). E stands for expenditure, while what is

[1] Fritz Machlup 'Relative prices and aggregate spending in the analysis of devaluation' and 'The terms-of-trade effects of devaluation upon real income and the balance of trade' in his *International monetary economics* London: Allen and Unwin 1966.

[2] See reference on p 50.

required to correct a balance-of-payments deficit is either 'expenditure reduction' or 'expenditure switching'. The two terms are, at least, parallel to Alexander's reduction in absorption and Machlup's substitution or reallocation of resources. The substitution of the word 'expenditure' for 'absorption' stresses the importance of domestic monetary (and fiscal) policies, touched upon on p 51. The purpose is to change the relationship between aggregate expenditure and income, which depends on output, so that the two are brought into line.

Absorption reconsidered. The crucial magnitude in Alexander's approach is *c*, the propensity to absorb out of a given income. He envisages the possibility that *c* may be larger than one, in which case devaluation cannot succeed if real income grows and direct effects of devaluation do not counteract the rise in absorption owing to the rise in income. He does not go into the question of why *c* should be larger than unity, but merely says that 'the existence of the business cycle makes it plausible that *c* may be larger than unity'. He does say however that the difference between the real production (equal to real income) and the real expenditure on goods and services may be termed 'real hoarding'.

From this it follows that real absorption can be lower than real production or income if there is real hoarding (or, one may add with Johnson, 'real' credit contraction), and higher if there is real dishoarding (or 'real' credit expansion). But hoarding means increased cash balances and dishoarding, reduced cash balances, so that there is a link between *c* and Alexander's first and most important direct effect of devaluation, the 'cash-balance effect'. It further follows that government fiscal and monetary (including interest rate) policies can influence *c*, as they can influence cash balances, and that, as a consequence, government action will be crucial to make devaluation work.

Devaluation may cause real output to rise, and as a result real absorption relatively to fall if *c* is smaller than unity for two reasons. One is what Alexander calls the 'idle-resources effect'; the change in prices because of devaluation improves the balance of payments, so that there is less diversion of demand abroad, which increases the domestic income through the foreign-trade multiplier if there are unemployed resources. But if currency flows are not neutralized (see p 93) there is also an inflow of currency, and therefore an increase in the money supply if the government does not intervene.

The other rise in real income may come from the reduction in what was called 'structural unemployment' owing to excessively low prices of traded goods (see p 43). Devaluation raises these prices, and employment in the traded goods sector expands. This development may also increase real cash balances (hoarding) so that absorption is relatively reduced. If on the other hand factors are sufficiently mobile to have moved into the non-traded goods sector there will be no rise in income, but only reallocation of resources between traded and non-traded goods.

Alexander's second income effect is the 'terms-of-trade effect'. He says that it is 'usually presumed, frequently with justification, that a devaluation will result in a decline of export prices in foreign currency greater than the decline of import prices in foreign currency'. A reason for this presumption is 'the fact that a country's exports are usually more specialised than its imports, so that a country's exports will be much more subject to the influence of devaluation than will the price of imports'. It can be presumed therefore that devaluation reduces a country's real income.

Alexander argues that a reduction in real income, if *c* is less than unity, implies a deterioration in the foreign balance because absorption is reduced by less than real income. Such a result would be true if a reduction in real income meant dishoarding, a reduction in cash balances. But a reduction in real income may mean that balance holders will want a reduction in real cash balances but not in nominal cash balances, as the same nominal cash balances are reduced in real terms when the price of imports rises. Therefore the most probable conclusion is that the change in the terms of trade means no change in nominal cash balances and as a result no change in absorption.

Conversely, Alexander believes that the general rise in prices because of the foreign-trade multiplier, if there are no 'idle resources', does not change absorption and the balance of payments at all. But surely, even if real income does not change, income in money terms does change and cash balances in money units will have to increase in order to preserve the same value in real terms. So a general rise in prices does lead to hoarding and hence to diminished absorption.

In other words, devaluation has to bring output, prices and the demand for and supply of money into line. Originally supply of money is excessive, hence excessive absorption. Any rise in output entails higher real cash balances, and any rise in prices higher nominal cash balances, which means that in both cases demand for money rises and finally catches up with the supply, provided, of course, that the government does not speed up anew the supply of money and thus start a new bout of imbalance.

Alexander's direct effects, which he mentions in addition to 'cash-balance effect', are *transitory* in his own words and therefore of little long-term importance. Redistribution of income is far less important than would be expected, because it matters, with respect to absorption, only in so far as it changes 'hoarding' and not savings and investment. Remember that investment is a part of *c*, the propensity to absorb.

On the other hand, inflation may originate from factor rewards rising faster than their productivity, which is usually the case under the recent combination of unemployment and inflation. Increases in factor rewards, primarily rises in wages, lead to a redistribution of income away from profits and towards labour. But as mentioned before (see p 72), factor rewards can rise so fast that they not only impinge on profits, but even erase them and turn them into losses, at least in marginal firms. In such a case firms can cover their costs in excess of revenue only if they draw on their reserves (dishoard) or borrow in the hope that, later, prices will catch up with rising costs. Dishoarding by firms in this context could be termed 'involuntary'. Such development does not bring much benefit to anybody; it limits investment, raises prices and accentuates the balance-of-payments deficit.

In this case income is no longer equal to output as Alexander postulates, so that *both* income and expenditure have to be brought into line with production. Devaluation can re-align prices and costs by re-aligning output and incomes at a certain level, but it cannot stop further cost-push inflation. As pointed out above (see p 66) it cannot stop further demand-pull inflation either. That is the task of government policy. Monetary and fiscal policies could easily stop inflation, but there is the danger that unemployment will follow if workers' attitudes do not change. Therefore incomes policy (see p 65) has been tried in many instances to change labour's behaviour regarding wage claims.

4.4 The transfer problem

Machlup[1] describes the transfer problem in the following way:

> If a country undertakes to make *very large payments* [italics supplied] abroad – for military expeditions, subsidies, war indemnities, foreign aid, loans, or investments – the question arises whether it will thereby exhaust its reserves of gold and foreign currencies (or, in the absence of disposable reserves have its currency depreciated without a definite limit), or whether its trade balance will adjust itself to the flow of capital and unilateral payments and thus produce the international means of payments with which the foreign commitments can be met. This, in a nutshell, is the transfer problem.

The words 'very large payments' indicate that there is only a difference in degree and not a qualitative difference between *ordinary* (see p 49) capital and unilateral payments flows and very large flows which cause a transfer problem. Sometimes a further qualification is added, namely that a transfer problem arises if very large payments abroad are to be made *in a short time.* In this case the problem is first to increase exports for a few years and then to return to normal foreign trade. But Professor Machlup deals, as an example of transfer problem, with the US payments crisis caused by *permanent* large outflows of military expenditure, capital and aid, so that, in his view, the problem also encompasses large flows over many years which do not start and end abruptly. (Large payments over a short time can of course be transformed into smaller payments over a longer time by an extension of credits and loans to the paying country.)

[1] F Machlup 'Capital movements and the transfer problem' part V in his *International monetary economics* London: Allen and Unwin 1966.

Professor Johnson[1] divides the transfer problem into two:

1) The first is whether the process by which the transfer is financed in the transferor country and disposed of in the transferee will affect each country's demand for imports (at unchanged prices) sufficiently to create the trade surplus and deficit necessary to effect the transfer.

2) The second part of the transfer problem is whether the adjustment mechanism will be effective in restoring equilibrium if the exchanges due to the transfer process itself fall short of, or exceed, the amount of transfer.

The transfer process consists in the handing over of purchasing power from one country to another. The question is who gives up purchasing power in one country and who receives it in the other. The situation will be different if the purchasing power stems from savings in one country and is paid out to owners of factors of production in the other, or if the government collects it in taxes from the population and hands it over to the foreign government. For this reason, 'the propensity to import from the paying country out of the transfer' may be entirely different from the ordinary propensity to import from that country.

Nevertheless, it is to be expected that the transferee country will spend some of the transfer in the transferor country and that the transferor country will somewhat reduce its imports from the transferee country. (There can also be multilateral trade, achieving similar results.) The final effect of this first spending will depend on by what percentage of the transfer the recipient country will increase its imports from the paying country and by what percentage of the transfer the paying country will reduce its imports from the recipient country. If both percentages add to 100 this first spending will fully effect the transfer; if they add to more than 100 the transfer will be over-effected, if to less it will be under-effected. There is however no way of knowing in advance precisely how the transfer will affect imports of the two countries. Also tariffs and transport costs can complicate matters.

Whatever imbalance is left after the initial spending the adjustment mechanisms, either the price-change mechanism or the income-change mechanism, have to correct. The working of the price-change mechanism depends on price elasticities of demand and supply (elasticities condition: see p 76, with supply elasticity included); the working of the income-change mechanism, on the propensities to import. The income-change mechanism cannot fully correct the imbalance as long as there is any propensity to save in the economy (see p 61). In that case it will have to be supplemented by government policy.

[1] H G Johnson 'The transfer problem and exchange stability' in R N Cooper (ed) *International finance* Harmondsworth: Penguin 1969.

The transfer can be so large that no adjustment mechanism can lead to its effective completion. It may be feasible but rather painful. However, even a relatively small adjustment will not be carried through if the government first provides the purchasing power for transfer from newly created money and then prevents adjustment from working by constantly topping up the money supply in order to achieve its other economic aims (see p 52). This seems to have been the situation in the United States in the late 1960s. In consequence, the US first lost a large part of her reserves and then had to bargain for exchange rate changes (see pp 132ff and 165ff).

further reading

S A Alexander	'Effects of devaluation on a trade balance' in Caves and Johnson *Readings in international economics*
B J Cohen	*Balance of payments policy* Harmondsworth: Penguin 1969
H G Johnson	*Macroeconomics and monetary theory* London: Gray-Mills 1971
H G Johnson	'The transfer problem and exchange stability' in Cooper *International finance*
F Machlup	*International trade and the national income multiplier* New York: Kelley 1961
F Machlup	'Elasticity pessimism in international trade'; 'Relative prices and aggregate spending in the analysis of devaluation'; 'The term-of-trade effects of devaluation on real income and the balance of trade'; Part V 'Capital movements and the transfer problem' in *International monetary economics*
G H Orcutt	'Measurement of price elasticities in international trade' in Caves and Johnson *Readings in international economics*

chapter 5

automatic adjustment and balance-of-payments policy

5.1 Insulation of the domestic economy

When reasons for fundamental disequilibrium were discussed in chapter 3 (p 45) it was said that any of the occurrences causing external imbalance triggers off an adjustment mechanism. However, this mechanism can be prevented from working and when this happens a fundamental disequilibrium arises. Governments tend to prevent the working of adjustment mechanisms because they interfere with other economic goals, particularly full employment and economic growth (see p 52), and thus tend to insulate their economies from the external balance. If an economy is insulated in this way the government has to inaugurate a balance-of-payments policy, that is to take deliberate measures to rectify external imbalances unless they are due to reversible or at least transitional causes (see p 44). It is also possible that governments rely partly on automatic functioning of mechanisms and partly modify them by policy measures.

The OECD report on adjustment processes[1] puts it in the following words:

> For many countries these automatic mechanisms tending to restore external equilibrium are an important reason why surpluses and deficits have not been larger relative to total external transactions and to GNP. They do not, however, generally dispense with the need for a deliberate economic policy. Left to themselves, they might seriously interfere with internal policy objectives. Even in terms of the balance-of-payments objective as such, their effect may be too slow and too small, or in some cases too quick and too large.

Adjustment mechanisms and their effects were described in chapter 4. They work either through changes in exchange rates or through flows of purchasing power from country to country. The exchange rate of a currency automatically depreciates and appreciates according to the relationship of the supply of and demand for foreign currency in the exchange market. The government may not want these automatic changes (on arguments for and against flexible exchange rates see p 115) to take place and therefore intervenes by selling and buying foreign currency in order to keep the

[1] See reference on p 52.

exchange rate alterations within limits. In this way it 'switches off' the automatic mechanism of a flexible exchange rate. It has either to allow the functioning of other mechanisms or deliberately to change the exchange rate by order as a policy measure, ie devalue the national currency or revalue it upwards. The same effect can be also achieved by imposing tariffs on imports and paying subsidies on exports to simulate devaluation, or vice versa for revaluation upward.

Even if automatic adjustment through exchange rates is eliminated, there can still be automatic adjustment through flows of purchasing power. As explained (see p 50), if there is a balance-of-payments deficit domestic currency is flowing out of the country, and if there is a surplus foreign currency is flowing into the country. How one currency is transformed into another and what effects this has will be discussed below (see p 93). In principle, an external deficit automatically reduces domestic money supply and a surplus expands it. As a consequence, other things being equal, commodity price levels change, or, if prices are inflexible downwards, the level of activity changes. But governments often object to having the internal development dictated in this way by the external balance and to 'importing', as it is often put, unemployment or either deflation or inflation. For this reason they may wish entirely to insulate the economy from foreign influences and to neutralize any inflow or outflow of purchasing power. The ways and means for such neutralization will be discussed in the next section.

This kind of insulation makes good sense if imbalances are only temporary, a result of cyclical development. Excessive imports at one stage are financed from gold and currency reserves and the reserves are again built up when exports prevail at a different stage. This arrangement only supports domestic attempts at stabilization.

The situation is different, however, if the reasons for disequilibrium are persistent. If nothing is then done to correct it a fundamental imbalance as described in chapter 3 does develop and the government is, in the end, forced to act. Of course it can always substitute deliberate deflationary policies for deflationary pressure caused by outflowing purchasing power, or deliberate inflationary policies for inflationary pressure owing to inflowing purchasing power. But governments are trying precisely to neutralize international purchasing power flows to keep deflationary and inflationary developments at home under control and possibly wish to use deflationary and inflationary policies for other purposes, primarily to achieve full employment and growth. Certainly, deflationary and inflationary policies may be used for balance-of-payments purposes, but on the whole governments are loath to do that. Therefore, all they can eventually do is to fall back on devaluation (or revaluation upward).

5.2 Functioning of the monetary authority

Whether the management of gold and currency reserves is a direct function of the central bank or of a separate agency (called in Britain the Exchange Equalization Account) is of secondary importance. What really matters is what happens to the domestic money paid to the exchange institution in exchange for foreign currency, or where domestic money that the agency needs for its purchases of foreign currency comes from.[1]

The crucial question is whether the inflow of foreign currency (a balance-of-payments surplus) adds to the domestic money supply and the outflow (a deficit) subtracts from it, or whether the flows in both directions do not influence this supply.

The exchange institution may a) borrow domestic money from and repay it to the central bank, or be endowed with its own fund of domestic money which it dishoards and hoards; or b) borrow domestic money from and repay it to commercial banks and the public.

In case a) any net inflow of foreign currency adds to the domestic money supply since the agency purchases it with newly issued central bank money or with money out of its own fund which is otherwise held idle. If there is a net outflow of foreign currency, domestic money is withdrawn from circulation, since the exchange institution sells foreign currency for domestic money. This domestic money is then repaid to the central bank so that it is cancelled or is added to the idle balances of the exchange institution. In this way the impulses of foreign currency flows are fully translated into increased or reduced supply of domestic money.

In case b) they are not, at least not necessarily. When there is a net inflow of foreign currency the exchange institution borrows the domestic money to pay for it from banks or from the public. This procedure sterilizes the inflow by paying the earners of foreign currency with money borrowed from the sale of government securities. If on the other hand there is net outflow of foreign currency, the reduction in domestic money supply because of the purchases of foreign currency from the agency with domestic money is offset by using this money to repay debts to banks or the public. Thus the influence of foreign currency inflows or outflows on domestic money supply is neutralized.

This arrangement works so long as the money borrowed by the agency is diverted from other uses and money repaid is put to other uses. If commercial banks are not fully loaned, or if the public lends money from idle balances, the effects of sterilization will not materialize for the simple reason that the banks do expand their credits or the public dishoards, ie puts idle money into circulation. In the same way the 'offsetting' does not work if money repaid is cancelled by the banks or if the public adds to it idle balances.

[1] See F Machlup 'Theory of foreign exchanges' in his *International monetary economics* particularly pp 31 ff.

All that this procedure of borrowing and lending amounts to is what is usually called 'open market' operations. In countries where the government securities market is not well organized, these operations may fail, and the attempts by monetary authorities to neutralize net inflows or outflows may be unsuccessful for that reason.

So far it has been assumed, at least tacitly, that external currency flows are a consequence of operations pertaining to current and possibly long-term capital accounts. However, monetary movements themselves may not be compensatory, but rather autonomous (see p 48). Interest rate arbitrage (see p 9) is one of the reasons why such autonomous monetary movements occur. Other reasons are the probability of devaluation or upward revaluation or political circumstances.

In the next section we will describe how a government may seek to bring about private currency flows in order to finance its country's deficits or surpluses. But autonomous monetary movements may occur against the wishes of governments and make the situation worse. That happens if there is an outflow of short-term funds from a country in a balance-of-payments deficit or an inflow into a country with a balance-of-payments surplus. These flows are often referred to as 'hot money'.

In such cases monetary authorities may try to neutralize the flows in exactly the same way as they try to do this in response to compensatory flows of short-term funds. Inflows may be prevented from influencing domestic money supply if monetary authorities try to borrow them themselves, to order that any foreign deposit should be re-deposited with the central bank or to prohibit domestic firms from borrowing abroad. Or they may introduce taxes on interest paid to foreigners, prohibit interest payments to foreigners altogether or even introduce 'negative interest' on foreign deposits; ie, foreigners would have to pay a percentage for the privilege of keeping money in the country.

On the other hand, monetary authorities may prevent the outflow of domestic short-term funds simply by prohibiting their transfer abroad or by imposing an 'interest equalization tax', a government levy reducing or eliminating interest differentials. It is of course more difficult to prevent foreign-owned short-term funds from leaving the country because such an attempt would lead to international complications.

In conclusion, it should be said that it is very difficult entirely to insulate an economy from the consequences of its external imbalance and of events abroad. Something will tend to 'seep through'. And whatever the influence on domestic money supply and domestic development, gold and currency reserves tend to be dangerously run down or to accumulate beyond reason, so that in the end the government will have to act.

5.3 Balance-of-payments policy

As stressed at the beginning of this chapter, a government that has succeeded, even if imperfectly, in insulating its economy from external imbalance has to embark on a balance-of-payments policy.

This policy may initially consist of financing (see p 56) the deficit by using official reserves or borrowing from other central banks or the IMF. A surplus country has to participate in such financing at the giving end. The decisions about these government-to-government operations are to a high degree political and are only partly sensitive to interest rates.

When however a government is trying to carry through its financing policy by attracting foreign private funds and official funds sensitive to interest rates, it has to combine its fiscal and monetary policy in such a way as to achieve this result.[1] The requirement is to maintain full employment by an expansionary fiscal policy and, simultaneously, to push up interest rates by a restrictive monetary policy sufficiently to attract the desired foreign short-term funds.

This combination of policies may facilitate the financing of a foreign imbalance, but it does nothing to cure it. On the contrary, it may make it worse because, for instance, the maintenance of full employment tends to encourage cost-push inflation, while high interest rates interfere with investment and hence possible improvements in productivity. Such perverse consequences lead to hesitations and imperfect operation of the fiscal-monetary policy mix. As Johnson put it:

> The deficit countries have in practice had to undergo more unemployment than they would like, and the surplus countries have been unable to prevent their surpluses from having inflationary consequences for their domestic price levels.

In addition, this financing approach puts interest rates and capital flows in the service of external imbalances caused by the wrong price signals (see p 67). As a consequence capital does not flow to the countries where it is scarce and therefore yields high returns, but to countries that run a balance-of-payments deficit because of their particular policies; and these may be rich in capital. Johnson discusses this question under the name of 'the welfare problem' and comes to the conclusion that under these circumstances, governments may as well use controls, since capital flows leading to welfare maximization will not occur anyway.

Financing then does not help in the longer run, so that governments have to use other means to tackle an external imbalance and bring about real adjustment. The question of which policy should be used for achieving which target is usually treated

[1] H G Johnson 'Theoretical problems of the international monetary system' in R N Cooper (ed) *International finance.* London: Penguin 1969.

under the heading of *the assignment problem.*[1] The term is specifically applied to the allocation of fiscal policy to the target of full employment and monetary policy to financing flows, but it can be given a wider meaning of generally assigning policies to targets in accordance with Tinbergen's[2] economic policy postulate that there must be as many policies as there are targets.

While fiscal and monetary policies can be considered two different policies as to the targets of full employment and *financing* of an external imbalance, they cannot be so considered when it comes to maintaining full employment and *adjusting* an external imbalance. Unless the exchange rate changes, adjustment requires a change in the price level or, if the price level is inflexible downwards, a change in the activity level. In bringing about price-level or activity-level changes, fiscal and monetary policies can only co-operate, which means that they cannot be used in different directions, one to serve external and the other internal equilibrium. More than that, with inflexible prices (and fixed exchange rates), full employment may be brought about by fiscal and monetary policy only when external balance is disregarded and vice versa.

However, as Harrod pointed out,[3] in some situations the same fiscal and monetary policies are required in the pursuit of external and internal equilibria. In fact, four situations can be distinguished as shown in table 13.

Table 13

external situation	internal situation	
	unemployment	inflation
external deficit	devalue or reduce factor rewards	deflate
external surplus	inflate	revalue upward or increase factor rewards

Clearly, when inflation is combined with an external deficit the remedy for both is deflation (or, euphemistically, disinflation). Similarly, unemployment and external surplus together require inflation (or reflation). But when the external and internal

[1] R A Mundell 'Appropriate use of monetary and fiscal policy for internal and external stability *IMF staff papers* 1962.

[2] T Tinbergen *Economic policy: principles and design* Amsterdam: North Holland 1956.

[3] In chapter VII 'Correcting an imbalance' of his *International economics* (revised text 1966). A more elaborate paper on the same subject is W M Corden 'The geometric representation of policies to attain internal and external balance' in Cooper's *International finance.*

situations demand that fiscal and monetary policies be applied in different directions, this cannot be done and new policies have to be introduced, working either through exchange-rate changes or changes in the domestic price level. A reduction of factor rewards may be impossible because of the resistance of organized labour, and an increase of factor rewards may be undesirable because it means that inflation is imported into a country that may nervously react to it. Thus the policy-makers are left with exchange-rate alterations.

Before passing on to consider by how much exchange rates should be altered, it may be necessary to bring Harrod's four situations up to date. In the last few years it has no longer been entirely true to say that wages are inflexible downwards because organized labour is now pushing money wages up faster than productivity increases. For this reason it is no longer impossible to have inflation and unemployment at the same time (see p 43). If wages rise faster than productivity, marginal enterprises have losses and reduce their activity or close down altogether. Investment is also reduced because profit expectations are low. The newly coined word for this situation is *stagflation*: stagnation with inflation.

The two internal situations in the table 13 must therefore be described in a different way. Instead of simply contrasting unemployment with inflation, unemployment exists in a situation when wages rise faster than productivity, and high employment when productivity rises faster than, or at least in step with wages. External deficits and surpluses have primarily become a consequence of differential rates of inflation. As a result, the remedies are no longer to inflate or to deflate, but to 'increase the rate of inflation' or to 'slow down the rate of inflation'. In the same way, the remedies are not to 'reduce factor rewards' but to 'try to slow down the increase in factor rewards', and not to 'increase factor rewards', but to 'speed up the increase in factor rewards'. Of course, the situation as it has developed is an insane way of running either the domestic or world economies, especially since it cannot bring any lasting advantage to anybody. Devaluation or revaluation should still correct external balances if everything else fails, but developments in different countries have become so erratic that adjustment can hardly keep pace with them.

5.4 The monetarist approach

Towards the end of the 1960s the financial world was heading for an impasse; governments were excessively reluctant to alter the exchange rates although fiscal and monetary policies hardly catered adequately for external equilibrium. Moreover, the British devaluation of 1967 did not show any sign of working in 1968. This situation coincided with a revival of interest in monetary policy, particularly in the effects of an expansion of the quantity of money as opposed to interest-rates policy. It was suggested that an appropriate expansion of the supply of money would be an expansion that kept commodity prices stable. Milton Friedman[1] even proposed simply the same modest increase in money supply year after year as he considered that the knowledge of how monetary policy worked was insufficient to warrant any more refined goal. At any rate, if the rate of expansion desirable from an internal point of view is known, it can be modified to take care also of the external disequilibrium.

This reasoning led to the so called DCE criterion. DCE stands for 'domestic credit expansion' which consists of an increase in lending by the banking system to the public and private sectors and in holdings of currency by the public. In fact, DCE consists of the rise in the entries on the asset side of a consolidated balance of the banks. Money, on the other hand, can be defined as the deposit liabilities of the banks *minus* deposits by (less lending to) non-residents *plus* holdings of currency by the public. The formula for the DCE criterion then reads

$$\text{DCE} = dN - B$$

where N = quantity of money (N is used instead of the usual M to avoid any possibility of confusion with M standing for 'imports'); B = balance-of-payments disequilibrium (deficit –, surplus +) and d implies change in.

Both N and B can be defined in various similar ways – for instance N as above and B as the "financing of the total currency flow" in the official UK balance of payments. But whatever the definition, the implication of the *DCE* criterion is that to keep domestic credit expansion in line with the policy aims, the supply of new money should be reduced if there is a balance-of-payments deficit and hence an outflow of purchasing power abroad, and vice versa if there is a surplus. This criterion which was urged on member countries by the IMF, then re-introduces the automatic functioning of the adjustment mechanism and to that extent infringes the pursuit of internal policy goals.

However, worse was to come. If in the late 1960s governments seemed too reluctant to use devaluation and re-valuation, in the early 1970s the question arose of whether alterations in the exchange rate could work at all. In Britain the balance of trade and the balance of payments had finally improved in 1969 and 1970, when a bout of exorbitant wage claims began to endanger the situation. Suggestions came from many quarters that the new Conservative government should inaugurate an

[1] See M Friedman 'The role of monetary policy' *American economic review* 1968 reprinted in M Friedman *The optimum quantity of money* Chicago: Aldine 1969. But in this paper Friedman advocates a floating exchange rate for the United States, because this continental country is so independent of foreign trade, amounting to about 5 per cent of the GNP, that it is not worth while trying to stabilize the exchange rate.

incomes policy. Such a proposal by Phelps-Brown was published in the business part of *The Times* of 19 November 1970. It called forth a letter to *The Times* by Johnson, printed on 23 November 1970, which read in part:

> Concretely, this country has been doomed to a bout of domestic inflation at some point, first by the devaluation of 1967, which initially reduced British real wages below the world value of British labour and secondly by the worldwide inflation of recent years, which has emanated from the United States. The exact timing of the socalled 'pay claims free-for-all', which I would regard broadly as a rational response by labour to the development just mentioned has of course been determined by political events in this country.
>
> In these circumstances, the Government might be wise to let things sort themselves out rather than rush in with some sort of incomes policy as many have been urging them to do. Such a policy of inaction involves, however, a serious risk of wages settlements overshooting, another balance-of-payments disequilibrium and the need to devalue again or let the pound float down; and it requires a willingness at the very least to let excessive wage increases result in unemployment . . .
>
> As long as this country is on a fixed exchange rate, its price target cannot be stability; it must be inflation or possibly deflation more or less at the world rate.

Few people would quarrel with the last paragraph, but the purpose of the suggested incomes policy was presumably not to promote absolute domestic stability but to prevent excessive wage and price rises from undoing the improvement through devaluation. We discussed (p 71) the need for a reduction in real wages to make devaluation work, an argument on which Johnson[1] comments as follows:

> This point has sometimes been put in terms of the positive charge that the standard model rests on 'money illusion', in the sense that it assumes that workers will accept a reduction in their real standard of living brought about by a devaluation which they would not accept in the form of a forced reduction of domestic money wages. An alternative version of this charge is that the standard model assumes that workers can be cheated out of their real marginal product by devaluation. The charge, however, is incorrect: if rectification of a balance-of-payments deficit requires that the domestic marginal product of labour in terms of foreign goods falls, because the price of domestic goods relative to foreign goods must be reduced in the foreign and home markets to induce substitution between these goods favourable to the balance of payments, it requires no money illusion but only economic realism for the workers to accept this fact. Applications of the standard model to the case of devaluation, however, do require the assumption of money illusion if the elasticities of substitution between domestic and foreign goods are in fact high (approximately infinite), and it is

[1] H G Johnson 'The monetary approach to balance-of-payments theory' in Connolly and Swoboda *International trade and money: the Geneva essays* pp 212–13.

nevertheless assumed that wages will remain unchanged in terms of domestic currency. For in this case it is being expected that workers will be content to accept wages below the international value of their marginal product, and that employers will not be driven by competition for labour in the face of this disequilibrium to bid wages up to their marginal productivity levels. The issue therefore is not one of the standard model wrongly assuming the presence of money illusion on the part of the workers, but of its possibly wrongly assuming low elasticities of substitution between domestic and foreign goods – which is an error in empirical assumptions rather than in model construction.

The passage from Johnson was quoted in full because it raises questions crucial for the further development of international economic relations. If trade unions are in fact realistic enough to accept changes in real wages necessary for re-establishing international equilibrium, the situation can be considered more or less satisfactory. But the concept of 'the world value of British labour' is so complicated that it is subject to serious doubt whether the workers and their representatives can really aim at the level of wages corresponding to it.

First, Johnson assumes that a devaluation will improve the profits of firms producing traded goods since he claims that they will 'bid the wages up' because of their 'competition for labour'. But with a balance-of-payments deficit, the currency of the country must have been overvalued so that exporting and import-competing firms must have had their profits depressed and some may have gone out of business (see p 43). Thus a devaluation, in all probability, only restores these firms' profits to the average level and brings back into business their unemployed capacities. Under these circumstances, the firms will not be ready to pay higher wages unless perhaps devaluation has been excessive and a surplus develops.

This last tentative statement raises the question of the 'world value of labour', deficits and surpluses. Presumably the workers are paid the world value of their labour only when they are paid their marginal revenue product while the balance of payments of their country is in equilibrium and the prices of traded goods produced abroad and at home are equalized calculated on the basis of an equilibrium exchange rate. Equalized prices mean that the elasticity of substitution is infinite. But if only balance of *payments* equilibrium were required the world value of labour would not be uniquely determined because it would change with the changes in capital flows (see the transfer problem p 87). Is it, therefore, required that the balance of *trade* (visible or also invisible) itself should be in equilibrium? If that is the requirement, a devaluation could eliminate a deficit on trade account, but could never turn it into a surplus so as to replenish the reserves or pay back the loans incurred to finance the previous disequilibrium.

For this reason the only solution would be to switch to freely floating exchange rates as Johnson suggests. But even then there should not be any capital flows adverse to wages. However, would trade unions be prepared to accept, without demur, any reduction in real wages and would they know what the wage corresponding to the world value of their labour was? One is entitled to doubt it.

It sounds much more plausible to claim that the trade unions are aiming at the minimum at the preservation of the achieved real wages and will resist any reduction even for reasons of international equilibrium. If that is so, and there is some indication that it may be, freely floating exchange rates cannot work either. In 1972–3 the British trade unions were vehemently protesting against the rise in food prices caused by the world surge in their level. As a consequence the British government prevented a further fall in the allegedly freely floating sterling (see p 112 and p 172) so as to obviate an additional rise in the prices of imported goods, although the British balance of payments moved into a heavy deficit.

Johnson nevertheless believes that the trade unions cannot cause inflation by self-seeking activities even though they have monopoly power. He wrote:[1]

> The other [form] is a strong propensity, even among professional economists who should know better, to blame inflationary developments on the immoral self-seeking activities of monopolistic industries and unions. The elementary economic theory of value teaches that monopolies, either firms or unions, will seek to set a relative price for their product that maximizes profits in real terms, while monetary theory suggests that the monetary price so determined will be adjusted by national maximizers in conformity with the general changes in the price level, so as to maintain the maximizing real price relatively.

This argument would apply to trade unions that had only economic monopoly power and therefore had to act within the rules of a market economy. It does not apply to trade unions that have political influence and want to break out of the market constraints. They can push up wages regardless of the economic situation and then blame the ensuing unemployment on the government. Whether public opinion believes or does not believe that the government had caused unemployment, it will demand that the government should see to it that unemployment is reduced to what are very low normal proportions. The government has no choice but to introduce inflationary monetary and fiscal policies that validate the wage demands granted by enterprises that by now expect the government to act in this way, and granted even by the government itself under political pressure.[2] Hence the view that the general level of money

[1] H G Johnson *Inflation and the monetarist controversy* Amsterdam: North Holland 1972 p 12.

[2] For a discussion of the role of 'power' in economic activity see K W Rothschild *Power in economics* Harmondsworth: Penguin 1971 and C P Kindleberger *Power and money* London: Macmillan 1970.

wages, and so of prices, is no longer set by central bankers but by trade-union fiat.[1]

What are trade unions hoping to achieve by behaving in this way? As pointed out, they believe that they can at the minimum prevent any fall in real wages, while at the maximum they expect that they can achieve a redistribution of the national income or even force up productivity. This is not the place to discuss trade-union hopes and expectations, but it should be said that, to a large extent, they are based on a misunderstanding of economic possibilities. Insistence on the preservation of real wages at a level achieved only as a consequence of a balance-of-trade deficit makes any international adjustment impossible and means that workers in one country want to live better at the expense of workers in other countries. Possibilities of domestic redistribution are highly overrated under the present conditions of steep progressive taxation and it is often forgotten that redistribution can mean reduced investment and consequently lower growth rates. In any case, substantial redistribution cannot be achieved through manipulation of wages but only through public finance transfers; redistribution through manipulation of wages only wrecks the market system.

But the wrecking of the market system is precisely what some people hope to achieve by means of wage claims unrelated to existing economic possibilities.[2] They appear to assume that they can replace the market system, which according to them does not work because it does not allow fast rises in workers' wages, by some kind of undefined planning system that will make it possible to fulfil everybody's wishes for high wages. This belief is based on credulity that does not take into account either realistic theoretical consideration or East European experience.[3]

Trade unions may have become more inclined to claim very high wage increases because international communications have improved beyond belief for both technical and social reasons and, thus, workers in some countries can see how much better workers in other countries are paid. In other words, we have moved into the era of the international comparability of wages (see p 151), although international mobility of labour may not yet be very high. This disregards the fact that wages can be comparable only if the productivity of labour is approximately the same in the area of

[1] P Wiles 'Cost inflation and the state of economic theory' *Economist journal* (1973).

[2] See *Financial Times* (22 June 1971), which reported that a research paper had been prepared for the Confederation of Shipbuilding and Engineering Unions which tries to refute the British Government's allegation that high wage settlements were the cause of the high level of unemployment. An appendix stated, referring to the Government: 'If they cannot run an economic system . . . then we can and they should get out of the way and allow the economy to be run on social, and that means socialist, lines. In the meantime we are not going to let our wages and real standard of living suffer.'

[3] See *Outline of international trade* p 33, and L Sirc *Economic devolution in Eastern Europe* London: Longman 1969.

comparability. If it is not, comparability only prevents adjustment, the purpose of which is to keep enterprises in countries with lower efficiency in business (see p 6).

Orthodox monetarists would deny that whatever their motivation trade unions could push wages up and thus create inflation. For inflation is held to be a monetary phenomenon and can therefore originate only from an undue expansion of money supply. It is true that inflation can hardly persist if it is not accompanied by expanding money supply, but the experience of the recent years shows that this latter will be forthcoming if the trade unions first push wages up. If the money were not forthcoming the restraint could stop cost-inflation but at the price of phenomenal unemployment.

The strict monetarists deny the possibility of this kind of 'political' cost-push inflation and try to explain the happening in terms of international monetary events. Here the United States looms large because it transacts such a considerable part of international trade, although the share of commerce with other nations is so small a part of its own GNP. The result is that the United States has a decisive influence on the world price level. And since there is at least a tendency towards international traded goods price equalization, the smaller countries import inflation from the world markets.

Obviously different economies are so interconnected that, with fixed exchange rates, inflationary and deflationary movements are transferred from country to country both through expenditure and money flows and through prices (see p 92). It is also true that the United States has been exporting inflation after 1945 if for no other reason than because its relative price level has not sufficiently lowered to effect the transfer of capital that the US government and residents wished to place abroad (see pp 87 and 134). This may explain inflationary pressure in Federal Germany, which had constant payments surpluses and had to use revaluation several times to fence off more imported inflation.

But it cannot explain inflation in Britain or even France. The rise in French wages by about 15 per cent in 1968 after the May students' revolt is a worse than usual example of non-economic wage increases granted with the full connivance of the government under political duress. Besides, France devalued several times and ran into a balance-of-payments deficit. The British case will be discussed at some length (see p 130). But the strong British tendency to deficits caused Laidler[1] to observe that 'the secular increase in the balance-of-payments deficit that took place throughout Britain was importing price stability over this earlier period'. Thus the UK and France must have made their modest (in comparison with the United States) contribution to

[1] D Laidler 'The current inflation – explanations and policies', *National Westminster Bank quarterly review* 1972 p 16.

the world inflation and exported it, although France was far more ready than Britain to devalue when need be.

Laidler himself conceded that, since 1949, the British inflation rate has been consistently above the US rate, but that it has taken two devaluations to permit this. He claims that devaluations made inflation worse because 'those involved in fixing wages and prices will anticipate a period of accelerated inflation in the wake of devaluation'. Devaluation is thus necessary because a country first has a balance-of-payments deficit, presumably caused by inflation; when it then devalues, it triggers off new inflation because devaluation raises the prices of traded goods whereupon the wage fixers ask for higher wage increases than before. To solve this problem, Laidler recommends flexibility in the exchange rate, but a rate which then declines also raises prices (see p 71). What makes this description of the inflationary consequences of devaluation less convincing is the fact that in Federal Germany at least there were steep wage claims after the upward revaluation of the mark in 1969.

Expectations have been cited as an explanation of wage claims in a wider context and it has been held that a formula based on inflation rates experienced in the past can be used to assess expectations and thus to predict the future path of inflation. But if expectations are accepted as a guide to wage claims, it is admitted that these claims are no longer within the framework of the static monopoly theory and that they can vary according to what the wage negotiators expect. If they can vary according to expectations based on past experience, they can also vary according to other objectives of the negotiators which are far less easy to assess and contain.

From this conclusion it would seem that incomes policy may not be as unhelpful as some monetarists claim. It may help to reduce expectations or break behavioural patterns (see p 86) based on the pursuit of wilder objectives. Such a policy entails an effort to explain to all those concerned the economic limits to what can be done. What makes it difficult to apply such incomes policy over longer periods is that it is almost impossible to determine appropriate changes in relative prices while aiming at keeping down the absolute price level. Even if the price level in a country is stable, this situation does not mean that there will be no movement of prices of individual goods: some will rise and some will fall but these movements cancel each other out. If, on the other hand, there is a rate of inflation amounting to a given percent of the starting price level, some prices of individual goods will move ahead of the average and others will lag behind. When a government tries to control the price movements, it is almost impossible to decide how prices of individual goods should be allowed to change so as not to vitiate the working of the market mechanism.

The monetarists are, of course, right when they claim that an incomes policy on its own cannot work and that it has to be supported by monetary and fiscal policies. If prices and wages are being kept under check while there is excessive money supply and government expenditure exceeds government revenue, sooner or later prices and wages must break loose and cost-push inflation may be thus turned into a demand-pull variety.

Some equations devised by Johnson very clearly show the interdependence between individual economies through changes in international reserves, provided the monetary authorities do not try to neutralize money inflows and outflows (see p 50 and 93). It is also assumed that the country is a price-taker (small) and that all goods are traded goods, so that the domestic price level will rise and fall with the world price level with which it is connected through the fixed exchange rate.

If we start from an external monetary equilibrium, an increase in the national income g_y will cause a rise in the demand for money g_{Nd}, which will depend on the income elasticity of demand for real balances η_y and the rise in world prices during the same period, g_p

$$g_{Nd} = \eta_y g_y + g_p$$

Interest rates are assumed constant, otherwise they would also appear in the equation.

On the other hand the change in money supply g_{Ns} depends on the rise in international reserves of the country g_R and on the rise in the domestic credit g_C. In the equation below, small r denotes the initial relationship between international reserves R and domestic credit C.

$$r = \frac{R}{R+C} \text{ and } (1-r) = \frac{C}{R+C}$$

Thus

$$g_{Ns} = r g_R + (1-r) g_C$$

If a very long-term situation is looked at, or if perfect world goods and capital markets are assumed, $g_{Nd} = g_{Ns}$ and

$$\eta_y g_y + g_p = r g_R + (1-r) g_C$$

If it is now assumed that world prices have not increased ($g_p = 0$), it follows that

$$\eta_y g_y = r g_R + (1-r) g_C$$

From this it first transpires that the balance of payments will be in equilibrium; that is, there will be no change in reserves ($g_R = 0$) when

$$\eta_y g_y = (1 - r)\, g_C$$

or in other words when the increased demand for real balances exactly matches the expansion in domestic credit, taking into account that the expansion has to compensate for the lack of new reserves and thus alters r, that is the relationship between R and C.

If the link between international reserves and domestic credit expansion is broken (see p 92), so that the whole demand for money has to be met from domestic credit, $(1 - r)$ must be omitted, and

$$\eta_y g_y = g_C$$

If g_C is greater than $\eta_y g_y$ or simply g_y, if $\eta_y = 1$ there will be a balance-of-payments deficit, because the excess credit will be used to buy foreign goods since domestic prices are linked to world prices and cannot rise. The same will however also happen if

$$(1 - r)\, g_C > \eta_y g_y - r g_R$$

This formula is really a more sophisticated form (since it includes η_y and r) of $DCE = dN - B$. What it says is that, with fixed exchange rates, monetary policy must be used to keep the foreign balance in equilibrium. More than that, the government cannot control the money supply ($M_s = R + C$), but only the proportion to which money supply is backed by foreign reserves and the domestic credit respectively. Undue extension of domestic credit will reduce reserves and vice versa.

This relationship is shown also, if it is assumed that the rate of growth $g_y = 0$:

$$r g_R = -(1 - r)\, g_C$$

$$g_R = -\frac{1-r}{r}\, g_C$$

If there is no growth, any expansion in domestic credit will cause a fall of reserves, which will be the larger, the larger is g_C and the smaller is r.

Johnson further developed this approach into equations indicating that a country's reserves will grow faster (will show less tendency to a balance-of-payments deficit) the lower its initial reserve ratio, the faster the growth of total world reserves, the higher its income elasticity of demand for money and its real growth rate relative to other countries, and the lower its international reserve ratio and rate of domestic credit expansion relative to other countries.

All these relationships seem understandable with the possible exception of the statement that a country will tend towards a foreign surplus (more reserves) if it grows faster. This is in contradiction with the Keynesian claim (see p 47) that higher real growth rates tend to move a country into a foreign deficit. The different conclusions are due to different assumptions: the usual macroeconomic assumption is that the supply of money required to maintain prices constant will be forthcoming and, implicitly, that the marginal propensity to import will remain the same. On the other hand, Johnson assumes that growth makes people want to increase their real cash balances (see p 86). If there is no domestic money expansion, cash balances will be raised at the expense of buying goods which leads to a tendency for the prices to fall. This tendency in turn produces a balance-of-payments surplus and, as a consequence, a rise in the country's reserves (cf p 51).

Most of what Johnson says can be brought in line with the general drift of argument in this book and is often implicitly contained in previous chapters. Johnson justifiably discards the traditional approach of price levels moving in different ways in different countries (see p 42), but then goes to the other extreme of making all prices in all countries equalized (via fixed exchange rates). Thus he assumes that all goods are traded goods which conceals the possibility that the prices of non-traded goods and, with them, prices of services and particularly labour, may move out of line because of domestic developments. The discussion in terms of internationally equalized prices of traded goods and non-equalized prices of non-traded goods and services and labour (see p 67) also makes it clear that for the elimination of a deficit it is not enough to stop further credit expansion but that relative prices have to be altered, especially as only relative prices can indicate to economic units what to do.

If economic agents are not prepared to accept market prices for products and factors (possibly mitigated by public finance transfers), the system will head for a break-down and there is nothing to replace it. Incomes policy therefore must be used to try to persuade those working against the constraints of the system that it is in their own interest to abide by it.

The monetarist policy would work very well if commodity and factor prices were flexible, but they are not. It would also work if unemployment could be used to bring factor prices into line, but unemployment is abhorred by the public including those who regret the inflexibility of prices. Therefore the policy-makers must try to influence those causing disequilibrium directly – which should also be an exercise in economic education. Of course, such incomes policy must – as stressed earlier – be accompanied by reasonable monetary and fiscal policy.

Monetary policy on its own could only try to dampen inflationary expectations – if these are all the countries are up against – without going so far as causing serious unemployment. This approach could take long years to achieve results and the chances are that it would be overtaken by some new upheaval leading to disequilibrium. What the monetarists say, in fact, is that we should have never erred away from the path of non-inflationary development. Whatever the merit of this proposition *in abstracto,* it seems too late to apply it in 1973.

5.5 Choice of the exchange rate

Since the alteration of the exchange rate remains the eventual solution (if there is any at all) for an external imbalance under the present conditions, it would be a considerable help if it were possible to calculate by how much the exchange rate has to be devalued or revalued if the government in the end decides on this adjustment method. An approach purporting to do just that was the *purchasing power parity theory* propounded by the Swedish economist Gustav Cassel after the First World War. This theory tried to explain the equilibrium exchange rate as depending on the price levels in the countries concerned.

Its absolute interpretation says that purchasing power parities, calculated as a ratio of prices for any pair of countries, will tend to approximate the equilibrium rate of exchange. And in its relative version the doctrine asserts that the change in the equilibrium exchange rate will be equal to the change in the ratio of price levels in two countries, if we compare two equilibrium positions which differ only in regard to the absolute price levels.[1]

When treating the question of international economic equilibrium (see p 41), we said that the domestic price/cost level and the level of activity are linked via the exchange rate to the world price/cost level and activity level. This would indicate that the exchange rate is dependent on price/cost levels, if the levels of activity, or in a dynamic situation the level of output, remains the same. The relative interpretation of the theory of purchasing power parity is therefore right in stressing that the two positions it refers to may differ only 'in regard to the two price levels'. This qualification alone would make the usefulness of the doctrine for practical computation problematic, as chances are that the level of activity and/or the output change over time. In fact, it is possible that the price levels remain the same, but that the exchange rate nevertheless has to change in order to maintain external balance if countries experience different real rates of growth or if there are capital movements, to mention

[1] See Bela Balassa 'The purchasing power parity doctrine: a reappraisal' in Cooper *International finance* and also F Lutz *The problem of international economic equilibrium* chapter 2.

only two most important 'other changes'.

But there are more complications. As repeatedly pointed out, the prices of traded goods cannot change because of foreign competition. They are linked with foreign prices of traded goods through the exchange rate itself, taking into account transport costs and barriers to trade. Thus, as far as prices of traded goods are concerned, the price level will not express the imbalance at all. On the other hand, the imbalance may be reflected in the prices of non-traded goods because the possible increased demand, which cannot pull up the prices of traded goods, will pull up the price of non-traded goods. But again, in order to link the rise in prices of non-traded goods with the necessary change in the exchange rate to establish equilibrium, we would have to know to what extent increased demand influences the price level of non-traded goods and to what extent it is responsible for excessive imports.

However, even if we could find that out, the link between the exchange rate and the price levels of non-traded goods would not be defined. Non-traded 'goods' are mainly services belonging to the tertiary sector. They are 'non-traded' because of the immobility or lower mobility of factors of production between countries. These services are on the whole far more labour-intensive than the products of the primary and secondary sectors, which also explains why productivity in the tertiary sector rises less quickly than in the primary and secondary sectors. But salaries and wages in the tertiary sector must be comparable with salaries and wages in the other two sectors; otherwise people would move into these sectors and the supply of tertiary services would be insufficient. As a consequence, the prices of the same services in countries with different income per head of the population (stemming from different efficiencies) vary while the prices of traded goods at least tend to be equal at the existing exchange rate. As a result, even wage rates cannot give us a clue as to what exactly the equilibrium exchange rate should be, as they are co-determined by the prices of both traded and non-traded goods, and the payments imbalance. The prices of traded goods tend to keep wages down, while the prices of non-traded goods and the imbalance pull them up.

All the considerations enumerated further indicate why it is so difficult to compare real incomes internationally.[1]

If the official national income figures in domestic currency are taken for the United States and United Kingdom and converted to the same currency at the official exchange rate (table 14), it appears that the British national income per head was 42 per cent of the US national income per head. Recalculating the national income at US or UK

[1] W Beckerman and R Bacon 'International comparison of income levels, a suggested new measure' *Economic journal* 1966; and Dan Usher *Rich and poor countries, a study in problems of comparisons of real income* London: Institute of Economic Affairs 1966.

prices changes the result to 64 per cent and 51 per cent respectively, mainly because in the first case the prices in the British tertiary sector are brought up to the level of US prices, while in the second case the US tertiary prices are pulled down to the British level. When the US and Soviet national incomes are compared, the calculation of the official rates is dispensed with because the rouble exchange rate is utterly artificial. The calculation at US and Soviet prices yields results similar to the US/UK comparison.

Table 14
Real income per head as percentage of the real income of the US

	at domestic prices converted at official exchange rate	at US prices	at local prices	geometrical average
UK 1955	42	64	51	57
USSR 1955	–	45	22	31

This exercise shows that there is no objective measure of real income. It cannot be said that the UK national income per head in 1955 was either 64 or 51 per cent of the US national income per head. This depends on whether we use the subjective evaluation of goods and services prevailing in the British or American situations. The calculation of a geometrical average is entirely arbitrary and serves only to merge two figures into one without any rational explanation of why it should be done in this particular way. Meaningful unique figures could be obtained only if there were perfect mobility of factors in addition to perfect mobility of all goods all over the world. In that case there would be only one set of prices, so that bundles of goods, representing national income per head in different countries at the same time, could be compared with each other.

Returning to the purchasing power parity, we find that here too no unique figures can be arrived at (table 15).

Table 15
Purchasing power parity calculated through GNP (£ in US $)

	official rate	at US weights	at UK weights
1955	2·8	3·14	3·68
1960	2·8	2·96	4·44

The general formula for calculating absolute purchasing power parity is

$$\frac{\Sigma p_2 q}{\Sigma p_1 q} = \text{purchasing power parity between countries 2 and 1}$$

We take a bundle of goods and services and multiply it by the set of prices in countries 1 and 2. When we divide the figure representing the bundle at one set of prices with the figure representing the same bundle at the other set of prices, we obtain a figure for the purchasing power parity between the two countries. But in order to avoid taking an entirely arbitrary bundle we take the quantities of goods and services in the GNP of one country, multiply it by the prices of the compared country, and divide it by the same GNP at original prices. Of course, the GNP of either of the two countries can be taken, and the results are different for reasons that should by now be clear. Not only are the results different, but in table 15 they move in different directions.

This movement in opposite directions foils even the hope that it would be possible to say, if not whether a currency is over-valued at the existing exchange rate, at least whether it is becoming more or less so. It is usually believed that a currency can be called over-valued if domestic prices, converted at the existing exchange rate, are higher than world prices, or if the calculation shows that the purchasing power of a currency is lower in terms of another currency than the existing exchange rate. According to table 15, in 1960 £1 could buy goods worth between \$2·96 and \$4·44, which would have meant that the dollar was overvalued *vis-à-vis* the pound at the official rate of £1 = \$2·80.

But the prices of traded goods tend to be equal everywhere, and prices of non-traded goods differ for reasons that have only partly to do with the exchange rate. The fact that purchasing power parities are higher than the official exchange rate may in this case simply be a result of the much higher US prices in the tertiary sector. At any rate, we know that the pound was over-valued in the 1960s because it had to be devalued in 1967. The only firm sign of over-valuation is an actual persistent balance-of-payments deficit. Of course, the pound could have been over-valued generally, but not with respect to the dollar; however, this seems improbable in view of the importance of US trade for Britain.

The conclusion must be that there is no easy way of calculating the equilibrium exchange rate. The only precise method would be to calculate it by means of a general equilibrium system of the whole world, which is naturally not feasible. Even if there were the computational capacity, the collection of data would take so long that the result would be obsolete when calculated.

Because that is so, it has often been suggested that equilibrium exchange rates should be arrived at by allowing the exchange rates to float for a while, This method for arriving at equilibrium exchanges rates when they are out of line was tried on a large scale in the second half of 1971. But there were soon complaints that the new rates would not be fair.

Britain, for instance, claimed then that the exchange rate brought about by floating while she had high unemployment, little growth and high interest rates would be detrimental to her future prospects because it would be too high. In 1973, on the contrary, the British government would not allow the sterling to fall further (see p 172) because this would further raise import prices and endanger the government's incomes policy.

Governments were also criticized for their open or surreptitious intervention in the markets that turned free floating into 'dirty' floating. Foreign exchange markets are nearly perfect markets as long as governments do not intervene. If they do, the governments of the big countries can certainly influence prices, in this case the exchange rates. They seemed to do it almost as a defensive reaction, since they expected other governments to interfere and could not allow them to load the dice in their own favour.

Thus the equilibrium exchange rate can be neither precisely calculated nor even exactly arrived at by 'floating'. It is in the end the result of a political compromise, at least in so far as the bigger countries are concerned. It is a result of political compromise because all countries can play the game. An important consideration therefore in particular in the US and the British case, is not to provoke or allow other countries to follow suit. With the pound the expected change in other currencies is specially important as the currencies of the sterling area used to move in step. In the 1930s countries used to indulge in 'competitive devaluation', each changing the exchange rate following the other and in this way undoing the adjustment possibly achieved. It seems that the percentage of the British devaluation in 1967 was the maximum devaluation expected not to bring too many other currencies down.

In spite of the scepticism in this section, the IMF seems to have developed a model for the calculation of equilibrium exchange rates and it used it in 1971 to calculate how the exchange rates should be re-aligned after that year's crisis (see p 168). The results were leaked, to the great irritation of the United States.

further reading

general books

W M Corden	'The geometric representation of policies to attain internal and external balance' in Cooper *International finance*
H G Johnson	'Theoretical problems of the international monetary system' in Cooper *International finance*
F Machlup	'Theory of foreign exchange' in his *International monetary economics*
M Michaely	The responsiveness of demand policy to balance of payments – postwar patterns New York: Columbia University Press 1971
R A Mundell	'Appropriate use of monetary and fiscal policy for internal and external stability' *IMF staff papers* (1962)
R A Mundell	'Capital mobility and stabilisation policy under fixed and flexible exchange rates' reprinted in Caves and Johnson *Readings in international economics*
E Sohmen	'The assignment problem' in Mundell and Swoboda (eds), *Monetary problems of the international economy*

domestic credit expansion

C A E Goodhart and A D Crockett	'The importance of money' *Bank of England quarterly bulletin* 1970
D Kern	'The implications of DCE' *National Westminster Bank quarterly review* 1970
F M Samuel	*Domestic credit expansion* Economic Research Studies no 1 London: Panmure Gordon 1969

monetarist approach

H G Johnson	*Inflation and the monetarist controversy* Amsterdam: North Holland 1972

H G Johnson	'The monetary approach to balance-of-payments policy' in Connoly and Swoboda *International trade and money*
D Laidler	'The current inflation – explanations and policies' *National Westminster Bank quarterly review* 1972
P Wiles	'Cost inflation and the state of economic theory' *Economic journal,* 1973

prices and exchange rates

B Balassa	'The purchasing-power parity: a reappraisal' in Cooper *International finance*
F Lutz	*The problem of international economic equilibrium* Amsterdam: North Holland 1962
W Beckerman and R Bacon	'International comparison of income levels: a suggested new measure' *Economic journal* (1966)
D Usher	*Rich and poor nations: a study in problems of comparisons of real income* London: Institute of Economic Affairs 1966
D Usher	*The price mechanism and the meaning of national income statistics* London: Oxford University Press 1969

chapter 6
adjustment systems

6.1 Fixed versus flexible exchange rates

It has been repeatedly pointed out that there are two possible arrangements with regard to exchange rates. Their determination may be entirely left to the exchange markets, when we speak of the system of flexible exchange rates; or the government maintains their movement within narrow limits through intervention in the exchange markets, which is the system of fixed exchange rates. At present there is some ambiguity in this terminology: under the IMF system exchange rates are fixed within limits for prolonged periods but may be changed by decree if a country finds itself in fundamental disequilibrium (see p 44). Sometimes this *adjustable peg* is considered sufficient to call the exchange rates flexible in contrast with the pre-First World War arrangement, when some of the leading exchange rates were in fact fixed for centuries. However, if the adjustable peg is called flexible, the daily flexible rates have to be termed something else, usually *freely floating* or *fluctuating* exchange rates. In this text the term *flexible* is used for exchange rates freely determined by the market, in principle without government intervention, and the term *fixed* is used for the adjustable peg.

When comparing fixed and flexible rates in this sense one has to be careful not to ascribe to the adjustable peg the characteristics of permanently fixed rates, but to keep in mind that, while the adjustable peg is fixed over long periods, it may then be abruptly altered. On the other hand, the pre-1914 permanently fixed exchange rate also did not mean that there was no flexibility in the system: if the exchange rate was fixed, the internal prices were adjustable up and also down. Upheaval then showed in changing internal prices; now it shows in pressure on the exchange rate. If there were fewer symptoms of upheaval then, that was because there was less upheaval in the economy, not because the system was better. It must not be forgotten that in the nineteenth century 2 per cent real growth per year was a respectable figure, while nowadays countries are aiming at 6 per cent and more. Growth, beneficial though it may be, requires restructuring and as a consequence causes economic and social strains, including the need for international adjustment. Even internally fast growth requires fast change in the production structures, and with external trade links the need for structural change tends to be intensified.

Sometimes it is said that flexible exchange rates (and this would refer to both floating rates and adjustable peg devaluation) cannot work because the elasticities are not sufficient. The question has been dealt with at some length (see p 73) and it transpired that elasticity pessimism is probably exaggerated. But if it applied, it would apply to permanently fixed rates also. Their adjustment mechanism is fundamentally the same – the alteration of the relationship between prices of traded and non-traded goods – but in this case through changes in the prices of domestic non-traded goods. Therefore a lack of sensitivity to price changes would lead to the impossibility of adjustment without unemployment in exactly the same way as in the case of adjustable peg or floating rates.

If the economy or economies did, in fact, become impervious to prices the government would have to take over the decision-making (see p 65); and government controls are often cited as the third adjustment system. But then governments could not rely on qualitative controls (price changes or multiple exchange rates) for the simple reason that they also require responsiveness to price changes. It would have to use wholesale quantitative controls, which would amount to central planning with all its inherent problems.[1]

Businessmen tend to favour fixed exchange rates because they *seem* to reduce their risks. It is true that cyclical fluctuations in exchange rates can be ironed out by the use of government reserves for intervention in the markets and that thus one source of instability and short-term risk is eliminated. But this does not do away with the long-term risks owing to fundamental disequilibria. Here the choice is between gradual adjustment through a moving exchange rate and an abrupt adjustment when the underlying circumstances change to such a degree that the existing exchange rate can be no longer preserved.

With freely floating exchange rates businessmen can avoid short-term risk by using forward markets (see p 8). But it is doubtful whether forward markets could be sufficiently developed to cater for all needs if rates were entirely flexible. Also, it is not clear what the price of forward cover would be and how much it would thus add to the cost of foreign trade and by how much it would therefore reduce international competition. The longest forward cover is at present usually three months, which is insufficient for many international operations. But in this respect the situation is no different with the adjustable peg. With that arrangement the exchange rate can also change in the long run if changing economic circumstances so require. At least a partial answer could be exchange rate insurance, which some governments are sponsoring.

[1] See *Outline of international trade* p 33.

When considering the long-term aspect, the risk resulting from the need for adjustment when there is a fundamental disequilibrium cannot be eliminated, but the question is whether adjustment should be immediate and continuous or delayed and sudden. If adjustment is delayed the price signals given to firms can be misleading. If a disequilibrium is allowed to persist some firms in surplus countries will enjoy an artificial prosperity, although this would be curtailed through a move back to balance, while some firms in deficit countries may be in the doldrums only because equilibrium is not re-established (see p 67). If then the alteration in the exchange rates comes suddenly after some delay, the ground may be cut from under the feet of the hitherto prosperous firms in one country, while the signal that firms in the other country were in the red may come fortuitously after these firms have closed down and their factors have been transferred elsewhere (see p 43).

In whatever way adjustment comes and price signals are changed, a re-structuring of the economy, and hence of firms, will be necessary in most cases. With a freely flexible rate adjustment this is a continuous process; with the adjustable peg it is a sudden discontinuity in development. This second method may be dangerous, because firms are allowed to live for some time in a fool's paradise and may then be awakened to the fact that the signals they were receiving were wrong and they are expected to carry through a major adjustment.

However, excessively fast adjustment can reduce or even eliminate the effectiveness of international competition. Exchange rates are a device to enable firms in different countries with different average efficiencies to compete with each other. If exchange rates are fixed, any increase in what is called *x-efficiency*[1] and technical efficiency in one country will cause competitive pressure in the other countries. If the improvement is on a sufficiently large scale it will also create an international imbalance. The firms under pressure may fight back by trying to improve their own efficiency and thus at least partly redress the balance. If the exchange rate changes as soon as there is an imbalance, it takes at least some of the competitive presssure off the firms in the other country and thus may considerably impede the transmission of efficiency, and therefore growth, through international competition.

The preceding passage about the role of exchange rates is an indication that they are not ordinary prices, meaning that there is a presumption that it is best to let them fluctuate. They are not ordinary prices because there are vast areas, as for instance the United States, where the same currency is used and no exchange rates are interposed. Nevertheless, hardly anybody claims that it would be advantageous to introduce exchange rates between various regions of the present large territories with a unified currency.

[1] Harvey Leibenstein 'Allocative efficiency versus 'x-efficiency' *American economic review* (1966).

More than that: a separate branch of study on optimal currency areas[1] tries to judge whether the present nation states are the best size for unitary currencies or whether currency areas should be organized on some different basis. Research so far is not fully conclusive, but it does point out that exchange rates have to be used in a particular way, and not just like any other price. Fixed exchange rates turn countries into unified currency areas as long as they last, and flexible exchange rates interpose some kind of filter which separates economic developments in different countries.

In fact, freely flexible exchange rates do give countries a considerable amount of freedom[2] to pursue their internal economic goals. In chapter 5 we discussed the attempts by countries to insulate themselves from world events by fixed exchange rates and neutralization of currency flows, but there the conclusion was that in the end they have to introduce adjustment. Freely flexible exchange rates insulate in a different way by providing continuous adjustment, which is however paid for by continuous changes of prices in foreign currency and therefore by possibly continuous re-structuring of the economy.

Freely flexible exchange rates, on the other hand, stop inflation (and for that matter also deflation and unemployment) from spreading from country to country, while under fixed exchange rates countries have to accept at least some inflation from abroad (but see p 71). However it is claimed that freely flexible exchange rates may foster domestic indiscipline. Whereas domestic inflation under fixed exchange rates immediately causes an external imbalance leading to a loss of reserves, it does not do so under flexible exchange rates since a change in the rate automatically corrects the imbalance. But what is worse from the viewpoint of governments: falling gold and currency reserves or a depreciating exchange rate? Obviously, falling reserves are dangerous as they are finite, but a falling rate certainly also has considerable disadvantages.

As it is an embarrassment, governments may be tempted to interfere in order to maintain exchange rates at certain levels. Thus, during the floating of some rates in the autumn of 1971, the governor of the Bank of England called for a return to fixed parities and said that 'the floating alternative was feared because it was believed that it would inevitably be associated with mounting exchange controls and trade restrictions to the detriment of international commerce.'[3] However, usually exactly the opposite is claimed: that the governments will have great difficulty in preserving fixed exchange rates and will for this reason resort to controls and restrictions to protect their reserves. It would be all right, the argument goes, to have fixed parities if the

[1] R I McKinnon – see bibliography at the end of this chapter.

[2] Samuel Brittan called his book advocating freely flexible rates *The price of economic freedom* London: Macmillan 1970.

[3] *The Times* (23 November 1971).

government would not maintain them by manipulating trade. In fact, with fixed exchanged rates, governments often find that they either have to interfere heavily with their domestic policies in order to maintain external equilibrium, or have to apply direct controls and thus avoid such interference, at least for the time being. It could be said that, with flexible exchange rates, adjustment may be too unpredictable and fast, and with fixed exchange rates too painful, for the government not to feel obliged to act in some way.

Finally, there is the question of whether speculation (see p 10) would be worse under fixed or flexible exchange rates, and whether speculation would be stabilizing or destabilizing. On the whole the scope for speculation is wider under flexible exchange rates since they may move at any time; but as they may move in either direction, up or down, speculators can easily burn their fingers. So speculators do in this case perform a useful function of ironing out cyclical movements. Under the adjustable peg, speculators are shooting at a sitting duck. By the time a parity is about to be changed the situation is so clear that it is an absolute certainty in which direction it is going to move. The guessing is only about the exact time. Over the last decade we have therefore seen enormous movements of 'hot money' trying to profit from the impending alteration of fixed rates. If he misjudged the moment, the speculator could withdraw his funds at little cost and place them again in the appropriate country when he thinks fit.

When one reads through arguments of this kind about the advantage and disadvantage of the adoption of alternative solutions, one begins to doubt whether economic theory has anything to offer. But when economists offer different solutions this does not necessarily mean that they disagree about theory, only that they expect different responses, either from the public or from the governments. Given different reactions and attitudes, different policies are required.[1]

6.2 The gold standard

Whatever the advantages and disadvantages of fixed versus flexible exchange rates, the latter were used only intermittently, while exchange rates fixed within narrow limits were the rule. Historically, their predominance in the last few centuries is understandable, as earlier gold coins were used, the value of which depended on their gold content, which thus also determined the value of one kind of gold coin in terms of another.

When the price-specie flow-adjustment mechanism was considered (see p 58) it was

[1] Cf F Machlup and B G Malkiel (eds) *International monetary management: the problem of choice* (report on the deliberations of an international study group of 32 economists) Princeton New Jersey: International Finance Section 1964;

described how this mechanism would react when gold coins were in circulation. When the leading countries passed from circulating commodity money to the credit money of banknotes backed by a fractional reserve of gold, the mechanism of price changes triggered off by purchasing-power flows continued to function, but in a more complicated form.

Banknotes have no *intrinsic* value, so that their value, or rather the value of units in which they were denominated, depended on the quantity of gold the central bank of a country was held to pay in exchange for them. In fact, one rule of the gold game, or one of the regulations defining what is called the gold standard, was that a central bank must always stand ready to convert its banknotes into gold and vice versa on application of any individual, and that it must do this at a rate that was called the *gold parity* or *mint parity* of a currency. Since the leading currencies were thus all defined in terms of gold, gold also linked them with each other. The exchange rate between two currencies was normally equal to the ratio of their mint parities. These arrangements amounted to a fixed exchange rate between leading national currencies, and therefore to a unified currency area within which money was not identical, but where one currency was easily convertible into another at a predetermined rate.

Currencies were not only convertible into gold but could be bought and sold for each other in exchange markets. There was no reason to convert them into gold as long as the market rates were in line with mint parities. However, if the market rate strayed away from the exchange rate aligned with mint parities as a result of a balance-of-payments disequilibrium, it could become advantageous not to buy or sell foreign currency directly but to use the possibility of converting currencies into gold.

If, for instance, the price of the pound sterling in the exchange market was falling, ie if less and less was paid for it in terms of dollars, a point came when it was advantageous to ask the central bank to convert the pound into gold at mint parity, ship gold to the United States and reconvert it there into dollars, again at the official mint parity. The point where this roundabout operation becomes profitable was the point at which the disparity between mint-parity-aligned par value and the market rate was more than the cost of shipping gold abroad, consisting of freight, insurance, interest rates during transit, commission, etc. The opposite would be true if the price of the dollar was falling in terms of the pound; in this case gold would be shipped from the United States to Britain.

The gold import point was the market exchange rate just sufficiently divergent from the mint par value to make import of gold profitable; the gold export point was the market rate which made export of gold profitable. The imports and exports would be carried out either by businessmen who needed foreign currency to fulfil their commitments or by gold arbitrageurs profiting from the divergence between market rates and mint parities.

Another rule of the gold game was that central banks had to adapt their monetary policy to the inflows and outflows of gold. They had to expand the money supply when gold was flowing in and to restrict it when gold was flowing out. This was, of course, also in conformity with legal reserve requirements as operated in those days.

Gold flowed out therefore when the market value of a country's currency in terms of other currencies was falling because the country had a balance-of-payments deficit. This made the central bank restrict the money supply and raise interest rates, which in turn tended to reduce commodity prices. This tendency boosted exports, so that the balance-of-payments deficit was eliminated when the pressure on commodity prices was sufficiently raised by the deflation triggered off by the outflow of gold. If a country was in surplus and the value of its currency was rising, gold inflow led to inflation and a tendency to rising prices, which eventually curtailed the surplus.[1]

At least, this is the theory of how the gold standard and the rules of the gold game worked. Its functioning depended on the link between the supply of money and the price and cost levels. The quantity theory of money claims this link to be direct, but even if such a simple kind of link is not accepted and the possibility of changes in the velocity[2] of money are taken into account, an indirect link between the supply of money and the price and cost levels must exist unless it is assumed that velocity changes can be infinite.

Regardless of the link between money supply and prices, it is often asserted[3] that during the period when the gold standard is alleged to have functioned many forces were at work that were not accounted for in the model. Thus it is said that deflation following gold outflow was not entirely reflected in falling prices, but also caused unemployment because wages even at that time were hardly flexible downwards. Often however gold flows did not occur, but were partly replaced by short-term capital movements, in fact international credit, which helped a country over the period of a deficit. At any rate it is easy to believe that the actual system was more complex than the theoretical model, but it seems to have worked tolerably well until the First World War.

[1] See p 43 for an explanation of how the terms 'rising' and 'falling' prices are used as shorthand for a much more complicated process.

[2] Velocity of circulation is a measure of the speed of turnover of a stock of money. W T Newlyn *Theory of money* Oxford: Clarendon Press 1971 p 79.

[3] See Herbert G Grubel *The international monetary system* Harmondsworth: Penguin 1969 and Robert Triffin *Our international monetary system* New York: Random 1968, the relevant passage also under 'The myth and realities of the so-called gold standard' in Cooper *International finance*.

6.3 The International Monetary Fund

Whatever the success of the gold standard system in the nineteenth and at the beginning of the twentieth century, it did break down between the two wars. Commodity and factor prices became more inflexible downwards (see p 52). Therefore governments had to pursue full employment policies to the neglect of external balance.

In this situation it was very costly in terms of employment to try to restore the pre-war parity of a currency after the wartime inflation, something that the British government tried in 1924–5. In the end a world crisis broke out and countries abandoned the gold standard in 1931. This was an era of confused internal and external policies, competitive devaluations, restrictions of trade, attempts to survive at the expense of other countries, of the so-called 'beggar-my-neighbour' policy. Everybody lost in the 1930s, international trade was almost halved from the previous peak level of about $56 billion.

The chaos lasted throughout the 1930s so that, even during the Second World War, the Allied powers considered it one of their tasks to prepare plans for post-war commercial and financial institutions that would establish the framework for orderly trade. The two main blueprints for the post-war financial system came from the United States, represented by Harry D White, and the United Kingdom, with Lord Keynes as spokesman. The British delegation consistently advocated a very 'liberal' system which would give deficit countries the right to borrow automatically within very wide limits, while the Americans were afraid that such largesse would lead to irresponsible behaviour by participating countries and that the United States would have to foot the bill.[1] Finally, the agreement on the establishment of the International Monetary Fund was signed at Bretton Woods in 1944.

The same conference at Bretton Woods established the World Bank, officially called the International Bank for Reconstruction and Development, the main task of which is to make or guarantee long-term loans for development projects in developing countries. In the 1950s two other agencies were founded to work with the World Bank: the International Finance Corporation and the International Development Association. The first was to help with loans to private enterprise in developing countries, the second to provide loans to the countries at lower interest rates and under more favourable repayment conditions that the World Bank itself could offer.

The 1944 payments organization may be called the IMF system. It took account of the changes in the period between two wars but tried simultaneously to apply some of the methods used under the gold standard in a modified way.

Internal and external economic developments remain separated from each other under the post-war system. Countries now hold reserves consisting of gold and key

[1] See Sir Roy Harrod *The life of Lord Keynes* London: Macmillan 1963.

currencies (see p 128). We therefore speak of a gold exchange standard.But changes in reserves are no longer intended automatically to influence internal money supply. Reserves, strengthened by the borrowed reserves available from the IMF, have the purpose of financing any deficit that comes about because the pursuance of internal goals is not consistent with the external balance. If the inconsistency is only cyclical, the use of reserves suffices to tide a country over the difficulties. In the case of fundamental disequilibrium, the IMF provides the possibility of a change in the exchange rate.

Private persons and firms may no longer ask central banks to convert their national currencies into gold, but a central bank is (or at least was until 1971) entitled to submit the national currency of a country to the central bank of that country for conversion. In practice that meant that the central banks would accumulate dollars which the United States was prepared to convert into gold at the official price till August 1971. Private persons, on the other hand, can in principle buy foreign currencies in the exchange market, while the central bank has the responsibility for ensuring that the market exchange rate remains within the prescribed limits from the par value. The margins had been one per cent up and down from the official par value, but this 'band' was widened to 2·25 per cent on each side in 1971. If, then, private persons decide to sell their foreign currency in the market, the central bank will have to intervene and buy up the excess of this currency which threatens to depress its exchange rate. As a result the central bank will acquire foreign currency that private persons are no longer prepared to hold and may submit it to the appropriate other central banks for conversion. Thus effects very similar to the effects of the gold standard are achieved by a roundabout way.

a *par values*

The Articles of the IMF require that each government should declare the par value of its currency in gold or in US dollars. The declared parity then has to be maintained by government intervention in its exchange markets within the limits of one per cent, or 2·25 per cent since 1971.

If a country finds itself in a fundamental disequilibrium (not more closely defined in the Articles, but described on p 44) it is allowed to alter its exchange rate. In order to make the initial adjustments of par values easier, the Fund rules provided for an initial change of up to 10 per cent without either consultation with or consent by the Fund Board. After this initial once-and-for-all alteration limit has been exhausted the Fund has to be consulted about any change in a country's exchange rate. If a country changes the par value without the consent of the Fund it can be barred from the Fund's facilities.

The difficulty of determining the right exchange rate for a country's currency has been discussed (see p 108). The additional difficulty is that this system of occasional adjustment of par values, called *the adjustable peg,* attracts speculation (see p 119) against the currency that is under pressure and whose par value may be altered. To impair speculation somewhat any alteration is surrounded by much secrecy, and often the measure is taken first and the Fund asked for its consent afterwards.

b *fund quotas*

Each member country of the Fund is allotted a quota determining its capital subscription, its borrowing potential and its voting power.

The initial quotas amounted altogether to $7·7 billion. There is a five-yearly review of quotas. After the admission of new members and an increase in quotas by 50 per cent in 1958, the sum total of quotas amounted to $15 billion in 1959. In 1965 the quotas were again raised by 25 per cent and some countries were allowed special increases, so that the quotas rose to $21 billion. In 1970 a new general increase by 35 per cent was introduced, bringing the quotas to $28 billion.

The quotas of the leading countries in 1970 are shown in table 16.

Table 16

	$ billion
United States	6,700
United Kingdom	2,800
Germany (Western)	1,600
France	1,500
Japan	1,200
Canada	1,100
Italy	1,000
India	940
Netherlands	700

The quotas are calculated on the basis of a country's economic size, foreign trade and gold and currency reserves. The communist countries, with the exception of Yugoslavia, are not members; nor is Switzerland.

The capital subscription of member countries has to be paid into the Fund: 25 per cent of the quota in gold and 75 per cent in the country's national currency.

c *borrowing from the Fund*

In principle, the member countries cannot draw, ie borrow, more than 25 per cent of their quota per year. When borrowing a country has to deposit the equivalent of the loan in its own currency with the Fund.

Any country can automatically draw until the Fund holdings of its currency amount to 100 per cent of its quota. This means that it can automatically draw as much as the *gold tranche,* the equivalent of its gold subscription to the Fund. It can also automatically draw the equivalent of other countries' borrowings of its own currency from the Fund.

Drawings bringing Fund's holdings of a country's currency above 100 per cent of its quota but still below 125 per cent, which is the so-called *first credit tranche,* are no longer automatic but are still easily granted. Any drawings over 125 per cent should be temporary and should contribute to monetary stability. The total borrowings of a country from the Fund are limited in so far as the Fund must not hold more than 200 per cent of any country's quota in its currency. Since 75 per cent of a country's quota are subscribed in the country's currency, a country can borrow up to 200 per cent minus 75 per cent – 125 per cent of its quota.

The countries using Fund facilities must accept regular consultation with the Fund's representatives and a certain degree of surveillance, scrutiny and criticism of the country's economic policy.

In addition to being allowed straightforward drawings on the Fund, member countries can also be granted *stand-by arrangements.* Under these arrangements they are given, against safeguards similar to those for straightforward drawings, the possibility of drawing amounts agreed upon from the Fund within certain periods. Very often such arrangements are by themselves sufficient to restore international confidence in a country's currency, so that actual drawing is not necessary at all. For this facility the countries have to pay a *commitment charge* of 0·25 per cent of the amount earmarked.

Following the first Unctad (United Nations Conference on Trade and Development) in 1962[1] a new special compensatory facility was provided for developing countries experiencing balance-of-payments difficulties because of fluctuations in export earnings from primary commodities. Buffer stocks under international agreements may also be financed by means of special drawings.

Repayment, technically *repurchase,* of a country's national currency from the Fund has to be made within three to five years. Its phasing depends on the country's currency deposits with the Fund and the movement of its reserves. At some stage the country also has to consult with the Fund regarding the implementation of repayments. For their outstanding drawings the countries are charged a commission of 0·5 per cent, an interest rate of up to 5 per cent, and under special conditions even more. per year depending on the size and duration of the overdraft.

As an illustration of drawings and repurchases from the IMF the UK account with the IMF is reproduced in table 17. It should be self-explanatory in the light of what was said in this subsection.

[1] See *Outline of international trade* pp 137 and 142

Table 17
UK account with the IMF

	1963	1964	1965	1966	1967	1968	1969	1970	1971	1972
gold subscription				−44				−38	−	(−33)‡
UK drawings		+357	+500	+44		+583	+354	+63	−	−
UK repurchases					−249	−77	−382	−141	−541	−21
Net drawings (−) of pounds by others	+5		−10	−29	−89	−	−2	−56	−13	−102
IMF holding of pounds*	522	881	1377	1358	1439†	1965	1950	1929	1374	1132†
UK IMF position**	871	512	16	205	594	68	83	404	959	1215

UK assets with IMF: increase − ; decrease +
UK liabilities with IMF: increase + ; decrease −

* Apart from the transactions in the first four rows, the IMF holdings of the pound are affected by administrative and operational changes and receipts.
** The amount the UK could draw without raising IMF holdings of the pound beyond 200 per cent.
† Includes maintenance of value adjustment.
‡ Revaluation of gold tranche in terms of sterling.
UK quota: before 1966 £696 million; later £871 million at $2·80 per pound and £1,017 million at $2·40 per pound; in 1970 £1,167 million. From March 1972 the unit of account of the IMF was changed from dollars to SDRs, which means to the dollar value before 1971. From the first quarter 1972, assets and liabilities are valued at current market rates of exchange.

Source: Financial statistics, under 'Overseas Sector'.

d *elimination of exchange restrictions*

In the same way as GATT,[1] or rather the original Havana Charter, was to eliminate restrictions on trade under the IMF agreement, the member countries were to liberalize international payments. Both institutions should in fact work hand in hand.

The first attempt at freeing the payments by Britain in 1947 ended in disaster in spite of loans from the United States ($3,750 million) and Canada ($1,250 million). The drive for convertibility was as a consequence postponed until 1958 when ten European countries liberated payments on current account. Later, some of them also freed payments on capital account, but short-term speculative movements remain a problem.

While the IMF agreement fosters convertibility, it does contain provisions for declaring a currency *scarce* and as a consequence for permitting governments to impose restrictions on the transactions in this currency. The purpose of the *scarce currency clause* was to put pressure on surplus countries to co-operate in the adjustment process. They are defined as countries achieving a credit position by means of trade restrictions or by means of excessively low par values.

Since an excessively low parity or *under-valuation* of a currency necessarily leads to a balance-of-payments surplus or credit position, this clause was aimed at surplus countries in general as a part of the wider question of how the burden of adjustment should be shared between deficit and surplus countries. In the wartime discussion, Keynes suggested that interest rates should not be paid only by deficit countries on their overdrafts but also by surplus countries that have accumulated assets on their accounts with the clearing union. Initially, this precaution was directed against the United States, then the only candidate for substantial surpluses, as was also the scarce currency clause, the compromise solution.

But as will be explained later (see p 132) the United States after a while ceased to be in its initial strong position. The two countries in a surplus position in the 1960s and later have been Western Germany and Japan. Certainly under the gold standard, which German economists and politicians may accept as a valid model, deficit countries were to deflate and surplus countries to inflate. However, Germany objected that her surpluses were a consequence not of normal ups and downs of internal prices, but of the undisciplined permanent inflation in debtor countries. The Germany government said it had no intention of importing inflation. Germany did revalue upward in 1961, 1969, 1971 and 1973, but the scarce currency clause has so far not been invoked either against her or any other country.

[1] General Agreement on Tariffs and Trades, *see Outline of international trade, p 124.*

6.4 Criticism of the IMF system

Until the early 1960s the IMF system had worked smoothly enough, but then shortcomings began to appear on all sides. Criticism crystallized around the following points: (1) fragility of reserve or key currencies; (2) insufficient liquidity or wrong composition of liquidity; (3) excessively slow or, paradoxically, excessively fast adjustment (but this second criticism merges with the point on liquidity shortage); and (4) the turbulence caused by speculative money movements.

a *fragility of reserve currencies*

The IMF system inherited from the interwar period the arrangement by which reserves of a country are no longer held in gold but in a combination of gold and convertible currencies. The two currencies used for this purpose, called *reserve currencies* or *key currencies*, are the pound sterling and the dollar. The pound sterling predominated until after the war but then the dollar became more important.

The key-currency reserves take the form of bank balances in the two key-currency countries or of short-term securities issued by governments. They are short-term claims on these countries, or rather on their governments or monetary institutions. (See p 24 on the balance of foreign assets and liabilities.) In contrast to gold, which does not bring any returns, balances or securities normally yield interest. This makes them a far more profitable method of holding cash, unless there are prospects that gold will appreciate or the key currency depreciate. The purpose of reserves is to tide the country over a balance-of-payments deficit, since they can be used to make payments either to the key-currency country itself (UK and US) or to other countries that hold their reserves in key currencies. If they are used for payments to key-currency countries themselves, this means that these countries can offer goods at competitive terms and are running a balance-of-payments surplus. If on the other hand the key-currency countries cannot offer goods at competitive terms, not only will their currency, held by foreigners, not return, but foreign holdings of short-term claims on them, or their debt, will increase.

If a key currency keeps running a balance-of-payments deficit and its money accumulates in foreign hands, confidence in its currency may be undermined as there is the danger that the currency will have to be devalued if the trend persists. This may trigger off attempts at getting out of the endangered currency into other currencies or gold. The accumulated key currency will under these conditions hardly be used to buy goods from the country since its uncompetitiveness is at the root of the matter.

Key currencies find themselves in a very delicately balanced situation that can easily turn sour. The key-currency country must run a deficit, in the first instance, so that other countries can acquire short-term claims against them. But if the deficit is prolonged or excessive and accumulated holdings of the currency are much larger than the reserves of the country (see p 31), confidence in the key currency can be sapped. If deflation is not acceptable for the key-currency country, the only way to stop further deficits is devaluation, which however only worsens the crisis of confidence.

The *fragility* of the gold-exchange standard is also underlined by comparing it to a double pyramid. First the key-currency country erects an inverted pyramid of credit money on the base of its monetary reserve, then other countries take a part of this credit money as a base to build another inverted pyramid. The French economist, Jacques Rueff,[1] claimed that this fragile construction was so entirely Anglo-Saxon that there was no French word for the notion of a gold-exchange standard!

French politicians and economists also objected that this system gave the United States and the United Kingdom the possibility of borrowing short and investing long. In other words they could use the loans in the form of bank balances held by other countries to buy up enterprises in these countries themselves or otherwise make long-term investments in them. (It has to be pointed out however that the French franc itself is a key currency in a limited sense. Within the French zone it plays the same role as the dollar and the pound sterling in the world.)

At any rate, the Americans and the British are far less sanguine with respect to the advantages of running key currencies, in other words of 'being bankers to the world'. Grubel calculated in 1964 that the direct financial benefits of the reserve currency function for the US dollar was \$3·3 billion a year, while the 'output gap' caused by this function was officially estimated in 1961 at \$40 billion.[2] The \$3·3 billion was the advantage gained through banking and other invisible services rendered in connection with the key-currency role of the dollar. The 'output gap' means the loss in activity level and growth because a key-currency country has to tread so warily and cannot put domestic issues first. Similar calculations could also be made for the pound sterling. But it is extremely difficult to decide how much of 'invisible exports' depends on the key-currency role.[3]

Whatever the advantages and disadvantages of the key currencies, and whoever gains in the final account, the system is not the result of any deliberate decision, but has grown up over the years. It would seem that everybody concerned must have got something out of it, at least in the short run, although they may not have quite planned the result.

[1] J Rueff *Le lancinant problème des balances de paiements* Paris: Payot 1966.

[2] Herbert G Grubel 'The benefits and costs of being the world banker', in *The national banking review* (December 1964) also in Officer and Willett (eds) *The international monetary system* Englewood Cliffs New Jersey: Prentice-Hall 1969.

[3] Benjamin J Cohen 'Sterling and the City' *Banker* (February 1970), also *Princeton reprint;* and *The future of sterling as an international currency* London: Macmillan 1971.

The system cannot now be dismantled overnight, if at all. The US and Britain have an overhang of short-term liabilities without corresponding short-term assets (see p 30), so that they cannot quickly liquidate the position. Of course, their total assets are larger than their total liabilities, but it would create financial chaos if they tried to force their residents owning long-term assets to sell them and put the proceeds at the disposal of the monetary authorities. On the other hand, it is not even certain that all those countries holding dollar or pound balances would want to liquidate them. Even if they were no longer used as reserves they could be useful as working balances. The problem of key currencies can be tackled only gradually.

The pound sterling. Till the First World War, the pound was the dominant currency because of the British economic and political role in the world. In contrast with the later position, sterling balances used by foreigners as commercial currency were to a large extent overdrafts, ie money on loan from Britain.

The two wars radically changed the situation. The United Kingdom lost a large part of its foreign investment, and therefore income from this investment, so that a far larger share of imports have had to be bought by exports since the Second World War. Further more, Britain had financed the two world wars to a considerable extent by inflation, that is by budget deficits covered by new monetary issue, because otherwise taxation would have to be raised excessively. This inflation (see p 122) made the pound exchange rate overvalued after both the First and the Second World Wars. As a result Britain had, in the end, to go off gold in the 1930s and to devalue in 1949. In this second instance the conditions turned out to be very inappropriate for such an operation. The Korean War made the world raw material prices rise, so that this rise together with the increase in prices caused by devaluation hit the British public particularly badly. Simultaneously, Britain had to increase defence expenditure, which prevented her from introducing the stringent monetary and fiscal policies that must accompany devaluation (see p 73).

The pound then re-emerged after 1949 at the parity of £1 = \$2·80 or 1 ounce of gold = 250 shillings. It was also used after 1945 as the leading reserve currency, not yet surpassed by the dollar; the official holdings of sterling balances amounted to the equivalent of \$7·8 billion as compared with the official dollar balances of only \$3 billion. The sterling balances had been inflated during the war when in particular India and Egypt acquired large quantities of sterling for wartime purchases. But the British reserves of gold and convertible currencies (ie dollars) were much smaller, which created problems of solvency even though total British assets abroad continued to be larger than total British liabilities (see table 7 on p 25).

The 1950s passed without too much trouble for the pound with the exception of the speculation against sterling after the Suez War. In the 1960s however there was a definite downward trend and attempts at improving the country's growth by expansionist fiscal and monetary policies resulted in a record balance-of-payments deficit in 1964. Britain's production is very import-dependent (the average import content of British manufactured goods is about 20 per cent), so foreign trade becomes a bottleneck for any growth spurt. However, this bottleneck could possibly be overcome if British costs were to rise less quickly than they have over the last decade or so.

The key-currency role of sterling made the British position more difficult. When there are balance-of-payments difficulties there is a fall in confidence in sterling and some foreign-held sterling balances tend to be converted into other currencies and assets. As an official publication[1] puts it: 'These fluctuations were rarely independent of the balance-of-payments position in the United Kingdom; but frequently they reflected movement in the United Kingdom balance of payments in an exaggerated way.'

After 1964 the situation improved, partly because of government efforts, partly because of drawing down of inventories, good harvests and improved terms of trade. In 1966 Britain was also given a stabilization loan of $1 billion with the explicit purpose of financing outflows of sterling but not the British deficit.

In spite of the improved balance of payments in 1965 and 1966, the rise in British costs, and hence the overvaluation of the pound, continued, so that in 1967 devaluation could not be avoided. In contrast to 1949, when all currencies of the sterling area followed sterling in devaluing against the US dollar, in 1967 the greater part of the sterling area did not move. This was among other things a reflection of the new trade patterns of the sterling area countries, which had become far less dependent on the United Kingdom.

Since the devaluation shook confidence in sterling and the sterling area countries had been diversifying their reserves anyway, it was felt that an international move was necessary to fend off precipitate moves out of sterling, which could leave the international monetary system in a chaotic state. The Basle Facility was therefore negotiated in 1968.[2]

Twelve leading central banks and the Bank for International Settlements provided $2 billion on which Britain would be able to draw over three years to meet falls in both official and private sterling balances belonging to sterling area countries. (The 1966 stabilization loan had applied to balances of all countries.) In exchange, the United Kingdom had to give dollar guarantees for the official sterling reserves held by these countries, which in turn undertook to maintain not less than an agreed proportion of their reserves in sterling. Furthermore, they agreed to deposit a part of their non-sterling reserves with the Bank for International Settlements on normal banking terms,

[1] HM Treasury *The Basle Facility and the sterling area* London: HMSO Cmnd 3787 1968.
[2] See HMSO publication cited in note 1

so that these funds could be lent to Britain. But there would be no restriction on their withdrawing their deposits. Any borrowings made under this facility within 1968 and 1971 could be repaid within ten years by Britain. Later this arrangement was extended for another two years to 1973.

This facility and other support for the pound altered to a considerable extent the functioning of the pound sterling as reserve currency. It became a kind of international operation and for a while the question was whether, in the end, a similar solution was going to be found for the pound sterling within the European Community, in spite of the British pledge to abandon the reserve role of sterling. The official pamphlet[1] still insisted:

> For the United Kingdom to attempt to 'pay-off' the balance in some form would have been quite impracticable and harmful to the world monetary system; in any case there was no sign that this was desired by Sterling Area countries.

By 1970 the British balance of payments was in considerable surplus following the devaluation, and the pressure had shifted to the dollar. The further developments of the pound will be discussed in the final chapter (see p 170).

The dollar. In contrast with the pound sterling, the dollar emerged from the Second World War in a very strong position. Although the United States gave the predominant share in the UNRRA[2] recovery programme and by herself provided the European Marshall aid, many goods were obtainable only from the United States, so that the dollar was a scarce currency even though it had not been declared such by the IMF. In addition many countries were trying to replenish their reserves. Since they were not prepared to increase their holdings of the pound, they increased their *official* dollar balances from \$3 billion in 1949 to \$12·6 billion in 1961 (see table 18). However, this increase in US short-term debt was backed by substantial gold reserves, accumulated before and during the Second World War. US gold reserves had been reduced from \$26 billion in 1949 to just under \$20 billion at the beginning of the 1960s, but they still almost exactly matched the *total* (official *and* private) US short-term liabilities (see table 9).

At the beginning of the 1960s attitudes to the dollar changed. An assumption of dollar scarcity was replaced by one of dollar glut. In fact, the previous trends did not change but doubts about the reliability of the dollar began to be felt around the world and in the US itself.

The doubts were certainly not at this time caused by the weak position of the US current account. In 1960 the surplus on goods and services transactions amounted to

[1] Quoted on p 13.

[2] United Nations Relief and Rehabilitation Administration.

Table 18
Reserve development* (billions of dollars)

end of:	1949	1961	1965	1967	1969	1972†
gold	33·1	38·9	41·6	39·4	39·1	38·8
of which						
USA	26·0	18·0	13·3	12·0	11·8 (+2·8)	10·5 (+0·24)
UK	1·8	3·3	2·3	1·2	1·4 (+1·05)	0·8 (+4·0)
official dollar balances	3·0	12·6	15·37	18·3	16·0	61·3
official sterling balances	7·8	7·1	6·7	8·2	8·9	8·5
EEC reserves	2·8	18·0	19·7	22·3	19·1	42·0
(gold + currency)			(14·8 + 4·9)	(15·0 + 7·3)	(13·8 + 5·3)	(15·1 + 26·9)
Japanese reserves	0·0 (+0·2)**	0·3 (+1·2)	0·3 (+1·6)	0·3 (+1·4)	0·4 (+2·6)	0·8 (+16·5)
USSR gold holdings			1·5			
gold production (West)			1·4	1·4	1·4	
Soviet sales			0·5	0·015		
other uses			1·75	3·0	1·3	
incl. China's purchases			(0·15)			
Soviet production	$150–175 million (maybe 3 times as much)					

Source: International financial statistics

* IMF holdings and facilities not included.
** government and banks.
† Change in the official gold parity of the dollar in 1971 (see p 169) conceals part of the movement.

almost \$4 billion, but at the same time the US balance of payments on liquidity basis (see p 21) was in deficit by almost \$4 billion also (see table 4).

This difference means that the surplus obtained through trade was used to pay for US private long-term and short-term investment abroad and for government economic and military aid and loans to foreign countries. The military expenditure for the US forces abroad however counts as purchases of foreign services and goods and is therefore included in the balance on goods and services itself.

Since the US deficit in the 1960s was due to capital and aid flows, it could be considered a *transfer problem* (see p 87). In spite of the US surplus on current account it was possible to say that US goods and services were not sufficiently competitive, ie the US costs were too high, to accommodate the sizeable outflow of capital and aid. The dollars earned by other countries were insufficiently used for buying US goods and services and were partly diverted to purchases from the recovering West European countries, which in turn added them to their reserves or even converted them into gold, thus draining the US reserves. The fall in the US reserves and increases in short-term official liabilities by 1961 were mentioned. Simultaneously, the reserves of EEC countries rose from \$2·8 billion in 1949 to \$18 billion in 1961.

Soon after his election in 1961 President Kennedy thought it necessary to take action in various directions. The government restricted its own expenditure abroad, for instance, by limiting the number of family members following US military personnel abroad through shortening the term of overseas duty, and by cutting the allocation of funds to US diplomatic and information services abroad. The administration also took measures to assure the return of aid dollars into the United States by *tying* the United States grants and loans to purchases from the United States. Capital outflow was to be curtailed by the *interest equalization tax,* which was to tax away the advantages of higher interest rates abroad (see p 94). The United States also started an export drive which included the Trade Expansion Act leading to the Kennedy Round of negotiations.[1] The government further wished to widen the trade horizon of the American businessman by providing information on export opportunities and facilitating trade with the Soviet Union and other communist countries. The American export drive even produced a so-called 'chicken war', when western European countries tried to stop the imports of American broiler chickens. Export financing was improved. It was also hoped the US balance of payments would be helped by inflation abroad and increased earnings from the large American foreign investment in the preceding period.

Judging by the increase in the surplus on goods and services, which rose to \$8·5 billion in 1964, the US trade measures were fairly successful. The same cannot

[1] See *Outline of international trade* p 125.

however be said with respect to government and private capital flows, the former rising from about $3 billion to $3·5 billion and above, the latter from just under $4 billion to $6·5 billion in 1964. The US administration felt obliged to introduce 'voluntary limitations' on capital exports, which reduced them somewhat in conjunction with rising US bank interest rates.

In the 1960s the US also took steps to protect the reserves by short-term financial measures. To boost confidence in the dollar swaps were arranged (see p 155) with other central banks, and for a while stand-by arrangements with the International Monetary Fund were also employed. Further, the US began to issue to other countries the so-called Roosa bonds, a Treasury paper with a guaranteed exchange rate, so as to dissuade other central banks from converting the dollar reserves into gold for fear that the dollar was going to be devalued.

In spite of such measures US gold reserves fell steadily. From $18 billion in 1961, they fell to $13·3 billion in 1965 and $12 billion in 1967. This was to a large extent due to conversions of dollars into gold by central banks. The French government pointedly switched a considerable amount of French reserves into gold at the beginning of 1965. As a consequence the share of gold in the French reserves rose from 71 per cent in 1963 to 91 per cent in 1966. The corresponding figures for some other countries are: Austria, 45 per cent to 57 per cent; Federal Germany, 54 per cent to 63 per cent; Canada, 31 per cent to 47 per cent. But at the same time Italy, Switzerland and the United Kingdom reduced the gold in their reserves, the UK, for instance, from 93 to 63 per cent.

Another reason for the reduction in US reserves was the constant private demand for gold. In order to prevent a rise in the gold price on the free market the central banks established in 1960 the so-called *gold pool* operated by the Bank of England. The purpose was to keep the gold price in the London market down to the official parity of $35 per fine ounce. But the private demand at this price was so heavy that it absorbed the whole new production outside the communist countries, amounting to about $1·4 billion worth of gold per year, and began to pull down total gold reserves of central banks, which fell from $41·6 billion in 1965 to $39·4 billion in 1967. In the end the central banks agreed to stop feeding the private gold market through the gold pool and to suspend all sales and purchases of gold, except among themselves. This so called *double-tier gold market* was started in 1968 (see p 154).

Just before that President Johnson was forced to introduce, for the protection of US balance of payments, mandatory limits on US investment abroad, both long- and short-term, a tax to force repatriation of profits from US investment abroad, voluntary restraint on US tourists abroad, etc. Despite these measures the US surplus on goods and services fell in 1968 and 1969 as compared with 1967 and US investment abroad was barely stabilized at the level of just under $5·5 billion. The overall balance was in surplus only because of the tremendous inflows of foreign investment into the United States ($8·7 billion in 1969).

Euro-dollars. While the United States government and the rest of the world were worrying about the US balance-of-payments and its influence on the dollar, a development was taking place that showed the underlying strength of the dollar. At the end of the 1950s, owners of short-term dollar assets began to re-deposit them with European banks, primarily in London and in Switzerland, without converting them into local currencies. These dollar-denominated deposits with European banks became known as *Euro-dollars.*

Originally, the re-depositing was due to the restrictions imposed on US banks, particularly the so-called *regulation Q* which limited the level of interest rates paid by US banks on short-term deposits and later also the restraint on US short-term loans abroad. As a consequence European banks could pay higher interest on dollar-deposits than could US banks, as they were not subject to US restrictions, and European-owned dollars could replace short-term credit not forthcoming from the other side of the Atlantic. Very often borrowers in the Euro-dollar market were American companies themselves.

It soon became clear that dollar operations of European banks were not entirely dependent on American government restrictions. In the meantime regulation Q was to a considerable extent abolished without any obvious reduction in Euro-dollar transactions. European banks, accepting narrow profit margins but knowing the market very well, could still do profitable business. In particular, European firms without regular US bank connections could borrow dollars from European banks.

If greater expertise were the explanation of the Euro-dollar market to a substantial degree, ultimate lenders could be American banks letting better qualified European banks do the job. In other instances Euro-dollar business is actually carried on by European subsidiaries of American banks. In 1973 the United States authorities further limited the validity of regulation Q and have reduced reserve requirements on foreign deposits. Furthermore, it has been said the the US administration will remove the controls of capital outflows as a consequence of the dollar's new flexibility gained in 1973 (see p 176). If the Euro-dollar market can survive these changes, the probability will be high that it has become a permanent institution.

The exact nature of the Euro-dollar transactions continues to be controversial. Some theorists consider that European banks act only as financial intermediaries, ie that they limit themselves to lending dollars deposited with them. Others claim that they handle dollars in exactly the same way as any other money deposited with them, in fact that they create dollars by means of a bank or credit multiplier in the same way as they expand credit in their domestic currency. It is certainly true that, for instance in 1969, the Euro-dollar credit available amounted to $37·5 billion, while

US banks' liabilities to overseas commercial banks were only $23·7 billion. This has been taken as an indication that there must have been some dollar credit creation, even if less than one would expect. In contrast, it is argued that banks can create credit only in a closed system, while the Euro-dollar system has considerable leakages, and that there may be other sources of Euro-dollars anyway.

The developments of Euro-dollar transactions have been followed especially by the Bank for International Settlements in Basel and estimates of their size are published in its Annual Reports. The Euro-dollar credits available to final borrowers amounted to $9 billion in 1964 but rose to $54 billion by 1971 and possibly to $85 billion by the end of 1972. Before final borrowers are reached European banks tend to lend dollars to each other, each taking a cut in the profit in the search for customers. As mentioned, the final credit in 1969 reached $37·6 billion, while the inter-bank lending added another $10 billion to this figure if one wishes to obtain the figure for gross Euro-dollar credit.

It can now be said that the Euro-dollar market was the beginning of a huge international money or credit market for which denomination in dollars is not essential. The fact that it was and still is, to a large extent, denominated in dollars is only a sign of the fundamental strength of the currency of the American economy which is still by far the strongest in the world. In turn, the market strengthened the dollar at a time when it was passing through what may be called marginal trouble. Even central banks, particularly of smaller countries, sometimes came in on the act and started placing their official holdings of dollars in this market, which is not surprising since the Euro-dollar interest rates reached 11 per cent, much higher than national rates. On the other hand this possibility of profits made it much easier to persuade central banks to hold dollars flowing out of the US in their official reserves.

But in spite of the predominance of the dollar the Euro-dollar market is essentially an international market in short-term funds. This feature is becoming gradually clearer as other strong currencies are joining the dollar in this particular international role. At the end of 1971, in addition to $54 billion ($46 billion in 1970) worth of Euro-dollars, there existed $27 billion ($16·5 billion) of other Euro-currencies; approximately $15 billion ($8 billion) German marks; $7·7 billion ($5·7 billion) Swiss francs; and $2·1 billion ($940 million) pounds sterling deposited in bank accounts outside the currencies' national territory (all figures in brackets refer to 1970). The total amount of Euro-currencies was then $71 billion at the end of 1971, which compared with official reserves of $130 billion (including IMF drawing rights). Even the term Euro-currency is not exact because it implies that a non-national currency is deposited in a European bank. A new term is needed because in fact it refers to all deposits in *any* bank outside its own country.

The Euro-currency system with Euro-dollars as the preponderant element has developed because it offers certain advantages over holding cash in other forms. The demand for Euro-currencies exists because of interest differentials, savings in conversion and reconversion costs and, very often, because it is possible to avoid constraints imposed on domestic currency holdings by central banks. On the other hand, banks themselves are often allowed to do business in foreign currencies which they could not do in the currency of their own country. Thus for most London banks, apart from clearing banks, Scottish and Northern Irish banks, foreign currency business is now more important than sterling transactions. A long-term capital market in Euro-currencies is also developing, concentrating on operations in Euro-bonds and loans in dollars or other non-national currencies.

Euro-dollars and other Euro-currencies certainly facilitate international trade because they provide a handy international vehicle currency (see p 2). In so far as they are used as working balances for normal transactions, they do not constitute any danger for stability. But as movement in and out of these currencies is easy, and as they often escape national regulations, they are also a channel for interest arbitrage (see p 9) and currency speculation (see p 10). As such they are highly volatile and contribute to the instability of the international situation. They also interfere with domestic monetary policies.

Therefore it is not surprising that financial authorities of the leading countries would like to bring the Euro-currencies under control. There were numerous proposals about how to do this, but it is clear that all governments would have to act together, since otherwise the market would simply shift to outside countries. It was suggested that central banks and the Bank for International Settlements themselves should stop investing in the Euro-market (the group of ten adopted this proposal in 1971), that foreign-currency deposits should also be subject to cash ratios, that there should be a prohibition of interest on all short-term deposits and that large-scale international open market operations should be started to mop up Euro-currencies. This last solution would require considerable interest payments and it is unclear who would take the responsibility for them. Individual countries can also act by prohibiting their companies from borrowing abroad.

The danger is of course that not only the volatile part of the market would be killed off or severely limited, but also the more valuable part that oils the wheels of normal international trade.

The dollar standard. The very wide use of the dollar as a reserve and commercial currency prompted some economists to say either that the world already is on a dollar standard or that measures should be taken to put it on a dollar standard. The meaning is that the dollar is or should become the means of final payment in international transactions in the same way as gold actually was under the gold standard, and theoretically at least under the gold-exchange standard.

The school that claims that the world is now on a dollar standard argues that this is so because US short-term liabilities have become so much larger than US gold reserves that the dollar is in practice no longer convertible into gold. This argument was, of course, strengthened when the US in 1971 officially suspended, temporarily (according to official statements), the gold convertibility of the dollar.

On the other hand, there were suggestions as early as 1965 that the United States should deliberately elevate the dollar to the standard status by doing two things: revoking the provisions on the gold cover for internal money circulation, and ceasing to buy any more gold for official reserves. Both these things did happen (see p 154), but the second was not a unilateral arrangement of the United States: all central banks agreed to stop adding to their gold holdings in 1968.

The present world financial situation could then be described as a (temporary?) dollar standard. This gives the US government tremendous influence on what happens in other economies, which can pursue independent monetary policies only by surrounding themselves with exchange restrictions. The position is the more dangerous as the foreign trade sector of the US is very small (see p 103), so that the US government can treat it with 'benign neglect' if it chooses to disregard the interests of other countries.

For this reason there is considerable resistance to an indefinite continuation of the *de facto* dollar standard. There are plans for the creation of a second financial centre, able to act as a counterweight to the dollar, in the form of a monetary union based on the European Economic Community. One idea was to use the pound sterling as the European reserve currency since on one hand the pound already has a tradition in this role, and on the other it is at present supported by European central banks anyway. This possibility was torpedoed by the French, who not only insist that the monetary basis should not bear the mark of any particular country, but demanded that the UK should divest the pound of its reserve role before it joined the EEC.

The other suggestion for the removal of the dollar standard is the development of an international currency in the true sense of the word as the SDRs (see chapter 7, pp 158 *et seq*). However, it must be stressed again that any attempts at a rapid removal of the dollar from its international pedestal would cause so much disruption that it could spell disaster.

b *deficiency of liquidity*

The IMF system was designed (see p 125) to increase countries' liquidity so as to facilitate their pursuit of domestic economic goals. Nevertheless criticisms soon abounded that liquidity was insufficient and that it hampered the development of international trade – so much so that the International Monetary Fund commissioned a report on this subject published in 1958 under the title *International reserves and liquidity*. IMF Annual Reports also devote considerable space to the problem.

International liquidity can be defined as the total amount of resources available to the monetary authorities of countries for the purpose of meeting balance-of-payments deficits. This is of course also the purpose of international reserves, so that, as a first approximation, liquidity can be identified with them.

But reserves themselves are not homogeneous: countries have at their disposal *owned reserves* (gold and reserve currency holdings including the new SDRs) and *borrowed reserves* (IMF drawing rights), which are again divided into *unconditional* and *conditional* drawing rights according to whether a country can use them only under the condition of repayment or whether it has to conform also with other requirements (see p 125).

However, monetary authorities can also use other resources to meet balance-of-payments deficits, although they are not described as reserves. They can borrow from other central banks even under previous arrangements. They can borrow from commercial banks and possibly from other institutions and private citizens. More that that: they can induce foreigners to place their short-term funds in their country although not necessarily in government securities. In fact, the balance of payments can be helped by private institutions or residents of one country lending to those of another country. Which of these short-term credits should be considered international liquidity and which should not? A firm answer to this question is as tricky as the answer to the question of which transactions are accommodating and which autonomous, and the two answers are connected (see p 17). It is hardly surprising that Machlup spoke of the fuzzy concept of international liquidity.

One thing is certain: no international liquidity would be required if trade were balanced. For balanced trading it is sufficient that national currencies should be convertible into each other (see p 2). International liquidity is required when there is a balance-of-payments deficit, which strictly speaking means only where there is a system of fixed exchange rates.

As a consequence it can be said that there is no direct connection between the reserves required and the volume or value of trade. On the other hand there is a more immediate connection between international liquidity and balance-of-payments deficits/surpluses. The need for international liquidity would then depend on the circumstances that determine the size of international imbalance.

The IMF team researching into international reserves and liquidity stressed these findings by devising a table showing the relationship between the value of world imports, representing world trade, and the value of world reserves, representing international liquidity. The table is shown (table 19) with the data for some years added (in brackets).

The figures for the post-war years are low because they do not include either reserve

Table 19
Gold and exchange reserves as percentages of the value of world imports

	the world		world without USA	
	total	gold	total	gold
1913	21	19	17	14
1928	42	32	35	23
1937	101	93	63	53
(1951)	(67)		(39)	
1959	57	35	32	15
(1960)	(55)		(43)	
(1965)	(43)	(25)	(39)	(22)
(1970)	(28)	(12)	(23)	(9)

positions with the IMF or, later, the SDRs. But even in 1972 these items would amount to only about 10 per cent of the total reserves and about 4 per cent of the value of world trade.

Table 19 shows, none the less, that before the First World War world trade could prosper on relatively very small reserves, while very high reserves between the two wars did not prevent international trade from being in serious trouble.

The conclusion reached by the IMF report of 1958 was that the environment in which international trade took place was more important for the size of reserves required than either the volume or the value of trade. If in 1913 the need for reserves was low, this was so because there was greater balance in international economic relations; stronger measures for adjustment were taken; there was more confidence between countries and hence more willingness to lend to each other; and finally, there was a very effective and well-organized network of private credit based on London.

In view of what has been said before, these conclusions seem sensible. The more balance there is, the less reserves are needed for covering deficits. The faster the adjustment, the more limited the deficits and again the less reserves required. In fact, if a system could operate bringing about instantaneous adjustment (as would the system of freely flexible exchange rates under ideal conditions) no reserves would be needed at all.

The better the international private credit facilities, the less the demand for governments to step in with their own credit arrangements. And governments will be more ready to extend credits to each other, the more confidence they have in each other's economic management. But at this point we return to the fuzziness of the concept of international liquidity. Which inter-governmental lending is a simple credit operation and which is an increase in liquidity? After all, acquiring short-term dollar or pound assets is also lending to the US and UK governments.

These considerations point to the importance of a particular kind of confidence: the confidence of governments in each other's management of external economic affairs. If a government requires limited and temporary credit it will easily obtain it. If it taxes its partners excessively, a crisis will arise. This is particularly true for the key currencies. Their availability in exorbitant amounts, like the excessive availability of any money, makes them less acceptable, *inter alia* because of the danger that their price will fall.

Thus the international liquidity problem is a question of fine balances; if there is insufficient liquidity, international transactions that might have taken place otherwise do not take place. Should there be too much liquidity, confidence in it may be undermined and a scramble may begin to get rid of it. This does not apply only to key-currency liquidity, issued by some national authority, but also to internationally issued liquidity (see p 128).

At this point it should be stressed again that holding international reserves is a kind of investment competing with other more profitable kinds of investment (see p 57). It is therefore undesirable to hold very large reserves. How large exactly they should be will in the final instance depend on the judgement of national governments, which will, one hopes, take into account all the circumstances or *environment,* as the IMF report calls it. The world need for reserves will be the sum total of national desires to hold them.

Nothing said so far should be interpreted as meaning that there could never be a shortage of reserves. If world price and income levels rise, they influence the volume and value of trade, and, *ceteris paribus,* the need for reserves. Similarly, if the value of currencies is diminishing and they are tied to gold, larger reserves are necessary to do the same work. International liquidity should also be sufficient so as not to force national governments into deflationary measures for fear of relatively small transitional imbalances.

But the IMF researchers into international liquidity thought that these reasons for the need for greater liquidity did not obtain and came to the overall conclusion that the existing liquidity was sufficient, at least in the late 1950s. In spite of this only a few years later, in 1962, the then secretary-general of the IMF, Per Jacobsen, went on record with a warning that the day of insufficient international liquidity could be approaching. His argument was based on the premise that the amount of US dollars in the reserves of various countries had reached its extreme level of tolerance and could not be expanded further. Therefore, some other asset would have to replace them if the world did not want to hamstring its trade. In fact, the IMF concentrated in the following years on the search for a new international liquid asset, which led to the introduction of SDRs in 1968 (see p 158).

The relationship between liquidity and confidence has been pointed out, so that it remains to indicate the link between liquidity and adjustment. No amount of liquidity can lead to a final solution for an imbalance of payments. Liquidity can help to finance a deficit (see p 56), but if the deficit is fundamental some kind of adjustment will eventually have to be brought about. For the same reason, the argument that there is sufficient liquidity but that it is badly distributed is less than convincing. If countries do not adjust, any amount of liquidity will end in the hands of the surplus countries.

If financing of deficits by the use of international liquidity is only a temporary measure, why has there been so much clamour for providing more reserves? Ample liquidity makes it possible to postpone adjustment and arguments for greater liquidity are precisely arguments for such a postponement.

It can be argued that adjustment is a painful process since it usually implies deflationary measures which, under present conditions, normally lead to unemployment. Therefore, considerable liquidity should be at the disposal of monetary authorities so that they can let developments take their course and reliably find out whether the international imbalance is fundamental and not merely transitional (see p 44). Only when it becomes clear that adjustment is absolutely necessary should they embark on measures interfering with smooth running of the domestic economy.

Another argument is that adjustment takes time (in the case of devaluation see p 81) so that reserves are necessary even if adjustment is automatic or if adjustment steps are taken immediately. Reserves are then necessary to finance the imbalance until adjustment bites, until the necessary structural changes take place.

In a similar way, it can be argued that structural changes can be the starting point and make adjustment unnecessary altogether. This can be achieved either by improved efficiency or by a change in the production structure. In this case, structural changes themselves act as a special kind of adjustment mechanism (see p 58). Therefore, the reserves should be sufficient for the competitive pressure between firms in different countries to take full effect and adjustment should be resorted to only when it becomes clear that structural changes on their own will not bring about a new equilibrium. There is a parallel between this argument and the argument that freely flexible exchange rates, by providing immediate adjustment, cut out the transmission of competition pressure between countries (see p 117).

Finally, Johnson makes the point that larger reserves help the monetary authorities to wait until the imbalance comes to an end through individual decisions that dishoarding (see p 57) has gone far enough and that they no longer want their cash balances to be further reduced. This makes it unnecessary for the authorities to frustrate the profit- or utility-maximizing decisions by individuals to move out of cash into commodities or securities.

Officially the British government, in the Keynesian tradition, consistently favoured the expansion of liquidity, while the French government opposed it, arguing that greater liquidity would only induce deficit countries (meaning the UK and US) to be even less disciplined in their policies.

c *adjustment and speculation*

The IMF articles provide for a change in the exchange rate as the means of adjustment if the imbalance turns out to be fundamental (see p 123). They were criticized on the ground that this device was used far too rarely, and was therefore accompanied by protracted international financial crises along with large-scale speculation (see p 119) in the form of huge hot money movements. While the IMF rules nowhere state it expressly, the atmosphere in the financial world was such that a devaluation was considered the last resort, implying a loss of face and faith with the countries' creditors whose claims are reduced in terms of other currencies and gold.

Precisely because the reluctance to devalue (and also to revalue, though for different reasons – see p 117) was a matter of public opinion and not of written rules, it was more difficult to deal with. It is relatively simple to change a legal provision but quite another matter to change the habits of public and governmental opinion. Against the feeling that it is wrong to reduce, in terms of other currencies, debts to creditors denominated in the devaluing country's currency, it can be argued that no gold guarantee has been ever automatically attached to these debts. It was only in 1968 that Britain gave a guarantee, and it was a dollar rather than a gold guarantee, for the official sterling balances within the framework of the so called Basle Facility (see p 131).

The shortcomings connected with slow adjustment and speculation are far more intractable than the shortage of liquidity. Maybe that is the reason why the official debate on IMF reform concentrated mainly on liquidity. But the problems of adjustment and speculation are at least as urgent.

further reading

exchange rates

S Brittan	*The price of economic freedom, a guide to flexible rates* London: Macmillan 1970
P Einzig	*The case against floating exchanges* London: Macmillan 1970
M Friedman	'The case for flexible exchange rates' in Caves and Johnson *Readings in international economics*
M Friedman	'In defence of destabilizing speculation' in M Friedman *The optimum quantity of money* Chicago: Aldine 1969
M Friedman and R V Roosa	*The balance of payments: free versus fixed exchange rates* Washington DC: American Enterprise Institute 1967
G Halm (ed)	*Approaches to greater flexibility of exchange rates* Princeton: University Press 1970
H G Johnson and J E Nash	*UK and floating exchanges* London: Institute of Economic Affairs 1969
S I Katz	*Exchange-risk under fixed and flexible exchange rates, the bulletin 83-84* New York University: Institute of Finance 1972
E Sohmen	*Flexible exchange rates* Chicago: University of Chicago Press 1969
J R Williams	*International trade under flexible exchange rates* New York: A M Kelley 1968
P Wonnacott	*The floating Canadian dollar, exchange flexibility and monetary independence* Washington DC: American Enterprise Institute 1972

optimum currency areas – monetary union

W M Corden	*Monetary integration* Princeton: University Press 1972

F Hirsch — 'The political economies of European monetary integration' *The world today* (1972)

H G Johnson and A K Swoboda (eds) — *The economics of common currencies* London: Allen and Unwin 1973

P B Kenen — 'The theory of optimum currency areas: an eclectic view' in Mundell and Swoboda *Monetary problems of the international economy*

R I McKinnon — 'Optimum currency areas' in Cooper *International finance*

R A Mundell — 'A theory of optimum currency areas' *American economic review* (1963)

D A Snider — *Optimum adjustment processes and currency areas* Princeton: University Press 1967

E Sohmen — 'Currency areas and monetary system' in J Bhagwati (ed) *Trade, balance of payments and growth* Amsterdam: North Holland 1971

International Monetary Fund

A L K Acheson, J K Chant and F J Prachowny (eds) — *Bretton Woods revisited* London: Macmillan 1972

H Aufricht — *The fund agreement: living law and emerging practice* Princeton: University Press 1969

R N Gardner — *Sterling-dollar diplomacy; the origins and the prospects of our international economic order* new edition New York: McGraw-Hill 1969

H G Grubel — *The international monetary system* second edition Harmondsworth: Penguin 1972

A Kafka — *The IMF: the second coming?* Princeton: University Press 1972

R Triffin — *The evolution of the international monetary system: historical reappraisal and future prospectives.* Princeton: University Press 1964

R Triffin — *Our international monetary system: yesterday, today and tomorrow* New York: Random House 1968

HMSO — *The international monetary fund* (three volumes) London: HMSO 1970

J H Richards — *International economic institutions* London: Holt, Rinehart & Winston 1970

M A G Van Meerhaeghe, *International economic institutions* second edition London: Longman 1971

the pound sterling

B J Cohen 'Sterling and the City' *The Banker* (1970)

B J Cohen *The future of the sterling as international currency* London: Macmillan 1971

B J Cohen 'The future role of sterling' *National Westminster Bank quarterly review* (1973)

P Einzig 'The declining use of sterling as a trading currency', *Westminster Bank review* (1963)

E H Feaveryear *The pound sterling: a history of English money* second edition revised by E Victor Morgan, Oxford: Clarendon Press 1963

Federal Trust for Education and Research *Sterling – European monetary co-operation and world monetary reform* London 1968

H M Treasury *The Basle Facility and the sterling area* Cmnd 3787 London: HMSO 1968

F Hirsch *The pound sterling – A polemic* London: Gollancz 1965

F V Meyer *The functions of sterling* London: Croom Helm 1973

Susan Strange *Sterling and the British policy* London: Oxford University Press 1971

the dollar

W Fellner 'The dollar's place in the international system' *Journal of economic literature* (1972)

H G Grubel 'The benefits and costs of being the world banker' *The national banking* (1964) also Officer and Willett, *The international monetary system: problems and proposals*

G Haberler and T D Willett *A strategy for US balance of payments policy* Washington DC: American Enterprise Institute 1971

G Haberler 'US balance of payments policy and the international monetary system' in W Schmitz (ed) *Convertibility, multilaterism and freedom, essays in honours of Reinhart Kamitz* Vienna: Springer 1972

H Lever 'The dollar standard' *New Statesman* (9 July 1971)

R I McKinnon *Private and official international money: the case for the dollar* Princeton: University Press 1969

R V Roosa — *The dollar and world liquidity* New York: Random House 1967

W S Salant — 'Financial intermediation as an explanation of enduring "Deficits" in the Balance of Payments' in F Machlup, W S Salant and L Tarshis *International mobility and movement of capital* New York: National Bureau of Economic Research 1972

the Euro-dollar

O L Altman — 'What does it really mean? – Euro-dollars' *Finance and development* (1967)

'UK banks' external liabilities and claims in foreign currencies' *Bank of England quarterly bulletin* (1964)

E W Clendenning — *The Euro-dollar market* Oxford: Clarendon Press 1970

D Kern — 'International finance and the Euro-dollar market' *National Westminster Bank quarterly review* (1971)

F Machlup — 'Euro-dollar creation: a mystery story', *Banca Nazionale del Lavoro quarterly review* (1970)

H W Mayer — *Some theoretical problems relating to the Euro-dollar market* Princeton: University Press 1970

A K Swoboda — *The Euro-dollar market: an interpretation* Princeton: University Press 1968

Reports on the developments in the Euro-currency market are regularly published in the *Annual Reports of the Bank for International Settlements.*

international liquidity

M J Fleming — *Toward assessing the need for international reserves:* Princeton: University Press 1967

R Harrod — 'International liquidity' *Scottish journal of political economy* (1966)

R Harrod — *International reserves and liquidity* Washington DC: International Monetary Fund 1958

C P Kindelberger — *Balance of payments deficits and the international market for liquidity* Princeton: University Press 1965

F Machlup — 'The fuzzy concepts of liquidity, international and domestic' in Machlup *International monetary economics*

P M Oppenheimer — 'What kind of mechanism for reserve creation?' *Westminster Bank review* (1965)

J. Williamson — 'International liquidity: a survey', *Economic Journal* (1973)

chapter 7

reform of the IMF

When it was announced in 1963 that both the IMF and the Group of Ten would commence studies on the functioning of the international monetary system, it was emphasized that any recommendation for reform should avoid a departure from fixed exchange rates and the established price of gold. Involuntary foreign lending[1] was also excluded later from the range of acceptable solutions. These provisos were required for the simple reason that any consideration of such changes could trigger off massive speculation. Nevertheless, it seems that the fear of speculative flows was not the only reason for them, but that the monetary powers did not in fact wish to alter these features of the existing system. Ironically, in 1971 changes on these lines, albeit in a limited way, were a part of the solution for the crisis (see p 169).

The Group of Ten developed as an *ad hoc* inner council of the IMF consisting of the ten financially strongest governments plus the non-member Switzerland as observer. These governments first co-operated in 1962 when they agreed in Paris on the General Arrangements to Borrow (see p 156). Although the group had no formal status within the IMF, it has been acting since as a consultation forum to prepare proposals for the full meetings of the IMF, where, incidentally, the members of the group have a majority of the votes. At the beginning of the 1970s pressure was applied by the rest of the members demanding that preliminary consultations should take place in a wider circle which would include representatives of other members. As a consequence the annual meeting of the IMF in 1972 formally established a committee to study the reform of the monetary system, which became known as the *Committee of Twenty.* Its members are appointed on the same basis as IMF executive directors by member countries and groups of member countries, so that the developing countries are now very well represented. They also have 30 per cent of the votes so that they could block any decision on the reform if they so wished.

[1] F Machlup *Involuntary foreign lending* Stockholm: Almquist and Wiksell 1965.

7.1 two solutions originally ruled out

a *flexibility of exchange rates*

The merits and demerits of freely flexible exchange rates have been discussed in chapter 6. Whatever their merits, and however spirited their advocacy by prominent academic economists and some financial journalists in the 1960s, there seemed to be hardly any chance for permanent flexible rates to be adopted by practical men: business people, commercial and government bankers and governments themselves.

Their attitude may have changed in the 1970s. Since the 1971 crisis, to be described in the last section of this chapter, *managed flexibility* ('dirty' floating) has been widely used, less for the establishment of new parities than as a weapon against speculation and loss of reserves or involuntary foreign lending (undesired accumulation of key currencies).

Fully aware of the unpopularity of complete flexibility in business circles, and mindful of the need for adjustment through exchange rates, a group of most distinguished teachers of economics published in 1966 a statement in favour of limited exchange-rate flexibility in the form of wider bands and shiftable parities.[1]

The wider band proposal aimed at increasing the margins from the official par value within which the authorities have to keep the exchange rate of their currency in the exchange market (see p 123). The 1966 statement suggested that the then 1-per-cent margin up and down should be replaced by one of 4 to 5 per cent on each side of parity, which would give an 8-per-cent spread for each currency, *vis-à-vis* gold or dollars in terms of which the par value is determined, and twice this spread for other currencies *vis-à-vis* each other. If dollar flexibility was considered important, which seemed plausible, then parities should be fixed only in gold, which would give the dollar the same double spread of 16 to 20 per cent *vis-à-vis* any other currency. The double spread is the result of the possibility that two currencies, commencing at the upper and lower limit respectively of their spread with regard to the unit in which their parities are determined, can move to the opposite ends of this spread, ie to the lower and upper limit respectively.

This arrangement, in accordance with which the prices of the currency in terms of another could vary by as much as 20 per cent, would introduce a considerable automatic adjustment. The relationship between domestic price levels would change by the same percentage as their exchange rates; ie, the prices of the country with exports lagging, converted into another currency, could be reduced by up to 16 or 20 per cent, which would foster its exports and hamper its imports (see p 64) and vice versa. Thus the need for reserves to tide over temporary imbalances would be less, while

[1] The statement is reproduced in W Fellner 'On limited exchange-rate flexibility' in Cooper *International finance.*

simultaneously movements of exchange rates, and as a consequence speculation, would still be kept within some limits.

Even with wider bands of flexibility around a fixed parity it remains possible for a currency to be pushed to the floor or to the ceiling of the range of flexibility if full adjustment requires an alteration in the exchange rate exceeding the band. The need for adjustment in excess of limited flexibility can easily occur if the currency's country indulges in policies leading to fundamental disequilibrium. In such a case the wider band could not prevent a crisis and one-sided speculation as under the narrow band. To prevent such developments the 1966 academic statement coupled the wider band proposal with a proposal for the introduction of shiftable parities (also called sliding parities or 'crawling peg').

Under this arrangement governments would be allowed to shift the official parities of their currencies up or down, year after year, by small percentages without any reference to the IMF. In the long run such small shifts would add up to a substantial adjustment without any abrupt jumps inviting speculation. Even the small changes in parities that could still tempt speculators could be counteracted by a policy of adequate interest rate differentials.

The 1966 statement suggested that the governments should be allowed to alter their official parities by 1 or 2 per cent down or up within a year. Another possibility would be to allow governments to adopt the average market rate of one year as the official parity in the next. The main idea is, in fact, that there should be frequent small changes in official exchange rates instead of the present infrequent sizeable alteration as a measure of last resort. In spite of such an arrangement it could happen that the tendency of a country to imbalance would be so strong as to make limited flexibility insufficient and require a radical alteration of the exchange rate.

However, the signatories of the 1966 statement recognized that some groups of countries may legitimately wish their currencies to be fixed in relation to each other, in other words to establish *monetary unions.* Theoretical reason for such firmer links between currencies, which at least in some respect turn them into one single currency, are now being investigated under the heading of currency areas (see p 118).

In this context it has to be pointed out that to have fixed exchange rates without provision for their alteration is to eliminate the easiest mechanism. Unless the development of prices, efficiencies and growth between such countries is to a large extent uniform, their governments have to fall back on price-change and income-change adjustment mechanisms, which may be very difficult to operate because of price rigidities and abhorrence of unemployment. Close links between the countries and the ensuing ease of communications could lead to demands for *wages parity* between countries (see pp 102 and 109) and even negotiations for uniform wages for the same kind of work over the whole monetary union by closely co-operating or unified trade unions. If price, efficiency and growth developments within the area were then still disparate, such unified wages would be a constant source of inter-area imbalances and tensions. Since all adjustment mechanisms would be blocked, this would finally require an intra-area, in fact international, regional policy.

b *increase in the price of gold*

The proposal to increase the price of gold, as expounded by Jacques Rueff, the theoretician behind the French official moves in this direction, aimed at two things: on the one hand the abolition of the gold-exchange standard through repayment in gold of dollar and pound balances held by central banks, and on the other a return to the gold standard and its discipline, in particular for the two key-currency countries. General de Gaulle himself seemed to go further and wished to reintroduce gold as the only international liquidity because of the intrinsic value – because it was commodity money and not credit money. He said that 'gold that never changes' bears 'the mark of no particular country' and is the money *par excellence.*

Rueff claimed in mid-1960s that the doubling of the price of gold would make it possible for the US to repay all her official short-term debts denominated in dollars because of the increased dollar value of her gold reserves. (Later the dollar balances shot up to such an extent that a doubling of the gold price would no longer be sufficient to bring this about.) An international financing operation could be mounted to help Britain repay official short-term sterling debts. Britain would have to borrow for this purpose from other central banks, whose gold reserves would have appreciated in terms of all currencies, and would have to repay this stabilization loan over a prolonged period.

Once the key-currency balances were eliminated central banks would no longer hold their reserves in this form, which would force all countries, including Britain and the United States, to react to any loss or gain of gold – in fact to behave as under gold standard, to submit to the discipline of gold. Such discipline was necessary because one could not expect the financial houses of countries to be kept in order by deliberate acts of politicians, who would yield to public pressure. And the electorates always push governments into inflationary policies since any attempt to cut back inflation causes unemployment. Rueff believed that the resistance to disinflation would be weakened if these government actions were not deliberate but were dictated by an automatic mechanism such as flows of gold.

Rueff's critics objected that it would be extremely difficult to choose a price for gold that would exactly fit the existing situation and would be neither deflationary nor inflationary. If the price were chosen in such a way (after the repayment of dollar and sterling balances) as to make the gold international liquidity, valued in national currencies, larger than total liquidity before, the result would be inflationary, and vice versa. Such undesired results could be avoided only if national monetary authorities acted judicially, which Rueff did not expect them to do.

Critics also thought that no kind of automatic mechanism could now make governments accept unemployment. This was precisely the problem that arose with inflexible prices and wages downwards (see p 122) and destroyed the original gold standard. mechanism. Of course, life would be much simpler if people could be persuaded to accept flexible commodity and factor prices, but there is no indication that attempts at such persuasion can work.

Some critics claimed that government management of monetary matters is far better than any kind of mechanism anyway. This does not seem very certain as, time and time again, government management seems to have got out of hand. But critics thought that it would be wrong to allow the creation of new international liquidity to be fixed by production costs of gold mines and forecast that such arrangements would be deflationary. Rueff retorted that extraction of gold would considerably increase under the influence of the raised price. However, even if the volume of extraction would not increase, the value would increase in terms of national currencies.

According to the opinion of the Oxford economist Oppenheimer, a rise in the price of gold would not only help to repay official dollar and sterling balances, but could assist in bringing about a new international equilibrium. If the present surplus countries had to cut their surpluses by the full amount of the eliminated US deficit, they could find themselves in a very difficult situation because of the tremendous setback for their export industries (see p 67). This would however have to happen, as surpluses are equal to deficits unless there is an injection of international liquidity that is not a credit to anybody. If a gold-mining country exports newly extracted gold its current account is credited for it and it does not run a deficit. On the other hand, the importing country adds gold to its reserves and runs a surplus. Instead of adding dollars to their reserves, the export surplus countries could add gold and thus mitigate the elimination of the US deficit.

This would favour the gold-producing countries, South Africa and the Soviet Union, and there are thus political objections to increasing the gold price. But what is the difference between buying gold and buying other products from these two countries?

And if it is objected that it is all right to buy but that the prices would have to be excessively favourable, the reply must be to ask what the correct price is. It was said that the gold price should be raised because it had not been changed since 1934 when the dollar was devalued from \$20 to \$35 an ounce, whereas meanwhile other prices have roughly doubled. However, there is no economic presumption that relative prices must remain the same over time; the price level is only a weighted average of all prices, so that some can lag far behind and others move well in front according to economic circumstances. True, gold has an 'intrinsic value' because it is in demand for its industrial and ornamental qualities regardless of whether it is used as money. But this 'intrinsic value' is determined by supply and demand, which would be drastically reduced if governments stopped using gold as a reserve even though individuals might continue to hoard gold as 'a store of value'. Were governments to dispose of their own gold hoard, its price would in all probability fall even below the official IMF price. In this sense it is justifiable to say that gold has its present value because it is exchangeable for money and not that money has value because it is convertible into gold.

There was and still is much controversy about what course speculation would take if the price of gold were raised. Events after 1971 showed that a small increase in the dollar price of gold triggered off additional speculation because further increases were expected. But this development is not incompatible with the claim that a large rise in the official price would make speculators take profits and desist from further speculation, at least for the time being, since further large rises could not be expected.

In connection with the US dollar it was mentioned (see p 135) that the major central banks operated a *gold pool* to keep the gold price in the free market in line with the official price of $35 per ounce. In 1968 this intervention was stopped, the free market cut off and, thus, a *two-tier market* was introduced accompanied by a statement by the central banks that they would not acquire any more gold for their reserves. As a consequence, the free market price rose to about $45 per ounce but then fell back to $35. In 1971 the United States first abolished the convertibility of the dollar into gold and then, among other measures (see p 168) raised the gold price to $38 and again in 1973 to $42 per ounce. The free gold price rose to $70 per ounce by mid-1972 and to $130 by mid-1973.

The two-tier market with higher free prices opens the possibility that some central banks would try to profit by selling in the free market. This would be contrary not only to the agreement introducing the two-tier system, but also to their obligations under the IMF, which – according to a narrow interpretation (but see p 177) – binds them not to deal in gold except at the official price. On the other hand, any big sales by central banks would probably bring the price down substantially anyway.

7.2 Debate on reform

Even before the official research into the reform of the international monetary system began in 1963 (see p 149), economists and politicians had begun to put forward their ideas about what to do. For a while 'reform plans' and counterplans proliferated, so that it was difficult to keep track of them. Simultaneously, some minor solutions were introduced by central banks and the IMF *de facto* as they seemed to be the obvious thing to do. However, the whole debate and *de facto* solutions concentrated on liquidity and perhaps confidence while little was said about adjustment and what was said took the form of exhortation rather than practical proposals, as for instance the 1966 OECD report on *The balance of payments adjustment process.* It has to be admitted however that official bodies like OECD were forums where government representatives met and discussed policies with a view to their co-ordination,[1] which should have also helped with adjustment. Furthermore the original IMF articles themselves contained provisions for consultation with and surveillance of countries in a weak international position aimed at putting pressure on them to take steps for adjustment.

But as co-ordination and pressure did not seem to work particularly well, new methods of adjustment appeared to be necessary and the 1966 academic statement 'On limited exchange rate flexibility' was one of the rare moves in this direction (see p 150).

a *extension of the existing IMF system*

The IMF kept adapting itself to new requirements by increasing its quotas as was foreseen in the Articles of Agreement (see p 124). But it was felt that the owned reserves and reserves borrowed from the IMF were not sufficient, in particular for the key-currency countries, so that the central banks built up a network for mutual help on a bilateral and multilateral basis. The United States was especially active in this field and arranged a network of *swap* facilities that can be activated at a moment's notice. A swap is an agreement between two partners, in this case two national banks, to exchange their currencies under the condition that some time in the short-term future they will re-exchange the two currencies at the same rate. For all practical purposes this arrangement is short-term borrowing with an exchange rate guarantee. Being short-term, the currency obtained in this way could be used only for defence against hot money movements.

But if hot money does not return to the original country within the time period of the swap, the foreign currency that must be returned to the foreign central bank may not be available. For this case, the American devised the *Roosa bonds,* named after the then under-secretary of the US Treasury – medium-term bonds denominated in the currency of the lender central bank to eliminate its exchange risk. In other words, instead of paying their commitments in dollars, which the central banks were no longer keen to hold, the Americans arranged claims on themselves denominated in foreign currency so as to obtain additional credit and not have to disburse their gold.

The battle against speculatory flows also took multilateral forms. In 1961 the members of the Bank for International Settlements arrived at the so-called *Basle Arrangements* under which very informal short-term credits are available between the participating central banks.

[1] See *Outline of international trade* p 131.

Later on, in 1962, the ten financially strongest governments in the world plus, later, Switzerland, concluded with the IMF in General Arrangement to Borrow. In distinction from the 1961 arrangement, this arrangement covered longer-term credits, which would be extended to the IMF if one of the ten countries had to call on the IMF for help and IMF would not have sufficient funds to comply with its request. These arrangements made the IMF an intermediary and guarantor, but they certainly did not do more than supplement the funds available through IMF quotas.

While so far we have been dealing with practical solutions of limited importance, aimed mainly at making it possible for countries to face short-term hot-money flows, some suggestions tried to extend the IMF gold exchange standard in such a way as to create greater international liquidity. At the beginning of the 1960s the officially held sterling balances were stagnating and dollar balances seemed to have reached the limit of acceptability. It was taking only one step to suggest that the solution would be to bring other strong currencies, German marks, French francs, Swiss francs, into the role of key currencies.

This plan worked out by Friedrich Lutz, was known as the *multiple-currency reserves* proposal.[1] It could be initiated by a move of the United States towards not cancelling dollar claims upon herself when in surplus, but accumulating claims on other countries in their currencies. However, it turned out that it was becoming more difficult for the US to return to surplus than originally expected. For the system to remain viable, co-operation of the new key-currency countries would be required at least in providing short-term credit instruments in which claims on them could be held. But the candidate governments did not show any great enthusiasm for such developments, since the role of a key currency provider could be even more burdensome for small economies, than for the United States and Britain (see p 129).

Multiple-currency reserves would naturally increase the scope for switches from one currency into another, which could prove very disturbing. Therefore, Posthuma proposed that central banks should undertake to keep various kinds of reserves in fixed proportions. Such an obligation would protect the United States from attempts to convert dollar claims into gold, and would amount to forced lending.

Bernstein developed the idea of fixed proportions into the Composite Reserve Unit (CRU) plan, according to which countries could obtain units of international liquidity consisting of a prearranged mixture of national currencies by depositing their domestic currency with the Fund. This plan was, for a while, adopted also by the French.

[1] F Lutz *The problem of international liquidity and the multiple-currency standard* Princeton New Jersey: International Finance Section 1963.

b *an international central bank?*

The practical changes and reform plans discussed in subsection a were concerned with central banks lending to each other, either directly or through the International Monetary Fund as intermediary. A step forward would be to let the IMF or another agency act as an international central bank with the right to create international money.

Two plans that aimed at precisely that were the original Keynes[1] plan for a Clearing Union and Triffin's[2] plan of 1959. Under both these plans countries would pay an initial subscription and, under both plans, key currencies would be abolished. But the essential features would be that, under both plans, deposits with the central institution would be considered as money.

The difference between the two plans concerned the method by which new deposits with the central agency would be created. According to Keynes countries would have overdraft facilities which they could use unconditionally if in balance-of-payments difficulties to make payments to other countries, which would thus acquire a claim on the central agency in the form of a deposit with it. The agency would have a passive role and could not initiate an expansion in deposits.

Triffin's plan was different. The Board of Governors of the IMF would actively purchase national government securities and pay for them by creating short-term claims against the Fund, in the form of deposits. The initiative would be with the IMF and it could expand international liquidity and place it in the hands of those governments which in its view needed it.

The units would, under both plans, carry a *gold guarantee* (under Keynes's plan because they were denominated in an international unit called 'Bancor') and they could be used only for payments between governments. The international agency would have no direct control over national monetary authorities so that it could not establish any legal reserve ratios or money supply ceilings for them. For this reason Triffin denied that the IMF would become a super-central bank under his scheme. It would be left to national central banks to figure out the right proportion between their international liquidity and domestic money supply. In so far as they would have access to more borrowed reserves they would feel freer in their policies.

While international liquidity in terms of the Keynes and Triffin plans is no longer a liability of an individual national central bank, it remains a credit facility, a liability of the international monetary agency, backed by a claim of the agency on a government or its central bank in the form of an overdraft or a government security.

In Keynes's plan the method of distribution of new liquidity would be according to

[1] Chancellor of the Exchequer *Proposals for an international clearing union* Cmnd 6437 London: HMSO 1943.

[2] R Triffin *Gold and the dollar crisis* New York: Yale University Press 1961.

the free demand at the going interest rate, but only up to a ceiling amount for each country. The surplus countries would have to accept claims on the international agency in payment for the transfer of goods and services to the deficit countries. Since these were their real savings (see p 161) one would expect that they would be paid interest on their deposits with the agency. Instead, Keynes proposed that they also should be charged interest to force them to contribute to adjustment. That penal interest rates should be levied on *lenders* is understandable under the conditions of international trade. In international trade surpluses and deficits are not a consequence of deliberate saving and borrowing, but of wrong price signals, to the elimination of which the surplus country should also contribute (see p 127).

Under Triffin's plan new liquidity would be created when IMF bodies decided, according to normal voting procedure, that government securities of a country should be purchased in the open market. These securities would bring interest, but simultaneously similar interests would have to be paid on government-held Fund deposits with which their securities were paid. As long as governments hung on to deposits or used them only for current transactions, so that they would fluctuate around the original level, their interest payments and receipts would approximately cancel out. This would be justified because there would be no transfer of real resources. If the deposit was transferred to another country the government would continue to service its securities in the hand of the Fund, but would lose interest payments on it. This would also have been correct since the transfer of deposits would have been used to buy resources.

c *solution adopted: Special Drawing Rights (SDRs)*

In 1967 the official discussion and negotiations about the reform of the international monetary system came to a head. The protagonists of two opposed schools, the United States and France, maintained their positions to the very day when a compromise was struck in Rio de Janeiro. Only a few days earlier Rueff still claimed that the liquidity unit proposed by the US would be 'a nullity posing as a currency'.

The United States wanted a reserve asset to be introduced that could be allotted to and owned by participating countries, while France insisted that the new instrument for international payments should be at best a credit facility. The compromise went so far as to talk about allocation of facilities leaving out any mention of credit or asset. Not surprisingly, the new international liquidity is neither a clear reserve asset nor a credit facility but shows characteristics of both. France also achieved a provision according to which the Board of Governors would have to take all decisions on allocation of the new reserves by a majority of 85 per cent, thus giving the six EEC countries the power of veto since they were entitled to 16½ per cent of the votes.

In 1969 amendments to the IMF Articles of Agreement came into force introducing

Special Drawing Rights (SDRs). The operations of the IMF have since been split into operations on *General Account,* handled in accordance with previous provisions (see p 124), and operations on the *Special Drawing Account,* subject to the new rules.

When they feel that there is a lack of international liquidity and that such a shortage could endanger monetary stability, the Board of Governors can decide by the qualified majority of 85 per cent that a certain amount of liquidity should be issued within the next five years. The amount is stated as a percentage of the Fund's total quotas but is denominated in units equal to the gold content of one dollar before its devaluation in 1971. On this longer-term basis the yearly amount is decided upon so as to prevent any short-term action under the influence of pressures of the moment.

The liquidity created each year is then distributed to participants, ie IMF members willing to take part in the SDRs transactions, again according to their IMF quotas. If there were no limitations on the use of SDRs, this allocation would give the recipient countries a benefit equal to the purchasing power of the liquidity allocated, ie equal to the quantity of resources it can buy, in the same way as national currency creation bestows a benefit on the Treasury, the face value of currency enters the general revenue of the government together with taxes. In fact, issue of new currency is a kind of tax on existing currency holders because the additional currency reduces the purchasing power of the currency in existence.

The 'benefit' mentioned is a consequence of the fact that, unlike commodity money, *fiat* money (and SDRs are, *pace* the French, fiat money) costs practically nothing to produce and service but has the face value ordered by a national government, or agreed upon by governments in the case of international liquidity. The value of commodity money is equal to its costs of production. The difference between the face value of fiat money and its costs of production is the 'benefit', technically called *seignorage.* If fiat money replaces commodity money we then speak of 'social seignorage'. The question arises to whom this benefit falls.

Within a state the solution is simple: as mentioned, the seignorage accrues to the general revenue of the government that uses it to provide public goods or to redistribute income. The same central government method could be used by an international agency, which would spend the new liquidity on international public goods[1] or for international redistribution in the form of aid as suggested by Maxwell Stamp.[2]

But international agencies have neither the same status nor the same influence as national governments and so these latter agreed, in their negotiations about the introducing of SDRs, to allot seignorage to themselves, proportionately to their IMF quotas. This appeared a sensible method, but appearances can be misleading.

[1] See *Outline of international trade* on 'International public finance'.

[2] M Stamp 'The reform of the international monetary system' *Moorgate and Wall Street* (1965).

SDRs are not ordinary currency, like dollars or pounds or German marks, but simply inter-central bank currency since they can be used merely for payments to other central banks. They cannot be used for payments to individuals or companies so that resources may be transferred from the public to a government, as in the case of national currencies. By means of SDRs resources can be transferred only from one government to another, or rather from one country to another – if the possibility of using them for payments to the IMF is not taken into consideration, since such payments will amount to a very small part of the SDRs issued. As long as SDRs are held by the government to which they are allotted, there is no increased command over real resources of others but there is seignorage, as the governments do not have to 'produce' their international money at costs corresponding to its face value.

Theoreticians distinguish between *liquidity to hold* and *liquidity to spend.* Liquidity to hold does not have the purpose of transferring real resources, but does it then have any purpose at all? It does provide countries with additional cash or liquidity balances – increased monetary reserves, in fact – to meet any fluctuations in their balance-of-payments deficits without having immediately to step on the brakes by introducing deflationary policies and especially by imposing trade and exchange restrictions. Of course, those who are unhappy about the slowness with which governments have so far used adjustment policies claim that the result of SDRs is only going to be even laxer policies on their part. As in the case of gold being used as international liquidity (see p 153), the creation of SDRs also makes it possible for the total of all countries' balance-of-payments surpluses to be larger than total balance-of-payments deficits, with all the advantages this may bring.

As the supposed aim of SDRs was to meet governments' transaction demand for 'international cash', there were strenuous objections against distributing them amongst developing countries which would spend them for buying goods and services from industrial countries.[1] This procedure would make SDRs liquidity to spend, seignorage would go to developing countries, and there would have been straightforward transfer of resources to them. It was maintained that questions of such aid should be kept separate from questions of liquidity, as most aid-giving countries want to preserve control over their gifts. From an international point of view it can be said that creation of liquidity coupled with aid would cause pressure for a maximum issue of liquidity which might be excessive.

When liquidity to spend is issued not by the central government, which uses the resulting seignorage to tax its residents, but by some other institution, normally banks, a commercial way of distributing seignorage must be found. Those who demand liquidity, bank overdrafts, to spend it have to pay interest as its free market price.

[1] On the so-called 'link' between SDRs and aid to developing countries see p 180.

The banks then pay interest or provide services such as cheque facilities to those who are prepared to hold liquidity (bank deposits) after having provided real resources in exchange. The banks pay lower interest to deposit holders than they charge to overdraft users to defray the costs of their administration. Interest payments transfer seignorage to those who provide real resources, ie to real savers. However, bank balances are credit money and not fiat money.

On the other hand, SDRs are acclaimed as an innovation because they are fiat money as opposed to gold, which is commodity money, and key currencies plus IMF ordinary drawing rights, which are credit money. They seem to be fiat money because they are not a claim on the IMF in the way bank deposits are a claim on a bank. If money is sometimes defined as the debts of an institution that are accepted as money, SDRs are international money because governments have agreed to accept them as money. In this respect they are similar to gold, which is nobody's debt either, the difference being that gold has to be 'produced' while SDRs are simply a bookkeeping entry into the IMF's Special Drawing Account.

While they are no legal claim on any central institution, their acceptability as money makes them a claim on the resources of the world economy as a whole. As a consequence of this arrangement SDRs are not generally convertible into gold or any other form of international liquidity such as dollars or pounds, and the IMF as the issuing agency need not provide any backing for them in the form of reserves, not even fractional reserves of gold. They cannot be used to change the composition of the international reserves of any countries unless the country has a balance-of-payments deficit, which means if that country has purchased more goods and services and investment from other countries than it has sold to them, so that it has to pay for such an excess of purchases over sales.

However, this payment is made according to a procedure that makes it look like convertibility. The government of a country with a balance-of-payments deficit demands (with the assistance of the IMF – see below) that other governments sell it convertible currency against SDRs. The national currencies thus obtained are then used for intervention in the foreign exchange market, so as to prevent the exchange rate of the country in deficit from slipping outside the allowed margins. Thus, in the end, SDRs are used to pay for excessively purchased resources through national currencies. This roundabout arrangement has become necessary because SDRs are only inter-governmental money and as such cannot themselves be used for intervention in the exchange market, ie payment for resources. This arrangement however does not mean convertibility.

It was stressed that the SDRs were the result of a compromise and therefore displayed the features of both fiat money and credit money. Their nature as fiat money predominates, but some characteristics of credit money survive.

First, there are interest payments. The rules provide for the payment of a moderate interest, initially 1·5 per cent, on actual holdings of the SDRs and an equal charge on their cumulative allocation. This means that if a country is spending SDRs it holds less than it has been allocated and thus pays an interest on the SDRs used for payments to other countries. If no use has been made of the SDRs allocated, holdings exactly match allocation and the interest cancel out charges (active and passive interests). If on the contrary a country has received more SDRs in payment that it has paid out itself, it holds more SDRs than allocated to it and thus earns the moderate interest on the difference. Those countries that provide real resources against SDRs are paid an interest on the transfer, but the interest is so low that it cannot possibly mean the transfer of the total seignorage to the transferor of resources.

In addition to the payment of interest, a main feature of credit is the obligation to repay it. Since SDRs are deemed to be an owned reserve, repayment as with a borrowed reserve is formally impossible. But it is replaced with a different obligation having the same effect, the obligation of *reconstitution.* The initial schedule on reconstitution roughly requires that each participant should hold so many SDRs at the end of the first five years after the first allocation and that at the end of each calendar quarter thereafter the average of its daily holdings will be no less than 30 per cent of its cumulative allocation. This reconstitution rule is a remainder of both the partial credit nature of the SDRs and their partial nature of liquidity to hold. This could be put in other words as follows: a participant has to repay real resources borrowed on the basis of SDRs in excess of an average 70 per cent of his allocation. Since the repayments must ultimately be in real resources, this rule pushes participants towards better adjustment policies.

While surplus countries, lenders of real resources, are partly protected by the reconstitution rule, they are further protected by the rule that no participant need hold excess SDRs above twice his allocation. The obligatory maximum holding is, therefore, 300 per cent of cumulative allocation. That is not all: surplus countries should contribute credits to deficit countries more or less proportionately. To achieve that, a government cannot unilaterally choose the country from which it obtains national currencies in exchange for SDRs but has to request the IMF to designate the country. The designation is to follow certain rules, the purpose of which is to assure that currency comes from countries that need to reconstitute their holdings of SDRs under the 30 per cent requirement, or have large surpluses and/or relatively large gross reserves. Countries with large gross reserves but without a large surplus can be designated so as to make the holdings of SDRs proportionate to other reserves. The designation can be used also as a weapon against those countries that use their SDRs not for covering deficits but for changing the composition of their reserves in contravention of the agreed additional Articles of the IMF on SDRs.

The members of the IMF are in no way obliged to be participants in Special Drawing Account transactions. They could opt out from the very beginning, as some of the smaller countries did, and they may terminate their participation at any time on condition of a mutual settlement in gold or convertible currencies, between the former participant and the Account. A country that does not want to accumulate SDRs in excess of its allocation but does not wish to leave the scheme by termination could correct its surplus imbalance. On the other hand the IMF can suspend any participant not fulfilling his obligations from the use of SDRs.

The IMF can decide not only to allocate new SDRs, but to cancel some of the allocated SDRs. Finally the IMF can by a 85 per cent majority liquidate the Special Account altogether.

The SDRs are denominated in units expressed in gold but are not convertible into it. Thus they have a gold guarantee, subject however to revaluation up or down by an 85 per cent vote of the IMF. The SDRs could be said to be 'legal tender' between governments. Legal tender within a country is a means of payment that the government declares has to be accepted by a creditor within its legal sphere in final payment of debt. In this sense SDRs have only some features of legal tender, because they have to be accepted in final payment only within the prescribed limits and only by participants. Internally, legal tender as such can be enforced by the government through its courts. Internationally there is no enforcement because the IMF cannot in any way oblige a government to accept SDRs within its undertaking. It has the sanction to suspend, but this may be too weak, in particular as any government may at any time terminate its participation anyway.

The acceptability of SDRs, therefore, depends entirely on the willingness of individual governments to accept them in payment. Should excessive amounts of SDRs be issued, individual governments could consider that they are not worth as much as the IMF proclaims they are in terms of gold, and hence other currencies, and therefore refuse their acceptance by terminating their participation in the Special Drawing Account. However, governments in concert take the decision on issue and also the decision fixing the value of SDRs in relation to gold.

The above description of the SDR system leaves out some details, as the purpose is to analyse their nature and not to present a full description of legal provisions. All provisions can be revised by the appropriate majority vote in the IMF, but some provisions expressly contain revision clauses.

In practice, the IMF decided that the first basic period for the issue of SDRs was to be three years instead of five, so that a new five-year issue decision should have been taken in 1972. The first decision on the three-year issue of SDRs was such that approximately \$3 billion worth of SDRs were created in each of the years 1970, 1971 and 1972. Taking into account the change in the dollar par value *vis-à-vis* gold in 1971, there were just over $10 billion worth of SDRs in existence at the end of 1972. The net use of SDRs, that is payments by means of SDRs, during the same period was approximately $2 billion worth.

The $10 billion worth of SDRs have to be compared with $39 billion worth of gold at the end of 1972 (change of dollar par value taken into account) and almost $100 billion worth of foreign exchange (mainly dollars themselves). Of course, the decision to issue the three-yearly amounts of SDRs was taken when foreign exchange reserves were worth as little as just over $30 billion (pre-1971 dollars). It is not without irony that the first SDRs were being issued allegedly to supply additional required liquidity when dollars were pouring into other countries' reserves.

As a consequence, in 1972 the IMF managing director, Pierre-Paul Schweitzer, was not in a position to submit proposals to the IMF Board of Governors for the allocation of new SDRs and no decision was taken in this respect at the annual meeting in September 1972. The procedure for allocation is that the managing director, with the backing of the executive directors, makes a proposal to the Board after having satisfied himself that it will be consistant with the SDRs provisions and after having conducted such consultation as will enable him to ascertain that there is broad support among participants for the proposal. But in 1972 the managing director had to report to the Board of Directors that the conditions for a proposal to issue new SDRs were not fulfilled.

This rather embarrassing situation had developed because the various official study groups or monetary reforms concentrated on liquidity and ignored adjustment. The SDR solution cemented this disregard. In 1971 a dollar crisis broke out which was fundamentally a crisis of adjustment and confidence but had consequences for international liquidity. Dollar convertibility into gold was suspended, while simultaneously dollar holdings more than doubled.

There are suggestions that the consequent difficulties should be solved by an extra issue of SDRs[1] into which central banks could convert their dollar and pound balances if they so wished, so that a large proportion of short-term US and UK debt would be funded, ie turned into long-term debt which they could repay over a prolonged period of time, the only way they can repay it. The extra SDRs would have to carry a higher interest to become comparable with central bank-held dollar and pound balances, which yield far more than the 1½ per cent interest on SDRs. The charges for these SDRs would presumably fall on the United States and the United Kingdom and would be correspondingly higher. The question would be what would happen to the SDRs as the United States and the United Kingdom gradually repaid their funded debt?

[1] See H N Goldstein 'Monetary reform – the Barber proposals' *National Westminster Bank quarterly review* 1972.

Would they be cancelled or would they pass into US and UK hands? Under the present provisions countries are allowed their normal allocation of SDRs to buy back their own currency, if the country holding this currency co-operates.

The suggestion for an extra issue of SDRs and funding of dollar balances does not rest on the assumption that central banks would stop holding dollars, and for that matter pounds, altogether. Certainly, national currencies as key currencies still have some attraction. They yield interest rates, but this could be corrected by increasing interest rates on extra SDRs. They are used as commercial currencies, including Euro-currencies, which makes working balances in them not only desirable but necessary. Some people think that SDRs should not be only inter-government money, but should be made international money available also to companies and individuals, who would then hold Euro-SDRs instead of Euro-currency. Furthermore, this would make it possible for central banks to intervene in exchange markets with SDRs instead of with key currencies.

Finally, SDRs are not convertible unless into resources of all the economies of the world provided governments do not refuse to accept them by terminating their participation. The generality of the SDR's command over resources may be a snag, particularly when coupled with the possibility of withdrawal. On the other hand, after the suspension of dollar *financial convertibility* into gold, it hardly makes sense to say that dollar balances are a debt of the US government. But it does make sense to say that foreign-held dollars are also legal tender in the United States and give holders command over US resources. Sometimes this command is called *market or commodity convertibility.* At any rate, this convertibility is not conditional and the US government could not suspend it in good faith. This command is specific, not general, which is possibly its strength. It is precisely because of this specific claim on US goods that governments and individuals are still prepared to accept dollars.

d *crises in the early 1970s*

The introduction of SDRs in 1969 may have solved the liquidity problem, but it has not even tackled the problem of adjustment that reappeared with a vengeance in 1971. After the turbulent time for sterling in the 1960s, it was the turn of the US dollar to be in serious trouble.

Arthur F Burns, chairman of the Board of Governors of the Federal Reserve System, described what happened in a statement before the Joint Economic Committee of the US Congress in February 1972:

> Despite much idleness of man and equipment, wages and prices continued to rise at a virtually undiminished pace. Moreover, the competitive position of the United States in international trade was deteriorating further, confidence in the exchange rate of the dollar was weakening, and a massive shift out of the dollar and into foreign currencies

Table 20
US balance of payments (millions of dollars)

March 1972 (credits +, debits –)	1969	1970	1970 II	1970 III	1970 IV	1971 I	1971 II	1971 III^{p}
balances excluding allocations of SDR's – seasonally adjusted								
net liquidity balance	–6,084	–4,688	–1,085	–892	–1,240	–2,684	–5,961	–9,472
official reserve transactions balance	2,702	–10,688	–1,621	–2,292	–3,694	–5,713	–5,910	–12,300
balances not seasonally adjusted								
balance on goods and services	2,011	3,592	1,300	–291	1,349	–1,513	228	–1,400
balance on goods, services, and remittance	745	2,182	925	–657	1,002	1,188	–140	–1,795
balance on current account	–899	444	487	–1,060	552	732	–670	–2,282
balance on current account and long-term capital[4]	–2,879	–3,038	–899	–1,535	706	–1,256	–3,615	–4,428
balances including allocations of SDR's:								
net liquidity	–6,084	–3,821	–1,704	–1,454	–152	–1,843	–6,596	–10,112
official reserve transactions	2,702	–9,821	–2,069	–2,612	–3,174	–4,718	–6,462	–12,679
balances excluding allocations of SDR's:								
net liquidity	–6,084	–4,688	–1,704	–1,454	–152	–2,560	–6,596	–10,112
official reserve transactions	2,702	–10,688	–2,069	–2,612	–3,174	–5,435	–6,462	–12,679

May 1973 (credits +, debits –)	1970	1971	1972^{p}	1971 IV	1972 I	1972 II	1972 III	1972 IV^{p}
balances excluding allocations of SDR's – seasonally adjusted								
net liquidity balance	–4,718	–22,719	–14,684	–4,508	–3,283	–2,385	–4,678	–4,342
official reserve transactions balance	–10,706	–30,482	–11,007	–6,127	–3,402	–999	–4,851	–1,759

Table 20 *(continued)*

May 1973 (credits +, debits −)	1970	1971	1972^p	1971 IV	1972 I	1972 II	1972 III	1972 IV^p
balances not seasonally adjusted								
balance on goods and services	3,563	750	−4,219	300	−803	−1,457	−2,292	333
balance on goods, services, and remittances	2,089	−779	−5,776	−100	−1,171	−1,853	−2,671	−80
balance on current account	356	−2,824	−7,983	−653	−1,801	−2,435	−3,169	−579
balance on current account and long-term capital[4]	−3,059	−9,281	−9,243	97	−3,615	−2,265	−3,781	414
balances including allocations of SDR's:								
net liquidity	−3,851	−22,002	−13,974	−3,466	−2,369	−3,043	−5,313	−3,249
official reserve transactions	−9,839	−29,765	−10,297	−5,882	−2,506	−741	−5,585	−1,465
balances excluding allocations of SDR's:								
net liquidity	−4,718	−22,719	−14,684	−3,466	−3,079	−3,043	−5,313	−3,249
official reserve transactions	−10,706	−30,482	−11,007	−5,882	−3,216	−741	−5,585	−1,465

Source: Federal Reserve bulletin.

[1] Adjusted to balance of payments basis; excludes transfers under military grants, exports under US military agency sales contracts and imports of US military agencies.

[2] Includes fees and royalties from US direct investments abroad or from foreign direct investments in the United States.

[3] Equal to net exports of goods and services in national income and product accounts of the United States.

[4] Includes some short-term US Govt assets.

[5] Not available.

^{p} provisional estimate.

NOTE – Data are from US Department of Commerce, Office of Business Economics, Bureau of Economic Analysis. Details may not add to totals because of rounding.

was getting underway.

In 1970 the US balance of goods and services improved as compared with 1969, but while in 1969 there was an inflow of private short-term funds to the tune of almost $9 billion (see p 136) and the reproductions of the US balance of payments 1969–71 and 1970-72 in table 20), in 1970 there was an outflow of such funds amounting to $6 billion.

Then in 1971 the balance on current account began to move into the red, even excluding US government grants. This was a sign for the flight out of the dollar to start gathering momentum. The flight seems to have been so unruly that it was statistically recorded to a large extent under errors and omissions (the difference between 'balance on current account and long-term capital' and 'net liquidity') instead of as short-term private flows, which are the difference between 'net liquidity' and 'official reserve transactions'. Errors and omissions not seasonally adjusted reached –$2,981 million in the second quarter and –$5,684 million in the third quarter of 1971, which is twice higher than the normal *yearly* figures. The result of the withdrawal of these private short-term funds was a flood of dollars into foreign official reserves. The reason was of course that, under the regime of fixed exchange rates, national monetary authorities have to buy up dollars or any other currency private holders are selling so as to preserve the exchange rate (see p 123). In fact, US short-term liabilities to foreign monetary authorities rose to $50 billion by the end of 1971 while foreign official reserves held $24 billion at the end of 1970, compared with only $16 billion at the end of 1969.

On 15 August 1971 the President of the United States proclaimed a ninety-day freeze of wages and prices, a temporary suspension of dollar convertibility into gold, a 'surcharge' of 10 per cent on the US imports and a 10 per cent reduction in foreign economic aid.

When short-term funds began flowing out of the United States in May 1971 strong-currency countries tried to defend themselves against the influx of 'hot money'. Thus, Austria and Switzerland revalued their currencies upward, while Germany and the Netherlands allowed theirs to float. After the presidential measures of 1971 most other important countries started floating, with the exception of France, which introduced a two-tier exchange rate system, keeping the official current-account franc within the prescribed parity to the dollar and letting the financial franc find its own level. Most countries also imposed administrative controls (see p 94), reduced interest rates and intervened in the market, which gave the 1971 floating the name of 'dirty floating' (see p 112).

Despite such measures the currency reserves of some countries increased substantially as indicated in table 21.

Table 21
Rise of reserves of the main countries in 1969–72 in billions of dollars at the end of the year)

	France	Germany	Italy	Japan	UK
1969	3·8 (0·3)	7·1 (2·7)	5·0 (1·2)	3·6 (2·6)	2·5 (1·0)
1970	5·0 (1·2)	13·6 (8·4)	5·3 (2·1)	4·8 (3·2)	2·8 (1·2)
1971	8·2 (3·6)	18·4 (12·3)	6·8 (2·8)	15·4 (13·8)	6·6 (5·1)
1972	10·0 (5·0)	23·3 (16·8)	6·0 (2·2)	18·4 (16·5)	5·6 (4·0)
Feb. 1973	10·6 (5·1)	29·5 (22·4)	6·4) (2·1)	19·1 (17·1)	5·9 (n.a.)

Figures without brackets indicate total reserves; figures in brackets reserves in foreign currency.

Source: IMF *International financial statistics*.

Japan's reserves more than trebled from 1970 to 1971, which confirmed that the yen was undervalued, though it was denied by the Japanese themselves. They claimed, as others did also, that their surplus was only temporary and that they were still too poor for a revaluation upward, which would also upset their delicate labour relations. But poverty is certainly no reason for financing US imports, which the underdevaluation of the yen forced them to do, and revaluation upward would increase the purchasing power of wages, which would probably not harm their labour relations. Germany was on the receiving end of large private short-term capital flows, as was partly also the United Kingdom. Both Japan and Germany, by the end of the crisis, had larger reserves than the USA.

On 18 December 1971 the Group of Ten plus Switzerland reached an agreement on the realignment of currencies known as the Smithsonian Agreement (after the Smithsonian Institution in Washington where the meeting took place). The United States abolished the 10 per cent surcharge on imports and promised, subject to a decision by the US Congress, a change of the US dollar gold parity from $35 to to $38 per ounce, which represented a devaluation of the dollar in terms of gold by 7·9 per cent. The currencies of other countries were realigned as shown in table 22.

As part of the agreement, the IMF announced that member countries would temporarily be allowed to widen their intervention margins from 1 to 2¼ per cent on each side of the par value or central rate (as provisional par values came to be called). The intervention margins of the pound *vis-à-vis* the dollar thus became $2·55 and $2·66.

Before the financial world could settle down again to normal business however the pound sterling got into trouble. In the third quarter of 1971 the UK surplus on visible trade account reached £181 million, fell to £80 million in the fourth quarter and turned into a deficit of £121 million in the first quarter of 1972. This development was taken as a sign that the continuing British inflation had eroded the advantages of the 1967 devaluation and that the pound was again overvalued. In his budget speech the chancellor of the exchequer boldly stated that the government would not allow the pound to interfere with its growth policy and would not hesitate to devalue if need were. This pronouncement and an untoward remark by a leading opposition politician, coupled with the deteriorating trade figures, sufficed to start a run on the pound in June 1972. Nor did it help that it was of course known that Britain would have to begin paying its financial contributions to the Europian Economic Community from 1 January 1973, which would necessitate balance-of-payments surpluses, thus making the sterling overvaluation worse.

The 1972 sterling crisis was complicated by the first move of the EEC member countries and candidate member countries in April 1972 towards a European Monetary Union. The intention is to pool a part of the member country reserves and to eliminate entirely the margins of fluctuation for the exchange rates of the EEC currencies with relation to each other, and as a first step it was decided to narrow the internationally permitted bands by half. This meant that the Community exchange rates could differ *vis-à-vis* each other from the official par values or central rates only by 2½ per cent instead of by 4½ per cent as allowed under the Smithsonian Agreement (see p 169).

The European currencies arrangement has become known as the 'snake in the tunnel' and is illustrated in figure 3. The European currencies are allowed to use the full limits of fluctuation around the central rate of the dollar up and down which represents 'the tunnel'. But while moving within this tunnel, they must not stray from the mutual central rates by more than 1⅛ per cent on each side or by more than 2½ per cent as the total spread, which is called 'the snake'. Thus if the market exchange rate of the strongest EEC currency is 2·25 per cent above its official central rate for the dollar, the market exchange rate of the weakest EEC currency must not be below its central rate for the dollar because the spread between the two EEC currency is not permitted to be more than 2·25 per cent. If the strongest EEC currency moves below its dollar ceiling, the weakest may move by as much below its dollar central rate.

The currencies have to be kept within the prescribed limits through monetary authority intervention (see p 6). But if one EEC country has been buying the currency of another EEC country to support it, the latter has to buy its own currency back against gold, SDRs and currencies in accordance with a formula based on the

Strains around Smithsonian

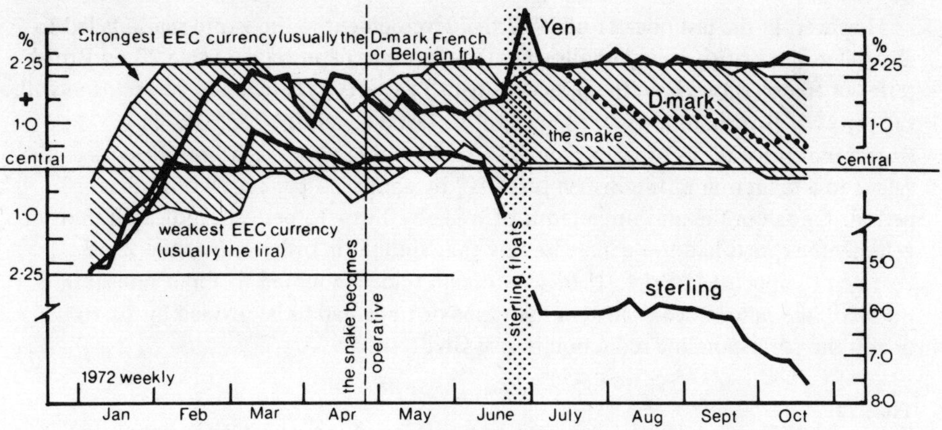

Figure 3. *Source: The Economist* (31 October 1972)

composition of its reserves. This rule is meant to prevent re-purchases of a currency in sole dollars which now abound in all official reserves.

As indicated in figure 3 the EEC monetary arrangement became operative on 24 April 1972, and Britain also joined in to prove its favourable disposition towards the European unification. But then came the pressure on the pound sterling in June 1972. In the week preceding 23 June the liabilities incurred by the United Kingdom monetary authorities to keep the sterling within the snake added up to about £2,500 million to be paid out of the country's reserves.

Rather than lose the whole of the reserves in a few more days, the government decided to abandon the EEC snake and float the pound, as the chancellor of the exchequer had predicted. Under ideal conditions, a country floating its currency (see p 118) need not lose any reserves, as any pressure on the currency can be compensated through changes in the exchange rate. In practice the reserves may not be so entirely expendable, as the government may not want the exchange rate to fluctuate without limits; but alterations in the exchange rate may certainly take part of the burden of financing deficits off the reserves.

In summer 1972 the pound sterling was drifting down towards its pre-Smithsonian dollar parity of £1 = \$2·40, which meant a devaluation, in line with the dollar, with regard to all other currencies. The British government did not seem to be excessively unhappy about this development, as it obviously hoped to regain some of the foreign trade balance lost through inflation. Late in October the pound even went as low as

£1 = $2·35.

However, in the last quarter of 1972 the development in the world markets led to a reversal in the British policy of allowing the pound to depreciate. Table 23 on British terms of trade[1] shows how the prices of British exports have fallen in comparison with the prices of British imports starting from the last quarter of 1972. The fall in the British unit price terms of trade from 111 to 97 within about eight months was equivalent to a reduction of the British real GNP by about 2·5 per cent within that period: the fall in the unit price terms of trade by 14 or 15 per cent indicated that the volume of exports had to be increased by that amount in order to buy the same volume of imports as before. If British foreign trade amounted to about one-sixth of the GNP, the percentage change in the terms of trade had to be divided by six to obtain the corresponding reduction in real GNP.

Table 22
British terms of trade unit value index numbers (not seasonally adjusted 1960 – 100)

	exports	imports	terms of trade
1970 Q 1	131	131	101
Q 2	134	132	102
Q 3	136	131	104
Q 4	139	131	106
1971 Q 1	143	131	109
Q 2	146	135	108
Q 3	149	137	109
Q 4	152	137	111
1972 Q 1	155	139	111
Q 2	157	140	112
Q 3	160	144	111
Q 4	162	152	106
1973 Q 1	166	164	101
February	166	165	101
March	168	169	99
April	171	173	99
May (*p*)	172	178	97

(*p*) = provisional estimate.
Source: Department of Trade and Industry (reproduced in *The Times* 5 July 1973).

Changes in the terms of trade have little to do with the merits or demerits of a nation or a government. They are a consequence of shifts in the world supply and demand which from the viewpoint of a nation are entirely random. Changes in the terms of trade would be affected only marginally by alteration of the exchange rate

[1] See *Outline of international trade* p 93.

(see pp 71 and 84). A devaluation must raise the domestic currency prices of both imports and exports *vis-à-vis* non-traded good prices (including labour cost), but it does not necessarily change the relationship between import and export prices measured by the unit price terms of trade. In 1967, at the time of the British devaluation, the British terms of trade stood at 105 for 1960 = 100, were reduced to 102 in 1968 and 101 in 1969, but rose to the yearly average of 104 in 1970 and 110 in 1971, when devaluation yielded full results.[1]

The British quite happily accepted the windfall gain in their real GNP when their terms of trade rose by more than 10 per cent between 1970 and 1971, but criticism of the government was heard when the opposite move started and compensation for the loss of real incomes was requested. Such compensation could not come from abroad, where at any rate the main gainers from the adverse British terms of trade were the developing countries exporting food and raw materials. Compensation could therefore come only through a redistribution of national income, which could however interfere with investment, an important source of long-term growth.

Nevertheless, the government thought it necessary to mitigate the effect of the unfavourable terms of trade by preventing any further fall in the floating pound exchange rate. As stressed above, a downward alteration of the exchange rate does reduce the incomes through a rise in domestic prices of importables and exportables, so as to bring the expenditure back in line with output (see p 71). Thus a further fall in the pound – necessary to keep the balance of payments in equilibrium – would compound the adverse consequences of the terms of trade. The British government therefore decided at the end of 1972 to support the pound by encouraging 'public bodies' to borrow from abroad. This expedient keeps the exchange rate higher than it would be otherwise and conceals the deficit, because borrowing by 'public bodies' (nationalized industries and local government) from abroad does not enter the deficit defined as 'official financing'. In other words, British consumption (expenditure) in the first half of 1973 was kept above what was warranted, by loans from foreign sources. At the beginning of August 1973 the Bank of England also raised for the same reason the 'minimum lending rate', from 9 per cent to 11½ per cent.

As the British devaluation of 1967 illustrated, the effects of a change in the exchange rate set in only after a while (see p 81). The situation may become worse before it begins improving, so that the plotted effect of devaluation on the balance of trade has the form of a J-shaped curve – first a short fall (increase in deficit) and then a sustained rise (move out of the red).

The development after the devaluation of the dollar in 1971 seemed to be following the established pattern. The US balance on goods and services heftily deteriorated in

[1] Calculated from *Trade and Industry*.

1972 (see table 5), and the Japanese trade surplus rose from \$7·8 billion in 1971 to \$9 billion in 1972. When these figures were published, they were however taken as a clear sign that the Smithsonian realignment of currencies was not working.

A run on the dollar ensued which required heavy support of the dollar exchange rate by European central banks amounting to \$6 billion on 6–9 February. On 12 February finance ministers of the countries most involved agreed that the dollar would be devalued by another 10 per cent in gold terms (1 oz of gold became equal to \$42·22), that other currencies would not follow, and that the yen would float. The Swiss franc had been floating since January anyway, as a consequence of Italian lira troubles which led to a two-tier market. Now it was decided that the split lira market would remain but that both the commercial lira and the financial lira would float, albeit separately.

In March 1973 another upheaval followed because previous events had shaken any confidence left in the dollar. This time it was decided that the EEC currencies would start a common float, with the exception of the pound sterling, the Irish pound and the lira. This implied that after March the Belgian, Danish, French, Luxemburg, Dutch and West German currencies would preserve (after the German mark had been revalued by 3 per cent) their mutual 2¼ per cent spread – remain within the 'snake' – but that they would not worry about the preservation of an exchange rate of the dollar fixed within limits – the 'tunnel' was abolished.

Figure 4 shows how, after 21 March, the snake first behaved reasonably, but then began rising off the dollar central rate in the company of the Swiss franc and even the pound sterling, while the Japanese managed to keep the yen steady mainly by pushing capital export. Within the rising snake, the German mark rose to such an extent that it had again to be revalued by 5·5 per cent on 29 June 1973, so as not to break out of the 'snake'. Of course, this need for revaluations for the currencies to remain within the 'snake' makes the whole idea of their close link problematic.

Table 24 demonstrates, even though excluding the June–July 1973 period, the tremendous change in exchange rates required and thus also both the disequilibrium existing before the change and the adjustment this change brought about. Obviously, the imbalance was left for too long and therefore required a lot of adjusting. In all probability, the intensity of the need for adjustment swung the pendulum too far the other way – the mistrust in the dollar and the pound sterling fed on itself – so that it can be expected to come some way back after mid-1973.

In fact, the deterioration of the dollar and pound rates *vis-à-vis* other currencies in 1973 seems to have been an automatic reaction – the dollar and the pound would fall further because they had been falling so far. The view was prevalent outside the market itself, amongst central bankers and journalists, that both key currencies were undervalued and were bound to bounce back.

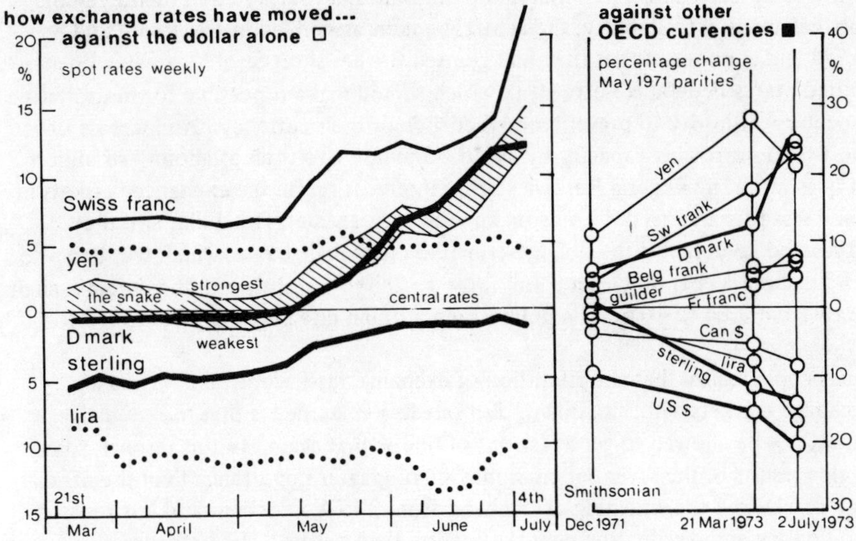

□ Most central rates are 11.1 per cent higher than their old Smithsonian (Dec 1971) parities (or, for sterling than $2.35); the D mark rate was 14.4 per cent higher than its Dec 1971 parity until 29 June and is now 20.7 per cent higher.

■ Changes in spot rates, weighted countries OECD trade in manufactures.

Figure 4. (*Source: The Economist*, 7 July 1973)

Table 23
Movement of exchange rates 1971–73* (percentage change on May 1971 parities)

	May 1972	November 1972	March 21 1973	June 5 1973
US dollar	− 9·6	− 8·7	−15·6	−19·0
lira	− 2·1	− 1·3	− 7·3	−13·8
sterling	+ 0·6	− 9·7	−11·7	−11·5
guilder	+ 1·6	+ 2·7	+ 4·6	+ 5·2
French franc	+ 0·4	+ 1·0	+ 3·6	+ 6·3
Belgian franc	+ 3·3	+ 4·3	+ 6·0	+ 6·6
yen	+13·5	+16·5	+27·8	+14·5
D-mark	+ 6·0	+ 6·4	+12·2	+17·8
Swiss franc	+ 3·9	+ 7·7	+17·4	+19·9

*Changes in spot rates weighted by countries' OECD trade in manufactures: the pound had floated to a low of around S2·35 in November, 1972; the dollar was formally devalued by 10 per cent in February 1973; and the D-mark revalued by 3 per cent in March.
Source: *The Economist* (9 June 1973)

To prevent further losses in dollar and pound rates, unwarranted in their eyes and possibly detrimental to stability, the central bankers assembled in Basle on 7 and 8 July 1973 and announced that they had granted further short-term borrowing lines to the United States Federal Reserve Bank which should make it possible for the American monetary authority to prevent a further slide of their currency. An increase of the short-term borrowing capacity by about \$6 billion to a total of about \$18 billion was in question. The Federal Reserve started interventions in the exchange markets in 1972 and was prepared to do it now on an even bigger scale. The dollar and the pound reacted favourably: the dollar-German mark exchange rate, which was down to 2·24 German marks per dollar on 6 July, rose to 2·40 by 11 July and the dollar-French franc rate from 3·84 to 4·16. The pound-French franc rate improved from 9·79 to 10·85.

Once people realize that the alteration of exchange rates works, but with a lag, the exchange markets will calm down. But one lesson learned is that the exchange rates must not be allowed to get as far out of line as that again. In this respect, some of the side results of the seventies crisis may be of greater importance than the official creation of SDRs – the widening of the band from 2 to 4·5 per cent and less resistance to floating and devaluation cum revaluation than before. The unfortunate experience during this period with the 'snake', the narrower band under the auspices of the European Monetary Union, may also persuade EEC countries not to insist on rigid rates even among themselves as long as developments vary considerably from country to country. These changes in rules and attitudes may go a long way to make the international monetary system work without constant upheavals.

The surprising thing is that the perturbed international exchange markets caused so little disturbance in the growth of international trade, although many experts would claim that changing exchange rates must hit international trade because of increased risk (see p 116). In the period 1960–70 the average growth rate of the volume of international trade was 8·4 per cent. In 1968 this rate was 12·5; in 1969, 11·4; 1970, 9·0; 1971, 5·8 and in 1972, 10 per cent, which seems to prove that the fall in 1971 was merely cyclical, not caused by the financial turbulance.

This does not mean that financial instability could not eventually harm world trade, if nothing were done to reduce it to more reasonable proportions. At the Smithsonian conference in December 1971 it was agreed that further study of how to reform the world monetary system was necessary and the United States particularly insisted that it should be given better access to the markets of the partner countries (especially agricultural markets and markets in Japan). The IMF prepared a report on 'Reform of the monetary system' and, also in 1972, established the Committee on the Reform of the International Monetary System and Related Issues, for short the Committee of Twenty (see p 149). The preparatory work is done by the deputies of the

Committee of Twenty.

The reform 'climate' has changed considerably since the reform debate in the 1960s. While then flexible exchange rates were officially excluded (see p 149) from scrutiny by bodies investigating the reform possibilities, floating has been widely used in the early seventies and flexibility is no longer as unthinkable as a solution as it used to be.

At any rate, much flexibility has been introduced *via facti* and the resistance to alterations of exchange rates has broken down. The question now is no longer whether adjustment should be achieved through flexibility, but how it could be done in an orderly way that would also prevent excessive delays. In the Committee of Twenty the Americans are pressing for some kind of new 'rules of the game' which would prescribe when deficit countries have to devalue and surplus countries to revalue (this symmetry is considered important – see p 127). It is suggested that changes in reserves should be the main indicator. But this book should have shown that such simple rules could be very irksome, as the reason for adjustment is fundamental disequilibrium (see p 44) and such a disequilibrium is not easy to define, let alone in terms of a simple indicator. Excessively clear rules on devaluation and revaluation would also open new one-way options for speculators. They would know when a currency is approaching a point when its exchange rate had to change and would act accordingly. On the whole, the reform committees talk about 'fixed but adjustable' rates with the addition that adjustments will be small but frequent, which should keep hot money at bay.

While the Americans worry about the symmetry between deficit and surplus countries, others are preoccupied by the asymmetry caused by the role of the dollar as intervention currency. This role makes it possible for the United States monetary authorities to sit back in 'benign neglect' letting the others buy dollars and accumulate them in reserves in order to keep the exchange rates in line. Until 1971 the United States undertook to convert such dollars into gold, but since then it is no longer able to do it (see p 168). To replace 'gold convertibility', the United States should also be held to support the dollar exchange rate by buying it in the American market for other currencies as it has started doing anyway (see p 176). This arrangement would offer a new kind of convertibility and is referred to as a 'multi-currency intervention system'.

In 1973 nobody is worried about the lack of international liquidity that figured prominently amongst the problems of the sixties, but the composition of this liquidity is the source of some soul-searching. First, what happens to the gold contained in the government's international reserves? In 1973 these reserves are immobilized because nobody is prepared to sell them at the official price of $42 per ounce of gold while the free market rate is well above $100. The suggestion is that monetary authorities should be allowed – as the IMF rules permit anyway – to sell their gold at market prices, but not to buy it. This move would further demonetize gold, probably absorb a part of unwanted dollars (if any – see below) from the world scene and bring the world free price of gold down.

Proposals are in circulation that the definition SDRs in terms of gold (see p 163) should be terminated and that they should instead be defined in terms of national currencies in accordance with some appropriate formula. This would bring the SDRs some way towards a 'composite reserve unit', but only with respect to their definition, not their use (see p 156). There seems to be agreement on the desire that SRDs should become the main component of monetary reserves. In so far as dollars and sterling abound it is also mooted that outstanding dollar and sterling balances could be funded by means of a special issue of SDRs (see p 164).

However, in spite of the continuing or even increasing fragility of the 'key currencies', it is questionable whether they could be easily replaced. Their replacement as reserve currencies would possibly not be difficult, but as trade currencies they will in all probability survive. In this capacity the SDRs in their present form cannot step into their place since they cannot be held by private persons or institutions. German marks and Swiss francs for instance look very attractive, but their money markets are not as well organized as the British and the American ones. Furthermore, the German and Swiss authorities have been doing their best to keep foreign liquidity out of their countries as they find it difficult to take the strain. In spite of this the German federal bank announced in April 1973 that the mark is overtaking the pound as the second reserve currency.[1] German monetary reserves have, as shown (see p 169) risen enormously, but so have German short-term foreign liabilities.

Once the international readjustment process settles, it is possible that private holders of international liquidity will return to dollars and pounds. Companies including multinational companies, and banks doing international business, must hold a part of their assets in the form of international liquidity so as to be internationally solvent. They will normally hold their cash in the currency easiest to handle, but will obviously watch the possible movements of exchange rates.

According to an estimate, international companies can mobilize about $300 billion at short notice. This figure illustrates the problem of hot money movements, although in the view of Lord O'Brien, former governor of the Bank of England, the cash management of big companies is not dominated by the search for short-term gain through currency speculation. But companies will try to pay in advance bills denominated in a currency about to be revalued and to postpone payments of liabilities in a currency suspect of devaluation. This tendency is at the basis of 'leads and lags' (see p 4), but is this operation speculation at all? The value of world imports in a quarter has now reached the mark of $100 billion, which shows what amounts are involved if there is

[1] *The Times* (24 April 1973).
[2] *The Times* (12 April 1973).

a shift of payments from one quarter to another. This problem will remain not only as long as there is more than one form of international liquidity, but as long as there is more than one national currency – and that may be a long time.

The study of speculative short-term money movements is amongst the tasks of the Committee of Twenty. The Committee is working on this problem at a time when there is a proliferation of measures to discourage capital inflow and encourage capital outflow. In consequence, suggestions that an international network of controls should be introduced is rife. But care is needed to police speculative movement without 'necessarily killing the goose that lays the golden eggs',[1] that is without impeding the legitimate international operations. It is very difficult to separate mere 'speculation' from economic activities that foster efficiency. If it comes to controls, it is better to control capital movements than trade transactions, but best to avoid both.

Flexibility of exchange rates is certainly a strong weapon against money flights from one country to another, but it works through abrupt swings of the exchange rates, which may in the end harm the world trade, although it has not done so far. A two-tier or split exchange market with separate exchange rates for commercial and financial transactions prevents the transfer of disturbances in the financial market to the commercial market, but requires that exchange transaction be supported by certificates on what kind of transactions they are. Such bureaucratic procedures hardly appeal as a long-term solution.

The problem of hot money movements can be resolved only if the problem of international maladjustment is tackled at the root. Large sudden changes in the exchange rates – either under the regime of 'fixed but adjustable rates' or of 'dirty floating', must be made unnecessary. This can be done only if the causes of international disequilibrium (see chapter 3) are reduced to a minimum. It is impossible to eliminate differences in growth rates between countries, as they are largely independent of policy measures. But it should be possible to reduce substantially the differences in the rates of inflation that are at present the main reason for fundamental disequilibria anyway.

The Dutch central banker Zijlstra said, speaking at a meeting of the Bank for International Settlement:

> The hub of the matter is that the power of particular groups and interests to push incomes and prices up has exceeded the power of governments and central banks to stop them doing so. I can see only one way in which this balance of forces can be reversed and that is by public opinion backing up anti-inflationary policies, not fitfully and partially, but strongly and persistently.[2]

[1] Lord O'Brien, *The Times* (12 April 1973).
[2] *The Times* (19 June 1973).

In this picture the developing countries – now an important part of the Committee of Twenty – seem to be insufficiently interested in the general functioning of the international monetary system. They are primarily interested in questions concerning their own short-term gains and losses like the 'link' (see p 160) or compensation for losses and sustained because of the changes in the reserve currency exchange rates. But the breakdown or defective working of the international trade and payments system would hit them as severely as the advanced countries and possibly more so.

conclusion

Outline of international finance deals with one of the most complex parts of economics. The reader may first be given the impression that, surely, a simpler and less crisis-prone way of dealing with international exchanges could be devised. However, on reflection he will begin to understand that a world price system cannot work without money and that, on the other hand, a high standard of living requires great flexibility which must be guided by prices. Unfortunately, high flexibility and its concomitant, complexity, make for a vulnerable system and it is the task of economists to find ways and means of reducing this vulnerability to the minimum compatible with flexibility.

Flexibility has nothing to do with greed or speculation, but is necessary the better to satisfy human needs. Increased efficiency is required for growth and neither can come about without change. Even if some advanced countries should become less interested in the material living standard of the individual and shift the stress to the 'quality' aspects, such as better environment, efficiency and hence flexibility and a highly sensitive system will still be required to provide the best 'quality' without unnecessarily reducing the material standard.

further reading

reform discussion

E M Bernstein — 'Further evolution of the international monetary system' *Moorgate and Wall Street* (1965)

W Fellner — 'On limited exchange-rate flexibility' in Cooper *International finance*

H G Grubel (ed) — *World monetary reform* Stanford: University Press 1965

R Harrod — *Reforming the world's money* London: Macmillan 1965

F Lutz — *The problem of international liquidity and the multiple-currency standard* Princeton: University Press 1963

F Machlup — *Plans for reform of the international monetary system* Princeton: University Press 1962 also in Machlup *International monetary economics*

F Machlup — *Involuntary foreign lending* Stockholm: Almquist and Wiksell 1965

F Machlup and B G Malkiel — *International monetary arrangements and the problem of choice* Princeton: University Press 1964

R I McKinnon — *Monetary theory and controlled flexibility in the foreign exchange* Princeton: University Press 1971

J E Meade — 'Exchange-rate flexibility' *The three banks review* (1966)

M Stamp — *The reform of the international monetary system Moorgate and Wall Street* (1965)

R Triffin — *Gold and the dollar crisis* New Haven: Yale University Press 1961

R Triffin — 'The international monetary system' *Moorgate and Wall Street* (1965)

G Walshe — *International monetary reform* London: Macmillan 1971

gold

P Einzig — *The destiny of gold* London: Macmillan 1972

F Machlup — 'Gold and foreign reserves', part 3 of Machlup *International monetary economics*

F Machlup — *The book value of monetary gold* Princeton: University Press 1971

P M Oppenheimer — 'Economic welfare and the price of gold' *Westminster Bank review* (1968)

J Rueff and F Hirsch — *The role and the rule of gold: an argument* Princeton: University press 1965

I Shannon — *International liquidity* Chicago: Regnery 1964

Special Drawing Rights

F Machlup — *Remaking the international monetary system* Baltimore: Johns Hopkins 1968

McCausland-Thompson — 'The place of SDRs in the international monetary system' *Bank of England quarterly review* (1968)

developments since 1971

German Council of Economic Experts — *Toward a new basis for international monetary policy* Princeton: University Press 1972

H N Goldstein — 'Monetary reform – the Barber proposals' *National Westminster Bank quarterly review* (1972)

G Haberler — 'Some observations on Japanese-American economic relations' *Banca Nazionale del Lavoro quarterly review* (1973)

G Haberler — 'Prospects for the dollar standard' *Lloyds Bank review* (1972)

H G Johnson — 'The Bretton Woods system, key currencies, and the "dollar crisis" of 1971' *The three banks review* (1972)

F Machlup — *The alignment of foreign exchange rates* New York: Praeger 1972

R S Ozaki — *The control of imports and foreign capital in Japan* New York: Praeger 1972

R Triffin — 'How to arrest a threatening relapse into the 1930s?' *Bulletin of the National Bank of Belgium* (1971)

postscript

While this book was being set, a tremendous upheaval occurred in the world markets which requires some comment. The first thing that needs to be said is that, when the dust settles down, the upheaval will in all probability look much less of a turning point in history than it was originally made out to be.

It should not be forgotten that the oil cuts started as a political exercise and that political counsels do not necessarily follow economic considerations. The Arab countries may well be prepared to accept an economic loss in order to score a political point.[1] However, even as a political weapon the oil embargo does not seem to be fool-proof. First, the Arabs are not the only suppliers of oil and there is no good reason why Iran and Indonesia or even the not-entirely Muslim Nigeria and non-Muslim Venezuela should follow them through thick and thin. It is true that the Arab peninsula countries are the only ones to have very large oil deposits, but in the present *political* game it hardly matters who will still have petrol in twenty years' time. What matters is who has it now and is obliged to sell it or not. While the thinly populated Arab countries could forgo their oil proceeds for some time, those with large populations like Iraq and Algeria could not and indeed have said so.

Furthermore, the Arab oil weapon could not reach with any strength the country they would like to hit most, the United States, which imports only a small amount of Middle East oil. It would not do the Arabs any good politically to strangle Europe and Japan – this would leave them on their own with the two superpowers while a large part of their trade, and hence prosperity, would be gone. In fact, even if they could also strangle the United States, they would desist since President Sadat, let alone King Faisal, cannot relish the prospect of having to cope with the Soviet Union without any balancing power. Strangely enough, the Soviet government itself does not seem to be very keen – except perhaps in radio propaganda – to have the Arabs hurt Europe and America beyond measure. Maybe they really need very badly American and European technical and organizational aid to help along their clumsily moving economy.[2]

[1] See Sirc, *Outline of international trade,* p 100.
[2] See *Outline of international trade,* p 33.

Finally, if the Arabs seriously used the *political* weapon of oil to damage Europe and America, they would have to expect a counter-attack at some stage. Before going under, if that is a possibility, Europe and America would probably find both the guts and the elusive unity to do something about it.

Thus oil does not seem to be the secret weapon first envisaged. What about the economic significance of the oil 'events'? Perhaps the answer should begin from the rises in raw-material prices after 1970 in general (see p 172). They are an example of structural changes in demand for and supply of individual goods causing international imbalance (see p 45), in fact perhaps the first such example since the dollar scarcity, when the United States was the only country capable of supplying some goods soon after the war, and the Korean war boom in 1950. This time abnormally increased demand for several goods and raw materials (bad harvests in the Soviet Union, exceptional growth of Japan etc) coincided with lagging supply, political upheaval in many producing countries and droughts which led to a soaring index of respective prices.

But this is not the end of the world. The production of most goods and raw materials can be stepped up and is going to be stepped up in response to price rises. Of course, the known reserves of some minerals are limited, but even in this case higher prices stimulate the search for substitutes, make salvaging and re-cycling pay or simply eliminate marginal uses. All this is bound to stabilize prices again, maybe at a higher relative level than before, but not at a prohibitive level. The producing countries will have a somewhat higher export revenue, which should help some developing countries, in so far as development depends on money, and the importers will have to bear with a setback equivalent to a few per cents of their GNP (see p 172). But this will not finish off the Euro-American economic civilization. It is fragile, but it is not all that fragile.

As for oil, the jump in its price was more sudden because oil economics was entangled with politics. Trying to punish the Europeans, the Arabs discovered that oil requirements are so inelastic that they could push the prices up almost as much as they wanted, and their customers would still come back for more. However it is highly probable that this is so in the short run only. While I am writing this, there are certainly innumerable forces at work to counter the rise in the price of oil: colliery production, which was uneconomic as long as oil was relatively cheap, will be stepped up; new ways of using coal will be found; shale will be exploited; nuclear power stations will come into their own, etc. The great advantage of the decentralized market economy is that it is extremely flexible and that no command from anywhere is necessary for things to start happening.

In opposition to this praise for the decentralized market economy, many people claim that the recent events have shown, on the contrary, the advantages of planning. Planners would have presumably foreseen that the Arabs were going to use an oil embargo and that the prices of oil were about to jump and they would have taken the necessary precautions. Unfortunately, judging by what is reported in East European countries where planning exists, the planners either failed to foresee what was going to happen or could do nothing about it, since it would not otherwise have been necessary for some communist countries to introduce petrol rationing, although they are far less vulnerable -- being less developed – than Western Europe. The explanation is that the planners did not know for certain what was going to happen, and had they known, at least some operators in the market economies would have known it also and would have rushed in. In fact for all we know, some operators may have guessed the developments and may have started the preparations for an oil shortage, which means that the reaction of market economies to the rise of oil prices will be all the more rapid. For in market economies nobody has to wait for the planners to decide what should be done first.

But neither the national planners nor business firms can know in advance precisely what is going to happen.[1] They have to take risks and change their activities in response to unexpected events. Therefore, there is such a premium on being flexible, and the *market economies* are so much more successful in spite of all the talk to the contrary. Risks also have to be taken, otherwise everybody would continuously sit on the fence and no opportunity would be used to advantage. Planning bureaucracies are very badly equipped for this particular task. If one wanted to eliminate risk, one would have to avoid dealing with foreigners whom one cannot control. That would mean autarchy which simultaneously eliminates advantages from trade for excessive fear of the real world.

Let us analyse the raised prices of oil from the viewpoint of economic theory. The section that applies is the optimum tariff theory.[2] The organization of oil-producing countries (OPEC) is acting as one country and raising prices as if it were levying an export tariff on them. The extent to which they can turn the unit terms of trade advantageously to their own favour depends on their own export supply and import demand elasticities and separate or joint elasticities of other countries.

The surprising thing is, that under the impact of the new resolve of OPEC, oil prices did not simply go up by a hefty, but nevertheless limited, percentage, as one would expect if monopoly power is suddenly applied, but were doubled and trebled within a few months. There seems to be something wrong with the actions and reactions of the oil suppliers and consumers. True, the oil market has been an imperfect market for a very long time : there has been a limited number of producing countries and a limited number of petrol multinationals, either producing on their soil or buying from them. The domestic prices of oil of the importing countries have

[1] See *outline of international trade,* p 37.
[2] See *outline of international trade,* p 110.

been highly influenced by domestic taxation. Under these circumstances, oil prices may have been on the low side and lagging behind the development of other prices. But OPEC has been in existence for quite a while and it is hard to believe that oil prices had been all that much below whatever the market could bear. Therefore, it can be said with some certainty that the doubling and trebling of prices was excessive and made possible only by the panic conjured up under the visions of what would happen if there should be no more oil at all. In the long run, the prices will probably come down or be overtaken by other rising prices.

Even in so far as the rise is based on a monopoly situation, the danger for the producers is that they will not preserve their solidarity. Monopoly works by limiting quantity to the point where quantity multiplied by price or by profit is maximum. With many participants in the game, the temptation is considerable to let the others do the limiting, and sell the largest possible quantity one can produce oneself at the thus established high price.[1] It is not difficult to imagine that the populous countries will try to let King Faisal and the Sheikh of Kuwait reduce the output while they profit from the high prices. Judging by the bilateral negotiations on barter deals between pairs of industrial and oil-producing countries going on at the moment, countries on both sides are out to do the best for themselves out of the situation. The EEC and OECD countries may be ill advised not to negotiate in a block, but so are the OPEC countries. Maybe in this way, the two blocks will simply dissolve again into so many countries trading at more or less market prices.

Monopoly power further depends on demand elasticity for a given good, closely linked to the existence or possibility of producing substitutes. As pointed out, efforts are in all probability under way now to replace Arab oil extensively as a source of energy and raw-material output. A higher price also means that it is more profitable to economize and reduce oil costs by using more labour or capital. Under the present circumstances, it is to be expected that the substitution for Arab oil will go further than warranted simply by the price rise and that it will continue even if the oil producers lower their price again. By using oil as a political weapon, the Arabs have given notice to everybody that they are not reliable suppliers and people whom they have frightened will keep that in mind. European governments would be well advised to increase gradually their petrol taxes so as to give an additional impetus to the search for substitutes. It may happen that there will be reserves of oil underground in the Middle East which nobody will want.

The optimum tariff theory usually envisages not only the possibility of substitution but also the possibility of economic retaliation. Without much doubt, the OECD countries could use their own joint monopoly power in many sectors to retaliate against

[1] See *Outline of international trade,* p 140.

the OPEC countries and redress the terms of trade. So far the possibility has been mentioned but no steps in that direction have been taken. It is perhaps thought that, in the slightly longer run wiser counsels will prevail anyway and the situation will return to normality.

One of the problems of the oil trade has been for some time that the oil-producing countries with low population do not know what to do with the proceeds of oil sales. They are either incapable or unwilling to use the money for development. They are incapable because they lack absorptive capacity[1] experience has clearly shown that capital is not a sufficient condition for economic development. Saudi Arabia and Kuwait can be called rich but underdeveloped countries. They may be unwilling because they do not want to disturb their traditional way of life or religious values.

The Arabian peninsula governments, therefore, have to invest their money in the USA and Europe. In a way, this does not resolve the problem because they then obtain returns on their investment which they still do not know how to use. This is a situation of real *embarras de richesse.* Nevertheless, they hold their money in the form of dollar and sterling balances (including treasury bills) and Euro-currency (see p 136) and more rarely in long-term bonds or industrial shares. The Arab governments have not as yet taken in a big way to holding balances in other currencies, nor have other countries been particularly keen on receiving the deposits of their money(see p 94). The size of the Arab short-term holdings in the world financial markets is estimated at something between $ 30 to 50 billion and it is generally thought that the switching of these billions around as hot money may have substantially contributed to the monetary troubles of the recent years.

On the other hand, the Arabs are complaining that their holdings of foreign currency are constantly losing value and even saying that it is far better for them to leave their oil underground instead of acquiring depreciating cash. We have pointed out that 'saving oil for future generations' could just make it useless. The complaint about the loss of value has substance : it highlighted the need for the money to recover its function of the store of value (see p 2); the falling into disuse of this function does distort economic activities. While it may be possible to silence small domestic savers continuously cheated out of their savings, it is not easy with powerful savers from abroad such as the oil sheikhs.

Until a general solution is found – if ever – for inflation, a special solution will have to be devised for the Arabs if their oil is needed and expected to flow. One suggestion is that the Arabs should be paid in special SDRs (see p 158) which would be defined in terms of a set of strong currencies (see p 178) but in such a way that revaluations would have more impact on their value than devaluations. But would they be content with the still low interest rates and would they consider even such SDRs sufficiently

[1] See *Outline of international trade* p 76.

safe (see p 163)? Another proposal is that the Arabs should invest more in American and European industries. Their shares may in the long run preserve the real value invested as they are related to industrial plant, but again they may not as their prices are also linked to expected profits. Profit expectations have taken a beating over the last decade under *inter alia* the impact of industrial unrest. One should not forget that the Frankfurt stock exchange is in January 1974 way below its peak in 1962. Therefore, portfolio investment would require more readiness to take risks than one could notice in the Arabs so far. So, in the end, the Arabs will have to fall back on the dollar and sterling balances despite past disappointments. Maybe they will want gold, or, in the case of sterling, dollar guarantees which the British have granted anyway (see p 131). For this very reason – that they have no choice – the Arab threat that they will withdraw their money from American and European banks is an empty one. Where would they take it without losing the larger part in the process?

One of the stranger side effects of the oil crisis is that individual oil-producing countries are now negotiating with industrial countries to exchange oil for the installation of industrial plant on a barter basis. There is perhaps a psychological and political explanation why these deals have to be done on a bilateral basis (see p 1), but there does not seem to be an economic one. Surely, the oil producers could have had before and can have now all the technical and organizational advice and plant and equipment – with the possible exception of military – they want from Western Europe and the United States, for the hard currency they cashed for their oil regardless of whom they sell it to in the first place.

Are the newly found partners going to cut prices mutually? This would leave them where they were before. Apparently the Arabs want to link oil prices bilaterally to prices of industrial goods and food, but it is improbable that they could enforce this idea of frozen relative prices for any length of time. The Arabs also seem to want bilateral negotiations between governments so as to cut out the petrol companies and their profits. In this respect they may have exaggerated ideas (as it so often happens) about both the multinationals' profits and the usefulness of their function as transporters and distributors. It would be strange if oil company profits were exceptionally high or their services inefficient, as competition in the oil business has been considerable.

Anyway, proposals have also been put forward to the effect that producer and consumer countries should meet and solve the problems on a multilateral basis, but some Arab governments seem to be frowning at that. Nevertheless, all things considered a multilateral solution will certainly be the best solution from their point of view also.

While the Arabs are thus worried about what to do with the money their oil earns, other countries are trying to figure out where they could possibly get the money from to pay for their oil imports. It is calculated that the oil producers' revenue from oil will go up by $ 60 million in 1974 if there are no savings of oil in consumer countries, and by $ 45 to 50 billions if there are consumption economies. The oil-producing countries may step up their purchases in the world markets by some $ 5 to 15 billion. This will give the whole world with the exception of oil producers – and possibly USA -- vast balance-of-payments deficits amounting together to between $ 30 to 40 billion. Britain will have a deficit of about $ 5 billion, Japan $ 6 billion, France and Italy $ 3·5 billion, Germany 2·5 billion, etc. How can these countries finance such a rise in their debts?

The normal reaction would be for the deficit countries to try and export more either by deflating at home or devaluing. Neither of these adjustment mechanisms can possibly work under the circumstances and deflation in particular may bring about a real depression at a time when economic activity in Europe and America is slowing down anyway. The adjustment mechanisms cannot work because the reduction in prices can attract customers only if there is some elasticity in their demand. A few Arab countries cannot step up their purchases by much at any price – their demand seems to be saturated at least for the time being. This means that the new deficits cannot be eliminated at all but will have to be financed, and will have to be financed eventually by the Arabs themselves. They will deposit their proceeds in the form of dollar or sterling or Euro-currency balances and these will be lent to the debtor countries. The IMF is considering the possibility of negotiating an Arab version of the general arrangements to borrow (see p 156) : the Arabs would deposit their money with the IMF, denominated in the new SDRs mentioned above and possibly at attractive interest rates, while the IMF would lend the money to the needy countries in the balance-of-payments sense of the word.

Of course, the higher oil prices will hit poor developing countries harder than the industrial world. It is expected that their deficit will rise by about $ 6 billion which is by about as much as the development aid they are given by OECD countries. The oil producers are talking about giving the third world some compensation for the losses caused by higher oil prices and about setting up an Arab development bank. There are also suggestions that Arab countries should extend long-term loans to the poor countries at very low interests, while the industrial countries would compensate them for the difference between these soft rates and market rates. This is a surprising suggestion : surely it is as much the moral duty, also according to Islam, of the countries with newly found riches to help poor countries as it is of the industrial countries. In fact their duty is much clearer and stronger. While the Europeans and Americans owe their standard of living primarily to their own technical and organizational talent and hard work, the Arabs are enjoying a windfall gain if there ever has been one, and are living on unearned income in the true sense of the word. It is hardly any merit that they sit on top of oil deposits which, furthermore, were prospected and opened up by Americans and Europeans. Moreover their oil would be of little use even nowadays if the Europeans and Americans were not buying it and giving other products in exchange. So they ought to play their part in helping the poor. It would be advisable for them to do it also for political reasons : the thinly populated Arab countries are necessarily an object of envy for their less fortunate neighbours. Britain had to rescue Kuwait from Iraq once.

The oil troubles speeded up the dollar and sterling recovery the reason being the expectation that the higher prices would have to be paid in these currencies and that the Arabs would hold at least part of their proceeds in balances of these two currencies. The dollar has shot up from its July 1973 low at 2·24 German marks per dollar to about 2·90 German marks per dollar in the first half of January 1974. The dollar-French franc rate became about 5·00 francs.

This firmly brought the dollar above its Smithsonian 'central rate' (see p 169) and, among other things, cancelled its 1973 devaluation (see p 174). The US monetary authorities thought that this rate was too high and expected foreign governments to intervene which would also reduce the outstanding short-term dollar overhang (see p 178). However, other governments do not seem to be in a great hurry to get rid of dollars at this juncture. The pound weakened *vis-à-vis* the dollar but strengthened with respect to other EEC currencies. Its effective devaluation from the Smithsonian parity improved from just over 20 per cent in October to 17 per cent at the beginning of January. But then domestic industrial trouble, foremostly the miners' ban on overtime working, and rumours of an election brought the pound down by mid-January to its lowest point ever *vis-à-vis* the dollar, to below 2·20 per £. But in terms of French francs, the pound was still equal to or better than, what it was in the summer, i e £1 = Frf 11.

The change in the monetary climate persuaded governments to reverse their controls on the inflow of money (see p 168). The Swiss for instance abolished their famous 'negative interest rates' (i e charges on some deposits by foreigners), and the Germans revoked limitations on foreign investment in Germany. On the other hand, the US authorities again allowed freer outflow of residents' money.

Through all these changes, world trade has further continued to grow (see p 176). Many experts say that this could happen only because the exchange rates of so many countries were freely fluctuating. There is a core of truth in this – flexibility is no doubt important, but was it actually necessary to let the dollar rate wander down from 2·90 German marks to 2·20 (that is by almost 30 per cent) and back again within a year? The oscillation was certainly not due to underlying economic circumstances

[1] *How well are fluctuating exchanges rates working?* American Enterprise Institute reprint of a statement on 21 June 1973 before the Subcommittee on International Exchange and Payments of the Joint Economic Committee of the Congress.

but to excessive human reactions. Maybe government intervention could have restricted the amplitude of fluctuations, but Milton Friedman[1] justifiedly points out the dangers of intervention : 'but whether a currency is overvalued or undervalued, whether an exchange rate is necessary or unnecessary, is a matter of judgement, not of objective, easily determined fact.'

On 15 November 1973, *The Times* published an article under the heading : 'Need to pay the Arabs spurred end to ban on gold sales'. This was a comment on the decision by seven governments led by the American to implement the suggestion (see p 177) that monetary authorities should be allowed to sell gold in the world markets but not to buy it at a price above $42.20 per ounce. This move certainly spells out the dissolution of the 'gold' part of the gold-exchange standard and frees gold as long as there is any in countries, reserves for ordinary payments. The free market gold price was above $120 per ounce in mid-1973, but fell back to just over the $100 mark just before the move by the seven governments and then to about $ 90 per ounce. In mid-January 1974, however, the gold price was up to $ 125 per ounce, after having touched $ 130 a little earlier.

The Nairobi IMF Conference in 1973 came and passed without any result except a promise of nations to each other that a one-piece reform plan for the international monetary system would be ready by July 1974. But by the end of 1973, the oil upset made many previously important looking questions (see p 177) irrelevant while some others had been solved *de facto.* Thus the convertibility of the dollar is no longer a burning problem and the question of gold has been settled. What is debated now is an SDR for the Arabs combined with an IMF Arab arrangement to borrow. The new situation may also demand the strengthening of the IMF's co-ordinating and supervising function. The flexibility of currencies is going to be preserved, but many IMF members wish that there could be some agreement on when floating is legitimate and how a government floating its currency should behave. It has also become clear that there is no time to wait for a single reform in one fell swoop, but that problems will have to be solved as they arise and as soon as partial agreement is reached.

All in all, it can be said at the end of a postscript to a textbook on finance that the situation looks grim in many respects, but that the world is not heading straight for the doomsday as yet. Maybe the advanced countries will have to take, because of the changed terms of trade, a cut in their real incomes of the order of 5 per cent before they can resume reasonable growth. But that they should take in their stride unless (and here is the main danger) some sections of the population continue to misunderstand economic conditions and insist on getting out of the economy more than was there even before the oil turn-about. Such behaviour could destroy the market system and its flexibility which has served us *all* so well.

index